Don Kirshner

Don Kirshner

The Man with the Golden Ear

How He Changed the Face of Rock and Roll

Rich Podolsky

Hal Leonard Books
An Imprint of Hal Leonard Corporation

Published in 2012 by Hal Leonard Books
An Imprint of Hal Leonard Corporation
7777 West Bluemound Road
Milwaukee, WI 53213

Trade Book Division Editorial Offices
33 Plymouth St., Montclair, NJ 07042

Credits for lyrics and photographs are on pages 279–283, which constitute an extension of this copyright page.

Printed in the United States of America

Book design by Michael Kellner

Library of Congress Cataloging-in-Publication Data
Podolsky, Rich, 1946-
  Don Kirshner : the man with the golden ear : how he changed the face of rock and roll / Rich Podolsky.
     p. cm.
  Discography: p.
  Includes bibliographical references and index.
  ISBN 978-1-4584-1670-4
  1. Kirshner, Don. 2. Concert agents--United States--Biography. 3. Music publishers--United States--Biography. I. Title.
  ML429.K555P63 2012
  781.64092--dc23
  [B]
                              2011052416
ISBN 978-1-4584-1670-4

www.halleonardbooks.com

To my wife, Diana, for her overwhelming patience and support

And to Jack Keller, whose spirit and devotion to the music
helped make this possible

Contents

Foreword

I've been in show business and the music industry for fifty years now, and I owe it all to Don Kirshner. He saw something in me that no one else did. He nurtured a career for me, as he has done for so many, including such great singers and songwriters as Carole King, Gerry Goffin, Toni Wine, Neil Sedaka, Howard Greenfield, Jack Keller, Bobby Darin, Connie Francis, Barry Mann, the Monkees, and Cynthia Weil.

The list is never ending. I can't list the people without writing pages upon pages of names of those who were blessed by this man with the golden ear. He changed the face of our industry by opening the door to independent record producers, allowing young record producers to be able to create and sell their works to major record companies. Prior to Donnie Kirshner, the major companies had their own in-house A & R men—artist and repertoire (fancy title for record producers), and outside producers were not let in.

The first such independent work was "The Diary" by Neil Sedaka, produced by Don Kirshner and Al Nevins for RCA Victor Records. Without that we would not have had such producers as Burt Bacharach, Phil Spector, and Leiber and Stoller as well as all the independent works of Motown, Gamble and Huff, the Beatles, Quincy Jones, and Michael Jackson. Don created this opportunity for them all.

Then came the *Don Kirshner's Rock Concert* television show, which for ten years gave birth to so many artists. Yes, not only do I owe him grateful thanks, but so do all the people mentioned above, and maybe I can go as far as to say that the record and music industries owe a shout-out of thanks to the man with the golden ear, Donnie Kirshner.

This is a must-read for all who love the music industry and the forefathers who made it all happen. Donnie is one of them.

—*Tony Orlando*

P.S. A grateful thanks to the author, Rich Podolsky, for taking the time to get it right on behalf of a great man, Don Kirshner.

Preface

I was born a baby boomer in 1946 and raised in the heyday of rock and roll. Like so many kids I grew up with, I dreamed of someday writing a hit song that would bring me high school's version of fame and fortune: instant, unwavering popularity.

And why wouldn't we have this dream? By the time I was a teen, music, for once, was being written and performed by people not much older than I was. These were stellar contemporaries we looked up to and wanted to be.

This revolutionary new trend, followed what seemed like an eternity, where former Tin Pan Alley songwriters penned a stream of benign, corny tunes—like "How Much Is That Doggie in the Window"—meant to appeal to the younger generation. Suddenly in the late '50s and early '60s, teenagers began writing songs for their peers, songs that mirrored their experiences and their feelings, and the kids all went crazy for it.

Many of us naturally came to idolize the songwriters and performers creating that music, and I was no exception. It was a fascination so powerful I never let go of it, even in adulthood. That fascination is what led me on a quest in 2005 to learn and tell the stories behind some of the best-loved songs from that time. It led me directly to the person who set that revolutionary trend in motion—music impresario Don Kirshner—and also to some of the illustrious songwriters he discovered and nurtured during the five years, 1958–1963, in which his legendary song publishing firm, Aldon Music, existed.

In researching this book I got to interview so many people I idolized at that time: songwriters Neil Sedaka, Jerry Leiber, Jack Keller,

Carole Bayer Sager, and Gerry Goffin; performers Connie Francis, Bobby Vee, Tony Orlando, and Gene Pitney; *Billboard* writer turned music executive Jerry Wexler (who passed away in 2008), along with his former partner at Atlantic Records, the legendary Ahmet Ertegun (who passed away in 2006); other former music executives, including Mitch Miller and Chuck Sagle; legendary DJs Bruce "Cousin Brucie" Morrow and Philly's doo-wop king, Jerry Blavat; and of course, Kirshner, who sadly passed away early in 2011.

Getting to meet these people—some in person, some by phone—was incredibly eye-opening. It was also quite humbling for someone who was an aspiring songwriter from an early age.

● ● ●

I always loved music, and was interested in songwriting even before my teen years, when that seemed like the ticket to irreversible coolness. At ten, I wrote my first song, aptly entitled "Mother." At the time no one could convince me that it wasn't a hit. I even went as far as trying to find some publishers in the Yellow Pages. Needless to say, my mother loved it, even though I couldn't carry a tune.

I didn't write my next number until I was fourteen, in 1960, a love song, no less, written in an effort to impress a girl on the next block named Hilda. Only nothing rhymed with Hilda. That one didn't get published either, but I really thought I was on to something. Fortunately for Carole King and Neil Sedaka and the other teenagers writing for Don Kirshner in New York, I wasn't ready to hop on a Greyhound bus and give up on making the JV basketball team.

Growing up in Northeast Philadelphia, I was kind of a stiff when it came to dancing. My awkwardness didn't bode well for my chances at popularity, but I had a saving grace: My father was a record buyer for Sun Rae, a chain of stores in Philly, and thanks to him I always had a lot of new 45s. That went a long way toward salvaging some degree of popularity.

I had a small Philco radio in my room, plugged in next to my bed. Every morning as I got ready for school, I'd listen to Joe Niagara, the

"Rockin' Bird," on WIBG. By the time we were sixteen, some of us had licenses and drove to school. On the way we'd blast WIBG and sing, "Duke, Duke, Duke, Duke of Earl, Duke, Duke . . ." while slapping the roof of the car to keep time. We were all so immersed in rock-and-roll culture. It infiltrated every aspect of our lives.

Then one day in the spring of '62, my father brought home a pile of 45s that were untried and untested. He didn't know if any of them were good, and assumed he might not recognize if they were since they weren't his style. So he asked me to play them and see if there were some I liked. I was thrilled by this task, which seemed like a fun game. I called it "Find the Hit." That night I listened to one bomb after another until one jumped out of the pile. It was Peter, Paul, and Mary's "If I Had a Hammer." It was sort of a combination of folk and country, and their harmonies were infectious.

I played it for my father and he agreed with me. He wound up buying it for the racks of his stores. Peter, Paul, and Mary were unknown at the time and hadn't cracked the Top 40 prior to this. Within a month or two, "If I Had a Hammer" was climbing the charts and it didn't stop until it hit the Top 10. I guess it didn't hurt that President Kennedy said it was his favorite song. But I was proud that I'd instinctively recognized the one hit in that pile my dad gave me.

From that point on, I started paying attention to the charts, via the Top 100 WIBG put out each week. Then one night my father came home and asked me if I wanted to go to a special dinner being thrown by one of the record labels. It was the spring of '62 and Cameo Parkway Records wanted to introduce a young singer named Dee Dee Sharp to the record buyers.

I put on a sport jacket, my father helped me with my tie, and we drove down to Center City. The dinner was at the Warwick Hotel on 17th Street. I was a little nervous because at sixteen I'd be the youngest one there by far, but my dad kept reassuring me that no one really cared. And he was right. We sat at a table about halfway back and everyone was nice. They seemed to get a kick out of seeing a teenager there.

For me the real treat was also seeing Chubby Checker, whose

dance craze, "The Twist," reached No. 1 twice, in 1960 and 1961. Checker was there because he and Sharp were releasing a new song together called "Slow Twistin'." He was decked out in a powder blue jacket lined with glitter and looking like he could lead Philly's famed Mummer's Parade.

When they sang "Slow Twistin'" to us, right there just a few feet away, I was knocked out. Then Checker told us that Dee Dee had a new dance song of her own, and she sang "Mashed Potato Time," which had all of us up on our feet clapping along to the beat. She was barely sixteen, just a few months older than me. It seemed like nothing bothered her. And it didn't. Soon the song became a new dance craze.

I had no idea the night would be that exciting. I was so grateful my father had invited me to join him. As we were leaving, a young DJ named Jerry Blavat introduced himself to my dad and a few other buyers. At the time, Blavat was still working out of his garage for a small Philly station, but he already had a cult following among teenagers. He talked a mile a minute and called himself "The Geator with the Heater." Please don't ask me what a Geator is.

And then I saw him—Don Kirshner. There he was, walking toward us, looking larger than life. Kirshner was only twenty-seven then, but his song publishing firm, Aldon Music, was the talk of the business. He had that *something* that made people want to be around him. My father even mentioned some of Kirshner's teenage songwriters at the dinner that night. In fact, Kirshner was there trying to get Cameo Parkway's owner, Bernie Lowe, to use some of the songs written by two of his teenage songwriters—Carole King and Gerry Goffin.

That was it: From that day forward I wanted to be in the record business. I studied it and found out everything I could. As the months went by, I learned more and more about Aldon Music and all the great young songwriters Kirshner developed, like Goffin and King, Sedaka and Greenfield, and Mann and Weil. Disc jockeys regularly lauded these writers by name, as if they were as illustrious as the recording artists themselves. To me that made them all seem especially cool.

Over many years, I pieced together the Aldon story—how it all began with a vision Kirshner had, which was unique for the time: that *teenagers should be writing songs for other teenagers.* In the years just following Elvis Presley's emergence on the scene, Kirshner knew there were kids hungering for music that really spoke to them. More than that, he knew there were other kids who were writing just the songs their peers wanted to hear. But those songs weren't being heard because the music publishers were content to play it safe with songs written by the old Tin Pan Alley writers. That just killed Kirshner. But it also provided him with a mission, and a place to make his mark.

● ● ●

I never did become a songwriter, but for the past twenty-five years I've wanted to tell this story. Then one day I decided I had to do it. I was sitting in a small Off-Broadway theater on Manhattan's west side watching a show called *They Wrote That?*

The show highlighted the great songwriting careers of Barry Mann and Cynthia Weil, with Barry and Cynthia singing their own songs, such as "Uptown," "Who Put the Bomp," "On Broadway," and "You've Lost That Lovin' Feelin'." The performance at the 199-seat theater wasn't sold out just by chance; the people in those seats knew who Mann and Weil were, and came ready to cheer. It was a great show. In fact, I loved it so much I was there for the second time.

Over the course of two hours, Mann and Weil told the story of how they met in 1961 while working for Don Kirshner at Aldon Music—or as Cynthia put it, how she "stalked" Barry and eventually married him. I think right there, at that moment, I decided it was time for me to write the Aldon Music story. Surely, I thought, the songwriters would want this great story to be told. I put together a chart of whom I thought the key players would be and started a timeline to include every hit Aldon ever published. Leading the chart was Kirshner, and then his discoveries: Goffin and King, Mann and Weil, and the first team he signed: Neil Sedaka and Howard Greenfield.

Next I started contacting everyone I knew in the entertainment world to try to locate these people. Within a fifteen-day period, I wrote letters to Carole King's production office and Mann and Weil's representatives, and I sent a personal letter to Gerry Goffin at his home in Beverly Hills—an address I found, remarkably, through the Internet.

While I traded e-mails back and forth with King's representatives and the reps for Mann and Weil, one of my friends came through for me with help I never expected: He put me in touch with Jeff Barry, the great Hall of Fame songwriting partner of Ellie Greenwich. (They wrote such hits as "Da Doo Ron Ron," "Be My Baby," and "Chapel of Love.") Barry wrote and produced for Kirshner, although not during the five years Aldon Music existed. He did, however, put me in touch with someone who had—Ron Dante. Also, Jeff Barry's assistant sent me the contact information for Neil Sedaka's publishing office. I immediately sent e-mails to both.

Dante got back to me first. Ron Dante's biggest success might have been discovering Barry Manilow and producing his early albums. But he was a very successful demo singer in his own right, whom Kirshner discovered in the early '60s, and who'd also tried his hand at songwriting for Aldon. He was the lead voice on '60s standards such as "Tracy" and "Sugar, Sugar." He was a terrific contact and the key to any luck I would have going forward.

Ron gave me an idea of what it was like to work with all of those great songwriters at the beginning of their careers. "It was difficult to think you were writing anything worthwhile when in the room next to you, you hear Carole King banging out 'Will You Love Me Tomorrow,' or Barry Mann on the other side writing songs like 'On Broadway.' It was unbelievably intimidating."

In addition to his memories and insights, Ron shared something else with me that proved invaluable: an e-mail address that proved to be the breakthrough I was looking for.

"I think this is the e-mail for Kirshner's office in Florida," he told me. "But don't tell him where you got it," he quickly added.

I immediately sat down and wrote an e-mail message that began: "Dear Mr. Kirshner, you are the hero of my book." In it I explained my plan to write about the Aldon years and all the great musicians and music he discovered. I also invited him to meet with me. When I was done, I sent the note off, out into the ether, and hoped for a reply.

While I was waiting, I got in touch with Sedaka's publishing office and spoke directly to a woman who managed it. She explained it would be difficult to interview Neil because his schedule was so tight, but I stayed in touch, hoping for the best.

Dante, as it turns out, also got me in touch with my most important contact on this journey. That would be Artie Kaplan, who worked at Aldon from 1960 on in many capacities. He was a songwriter and music contractor, hiring all the musicians to play during a recording date. He played the sax on at least a dozen big Aldon hits, including his famous solo on "The Loco-Motion." And he was also a song plugger, helping out on the promotional side. In other words, he did just about everything at that office, knew everyone who worked there, and was still in contact with many of them. Better yet, his memory of those days was nearly flawless, and Kaplan was also anxious to have this story properly told.

He put me in touch with songwriters Jack Keller and Gerry Goffin. Keller was like the fifth Beatle. Nobody knew his name, only the dozens of hit songs he wrote. He had written several No. 1 songs for Kirshner and had more than a dozen hits co-written with Greenfield or Goffin. He was enormously helpful to me in so many ways.

Goffin and I spoke at least two dozen times. His memories of his early relationship with Carole King and their struggle to get their first hit were infinitely important to this project.

Then one afternoon in February 2005, the phone rang. "Is this Rich Podolsky?" the caller asked. "Yes," I said, "who's this?"

"This is Don Kirshner," he said.

I felt chills go through my body. I took a big gulp and said, "I can't believe I've finally found you!" I felt so fortunate that I was there to receive the call. After many, many short conversations, and some lobbying from some of his friends I had contacted, Don finally agreed to work with me. Until that point he hadn't cooperated with any other author.

Our conversations were plentiful and long lasting. Every Sunday morning for six months we'd chat over coffee and bagels, 1,300 miles apart. As the story developed, I had so many questions and holes to fill, and Kirshner obliged by answering nearly every one.

And so it went. Nearly everyone I put a feeler out to got back to me: Connie Francis, Bobby Vee, Jerry Wexler and Ahmet Ertegun (both now gone), and Tony Orlando, who still thanks Kirshner in every show he performs.

I constructed what I called the "Aldon Timeline" and kept filling in the pieces; then I started listing every Top 40 song Kirshner published in those days. The list is simply packed with one huge hit after another.

Aldon Music existed from 1958 to 1963, when Kirshner sold it to Columbia Screen Gems for $3 million, moving all of his songwriters over there with him. In its brief five-year existence, Aldon put out more than 200 hits. And what great songs they were. Songs like "Will You Love Me Tomorrow," "Up on the Roof," "Uptown," "Breaking Up Is Hard to Do," "Where the Boys Are," "I Love How You Love Me," "The Loco-Motion," "On Broadway," and "Take Good Care of My Baby."

Those five years represented rock and roll's last gasp of innocence. They were the last songs written before the Beatles changed the landscape of American music forever.

But they were great years for me and 60 million other baby boomers. And now I finally get to tell the story.

Don Kirshner

Introduction

Don Kirshner had barely turned twenty-one in 1955 when Bill Haley's "Rock Around the Clock" officially ushered in the rock-and-roll era.

Many heard the song for the first time during the opening sequence of Richard Brooks' award-winning film *Blackboard Jungle*. Glenn Ford played a teacher and Sidney Poitier a student at a New York City high school where discipline did not exist. The film's popularity, plus Haley's driving beat kept "Rock Around the Clock" on the charts for an amazing twenty-four weeks, and at No. 1 for eight of those. That year, only twelve of the Top 100 songs were classified as rock and roll. But the staying power of Haley's hit was a forerunner of what was to come.

In the world of popular music, the song's overwhelming success was a game changer. Prior to that the airwaves were largely filled with safe, middle-of-the-road pop, along with some country and swing sounds. Rock and roll had begun to weave its way onto the airwaves a few years earlier with songs like Joe Turner's rhythm-and-blues classic "Shake, Rattle, and Roll" and the emergence of doo-wop harmony on songs such as "Earth Angel" by the Penguins, but they were few and far between. When Don Kirshner and his friends heard those songs, they were dying for more.

The first time Kirshner and I spoke on the phone, in 2005, he talked about those early years of rock and roll and the influence they had on him: "I loved to listen to Fats Domino, Dinah Washington, Chuck Berry, and Little Richard," he said. "They were the pioneers of the new music."

Rock and roll had its roots in the South with the blues. In the late forties, it came bubbling out from under the surface with a unique driving sound. It was played by artists like Louis Armstrong, Big Mama Thornton, and Joe Turner and was known in the trades as "race music"—developed by black artists intended solely for a black audience. Despite that, two white men in two different places heard that sound and were moved by it—so much so that they each, in their own way, became instrumental in making it available and popular with all audiences.

One was Jerry Wexler, a writer for *Billboard* magazine in the late '40s and early '50s who disliked using the term *race music*. In 1949 he boldly changed the name in *Billboard*'s pages to rhythm and blues. The name caught on, and at Wexler's urging *Billboard* kept a separate list of R & B hits along with country and western and of course pop music. A few years later, he joined Atlantic Records as a producer and was influential in the recording careers of such greats as Aretha Franklin, Ray Charles, Wilson Pickett, Dusty Springfield, and the Allman Brothers.

The other was Alan Freed, a white late-night disc jockey in Cleveland catering to mostly black listeners. He began playing records by Little Richard and Clyde McPhatter and found, surprisingly, that he was getting a response from white teenagers who loved to dance to the new R & B sound. In his time at the increasingly popular WJW station, Freed coined the term *rock and roll*. It was a perfect name for this music, one the kids could clearly relate to. And so he watched his audience quickly grow. Soon Freed was recruited to New York where, as a disc jockey on WINS, one of the country's most successful radio stations, he became a pied piper to nearly every teenager in the city.

Rock and roll's competition for airtime in the early '50s came from songs only your grandmother could love—songs like "The Ballad of Davy Crockett," Mitch Miller's "The Yellow Rose of Texas," Perry Como's "Hot Diggity (Dog Ziggity Boom)," and Patti Page's "How Much Is That Doggie in the Window." All four of these reached No. 1 on *Billboard* and were written by middle-aged songwriters entrenched from the old Tin Pan Alley days.

This drove Kirshner crazy. He knew that he and his teenage friends should be writing the songs for the radio—not those middle-aged songwriters. Kirshner and his peers could write the music and lyrics that their own generation could relate to, and then sell the rights to them for contemporary artists to perform and record. He knew in his bones that these new songs would be hits. Driven by this idea, in 1958, Don teamed up with a veteran of popular music named Al Nevins to start a rock-and-roll song publishing company—something unheard of at the time.

Up to that point, Don had been an unsuccessful songwriter whose writing partner was Bobby Darin, before anyone knew who Bobby Darin was. Nevins, who at forty-one was nearly twenty years older than Kirshner, was from another era. A successful performer in the '40s, Nevins had started a popular trio called the Three Suns, who became recording stars and had a very successful nightclub act along with a national radio show on NBC. With the emergence of Elvis in 1955, though, Nevins understood that music was changing in a big way.

For Kirshner, it couldn't change fast enough. While he and his friends were hungry for more rock and roll on the radio, existing music publishers were in no big hurry. They were still getting mileage out of the tried and true musical styles of the day—the light standards being played on *Your Hit Parade*—and so were more inclined to play it safe than to take risks with change. Ultimately, though, that reluctance worked out for Kirshner. It helped set the stage for him and Nevins to take music publishing in a whole other direction.

In 2006, two years before his death at ninety-three, I interviewed Jerry Wexler by phone from his home on the west coast of Florida. I'd gotten his number from David Evanier, author of *Roman Candle: The Life of Bobby Darin*. Evanier felt it was imperative that I interviewed Wexler and gladly gave me his number.

I couldn't believe that I was about to talk to this legendary music producer. It had been at least twenty years since Wexler's days at Atlantic Records, where he was instrumental in the careers of so many of the most popular bands in rock-and-roll history—a distinction that in 1987 earned him a place in the Rock and Roll Hall of Fame. Despite his age and a certain fatigue in his voice, Wexler was sharp as a tack as he explained to me the evolution of the song publishing business. He sounded like a Harvard professor giving a lecture on the history of the music business.

"In the '20s and '30s and even the '40s, selling records wasn't nearly as important as selling sheet music," Wexler said. "It was the era of the song plugger," someone from a publishing house who brought music to bands and tried to influence them to play it on the radio. Once those songs became popular, people would run out and buy the sheet music.

In the '20s, Max Dreyfus' song publishing company, T. B. Harms, became the most powerful and influential in the world. He began in 1917 by hiring Jerome Kern as a songwriter and song plugger. Soon he added George and Ira Gershwin along with Cole Porter and Richard Rodgers. He put them all under long-term contracts, purchasing their copyrights, and had them write on pianos he placed in cubicles at his downtown office. The strategy turned out to be brilliant—so brilliant that Kirshner and Nevins would later revive it at their publishing firm.

Song publishing quickly grew into big business, especially when silent films gave way to "talkies." Following the enormous success of *The Jazz Singer*, the movie studios began frantically searching for song product with the public thirsting for more musical films. Dreyfus sold his company to Warner Bros. for an incredible $11 million in 1929, shortly before the crash.

By the '50s, however, producing and distributing records became much easier and more profitable, and the goal of the song publisher shifted. Now the object of the game was to sell the rights of their songs to record companies.

Kirshner thought that under the right circumstances, he could duplicate what Max Dreyfus had done. "I needed a base, I needed an ability to do what Max Dreyfus did," he told me. "I had grown up with all the films about songwriters and song publishing: *Night and Day*, *The Gershwin Story*, and all those things with Robert Alda like

Rhapsody in Blue. I was an usher at the Coliseum on Broadway taking people into the theater, never dreaming that someday it could be me. I would groove on those kind of movies. Then when I wrote my first song, I realized there was a whole marketplace out there that was untapped, and someone was going to pluck it. And I was going to be the guy to pluck it."

By the time Kirshner and Nevins put their first names together in 1958 and started Aldon Music, the teenage public was clamoring for rock and roll. The stage was set for them. As music publishers, although very different, the two became perfect partners.

"Nevins and Kirshner were the most improbable quinella in history—but fantastically successful," Wexler recalled. "Al Nevins was an old hand and Donnie sprang out of nowhere like Minerva from Jupiter's head. Like where did this guy come from with this notion that he'd put a bunch of songwriters in separate rooms with pianos and say, 'play; bring me songs'? It was brilliant because it was a part of history that had been abandoned." Although Kirshner didn't invent it, he had the good sense to reinstate a formula that had already proven successful.

"Somehow Donnie and Al did it," Wexler said in awe. "You could say, sure they had great songwriters, but they had the format. Look, these kids were running around with songs—anybody could have picked them up. Anybody that had the vision. It was Al and Donnie that had the vision to put them under contract and give them a weekly stipend."

And what a vision it was. Aldon Music was in business only five years, from 1958 to 1963—a crucial little pocket of pop music history. It was the era between the appearance of Elvis on the scene and the emergence of the Beatles. It might even be argued that those hits—and Kirshner's and Nevins' vision—helped pave the way for the Beatles' arrival here, preparing young audiences for what was coming next.

Not only did these two men publish some of the century's greatest songs, but they also discovered and introduced some of its greatest songwriters. Without Kirshner and Nevins, we might never have known the likes of Carole King and Gerry Goffin, Neil Sedaka and Howard Greenfield, Barry Mann and Cynthia Weil, and Jack Keller.

This is about how Kirshner and Nevins did it—and the stories behind those great songs that they published. Songs that changed the face of music. Songs that today 60 million baby boomers can sing word for word.

For Don Kirshner it all started one cold and blustery day in 1955 at Kurtzman's Candy Store.

Splish Splash

Well, how was I to know there was a party going on?

Twenty-year-old Don Kirshner sat on a corner stool in his "office," Kurtzman's Candy Store in the Washington Heights section of New York City. It was a bone-chilling day in March 1955, and while he waited for his friend Natalie Twersky, he sipped an egg cream and read the *Daily News*.

The front page trumpeted how the U.S. was losing the Cold War to the Russians, but Don quickly turned to the back page and a story about the Yankees. Manager Casey Stengel had the Yankees ready to regain their proper place atop the American League, after finishing second in 1954. When Stengel first came to the Yankees in '49, the team won the World Series an incredible five straight years.

Don was in awe of Stengel's managerial skills. As a kid, he had hoped to be a Yankee. Tall and powerful, he even got a tryout for the Dodgers as an outfielder. He did fairly well that day—even hammered one into the left-field seats. But it wasn't enough to get a contract. That's when he turned his full attention to songwriting.

Suddenly the candy store's door burst open, sending a blast of wintry air down the line of stools. Don brushed aside his dark, wavy hair. He looked up to see his friend, a petite brunette whose ponytail swung side to side as she hurried to his side.

"I'm telling you," she said, "he is the most talented human being I've ever met!"

"I believe you," Don said, and laughed. "Now slow down and catch your breath!"

She hopped up on the stool next to his and then glanced over her shoulder. She turned back to Don. "There's just one thing," she said. "He . . ."

"What?"

"He looks bad. Don't judge him by that. He's had a rough couple of years. Lately he's been cleaning latrines to earn a few bucks."

"I don't care what he looks like, so long as he can write music."

Don already had one song published, "All of My Dreams," which he wrote the lyrics for after hearing his friend Morty Berkowitz's original melody the summer before. When the song was completed, he tried to sell it to Frankie Laine, which took a lot of nerve because Laine was the biggest pop star in the world at that time, and Don was just a bellboy at a beach club on Long Island. When he approached Laine at the club, Laine wasn't interested, but Don was undeterred; despite his young age and lack of experience, he already knew that the music industry would be his life. All he needed, he thought, was a partner to write more songs. Maybe Natalie's friend would—

The shop door opened, slowly this time. *Jesus,* Don thought, *she wasn't kidding.* The boy's shoulders were hunched against the cold, and he was frail. The black peacoat hung off his body. As the kid moved closer, Don could see that his wool scarf was badly stained and in tatters. He wasn't dirty; he just looked like he couldn't afford decent clothes. *So we're both broke,* Don thought, gazing his eyes toward the ceiling.

Don still lived with his parents, at the corner of 187th Street and Fort Washington Avenue. Upstairs lived a kid named Henry with his parents, Mr. and Mrs. Kissinger. Don's family had moved there from the Bronx, near where his father had a tailor shop around the corner from the Apollo Theater in Harlem.

"So, Donnie," Natalie said, her eyes sparkling, "this is Walden Robert Cassotto."

"Call me Bobby," the kid said.

"Sure. Bobby." Don stuck out his hand for a shake. Cassotto's hand was all bones.

"Natalie's raved about you." *I'll have to hear this guy to believe it,* he thought, releasing the bones.

"Well, let's go to my apartment," Natalie said. "I've got an upright." She lived on the fifth floor of a walk-up apartment building. Again Don looked at Bobby Cassotto, wondering if he would make it up the stairs. He was eighteen, Kirshner thought, but he looked thirty.

Soon they were in Natalie's living room. They took off their coats and flung them on a chair. Don flopped onto a sofa. "Let's hear what you've got," he said. He'd had enough small talk during the walk over.

Bobby pulled up the piano bench in front of the Twerskys' upright. He blew on his hands and then began to play a couple of old standards: "You Must've Been a Beautiful Baby" and "I Can't Give You Anything but Love."

Don's first reaction was, *you gotta be kidding me.* He sent a sidelong glance at Natalie. She was focused on Bobby, though.

But the longer Don listened, the less they sounded like old songs and the more they sounded like the new swingin' sound from artists like Frank Sinatra. *Maybe this kid is special after all,* he thought.

Then Bobby started to play "Won't You Come Home Bill Bailey," originally written in 1918. *Not another one of these,* Don thought. But it didn't sound like any version he had ever heard before. As the song progressed, Bobby became more animated. He shoved the bench out behind him with his legs, and half standing behind the piano, he belted out the lyrics while he pounded on the keyboard.

I'll do the cookin' honey, I'll pay the rent
I know I done you wrong . . .

His brown hair fell across his face in waves as he played. His blue eyes were now twinkling. As he went from one verse to the next, he had made an amazing transition. Now Don settled back and couldn't wait to hear what was next.

Jesus Christ. It wasn't just that the kid could sing, but he had something that grabbed you right away. He had style and the kind of showmanship that only the greats like Jolson seemed to have, Don thought.

Don was overcome with excitement. As if by magic, the scrawny kid he'd just met at Kurtzman's had transformed into a star. Don had seen great performers on TV and at the Apollo, but he had never seen anyone like Bobby.

At the end of the song, the kid straightened and turned around. Don jumped up from the sofa and quickly gathered his thoughts. His brown eyes were smiling at Bobby.

"Stick with me, kid," he said, and grinned at Natalie. "I'll make you the biggest thing in the business."

"Groovy," Bobby said with a wink.

Kirshner, the son of a tailor, who didn't have a single connection in show business, meant what he said, although he didn't have any idea how he would bring it about. What he did know was that Bobby had the goods and that he himself had the chutzpah to make things happen.

• • •

If you knew Don Kirshner in 1955, you knew there were two distinct sides to him. There was the guy who was so sure of himself, so confident, that you always wanted to be by his side. And there was the soft side, which is probably why so many of his friends called him *Donnie*. Donnie was always there for you with a smile and a word of advice. He could make you laugh when you were mad or soothe your pain when you were going to cry. He was a unique combination of a driving force and your big brother all rolled into one. So when he asked Bobby to be his partner, it was very hard for the kid to resist.

Cassotto was born in 1936 and raised in the Bronx during the height of the Great Depression. He wanted for everything, received very little, and his Italian family survived with the help of Home Relief. His father was a small-time crook who fell out of favor with the mob and disappeared, leaving his family penniless. The only thing he left Bobby was a piano, which was a present from mob boss Frank Costello.

Bobby was raised by his grandmother, Polly, who he thought was his mother. Though poor, she still managed to take him to Vaudeville shows at the old Bronx Opera House. At one of these shows, he saw Sophie Tucker perform and decided he too could do that some day.

He was just five feet eight inches tall and pencil thin when he met Kirshner in 1955, just before graduating from Bronx Science. You'd never know he was dead broke because he carried around an attitude that was somewhere between 1950s beatnik cool and 1960s Harlem swagger. He liked everyone, hated no one, and was easily liked in return. It's no wonder Kirshner took to him so fast, and vice versa.

Don and Bobby became fast friends and started writing songs together wherever they could. Bobby seemed comfortable writing either the lyrics or the music, so when they sat down to discuss the partnership, Bobby asked Don which he preferred.

"Jesus, Bobby, I never learned to read or write music," said Don, "so I guess it's pretty clear that I'll be writing the lyrics."

"Just as long as you don't sing them too, Kirsh," Bobby said with a giggle. "We've all heard you sing."

Even though the Kirshners didn't own a piano, they'd often write at Don's house, which was where Bobby could get a solid meal. Sunday dinners were a must.

"Sit down. Enjoy," Don's father, Gillie, told Bobby. "Stay for dinner. My wife's making your favorite: old-fashioned chicken soup, with brisket and mashed potatoes." Don's father was born in Poland and still spoke with an accent from the old country, even though he'd been in America most of his life. His mother, Belle, was from the Bronx.

Bobby ate like there was no tomorrow and was a regular at the Kirshner dinner table. Although he enjoyed writing with Don, Bobby didn't want to restrict himself to composing; he wanted to be a performer and recording artist too. And he was in a hurry to get there. As a kid Cassotto contracted rheumatic fever, which severely weakened his heart. He wasn't sure how much time he had left, which is why he blurted out one day, "Kirsh, I got to make it by the time I'm thirty."

If he were going to make it at all, he'd need a catchier name than Walden Robert Cassotto or even Bobby Cassotto. One night Cassotto was looking for a cheap place to eat in Chinatown. Looking up he saw a neon sign for a Mandarin Chinese restaurant with the letters *MAN* burned out. The remaining lit-up letters spelled out *DARIN*.

"That's it!" he said. "That's going to be my new name: *Darin, Bobby Darin*."

In the first years of their collaboration, Bobby and Don had suffered more than their share of tough times. To make ends meet they'd often take undesirable odd jobs. Don worked as an usher at a nearby movie theater and Bobby cleaned latrines. Often, to save money, they'd find themselves at Romeo's Cafeteria on Broadway, right next door to the Brill Building. Romeo's was the one with the big white chef's hat outside and the linoleum tables inside. On this particular day, Don and Bobby were settled in at a table near the rear of the joint.

"How much is a plate of spaghetti?" Kirshner asked the waiter.

"Thirty-five cents."

Reaching into his pocket, Don pulled out a few coins. "I've got some change. How much you got?" he asked Bobby.

"More than a dime and less than a dollar."

Don turned back to the waiter. "All right," he said. "A plate of spaghetti, with two forks and two spoons and don't forget two glasses of water."

Bobby chimed in as the waiter started walking away: "And the bread! Don't forget the bread, man." Then he turned to Don and asked, "Do we have enough to leave a tip?"

"If we do, it's that waiter's lucky day."

Kirshner took a deep sigh, and observed, "Here we go, Bobby. We're broke again."

Bobby interrupted, "It's not like they don't like us, Kirsh."

"It's *you* that they like," Don said. "You're gonna make it big someday. You're gonna be that big star you always dreamed of."

"Kirsh. Things aren't all that swingin' right now."

"With a talent as big as yours," said Don, "you're bound to hit. And when you do, the whole world will dig it. And when that happens, I'll find my own thing."

"Geez, Kirsh. I never thought of that."

"Don't worry."

"Well if I hit, you hit too. We'll figure something out."

• • •

The first money they earned together was for a jingle they wrote for the Orange Furniture Store in Newark, New Jersey. As Don and Bobby made the rounds in town, they became the best liked, unsuccessful songwriter team in New York. The radio guys would send them to the trade guys and the trade guys would send them to the advertising guys. One day an advertising buddy told them there was a department store in Newark that needed a new jingle for a radio ad. If they could come up with one, it would pay 500 bucks. It's amazing what one can write when he's hungry.

For value you can't beat
Start talking to your feet
Hop a bus and come with us
To 205 Main Street
We're going to Orange Furniture Store!

Bobby and Don eventually gravitated to Broadway, which was electric with the buzz of people in the business. How exciting it was, even if you were broke. They'd hang out at Hansen's Drug Store at 51st and Broadway, or Horn & Hardart's Automat on 57th Street, or Romeo's at 52nd Street and Broadway.

Hansen's had a long counter with a few tables and the gang would gather and eat on the cheap. Two members of that gang were Steve Lawrence and Eydie Gorme, who had always hung out at Hansen's when they were first looking for work. Now that they had made it, they didn't forget their old friends. Often they'd come by to offer encouragement and pick up a check.

Other times Don and Bobby would hang out at the Turf restaurant next to the Brill Building, where working musicians went after cutting a demo. Sheet music was plastered all over the wall. The restaurant had ten-cent beers and a clam bar. When the check came, no one would reach for it, hoping somebody they knew would come along and pick it up.

After working together for over a year, Don and Bobby accumulated twelve songs they considered to be good. They'd worked really hard and both felt strongly about their numbers. They were so proud of their work, they had the confidence to try and sell them to the major publishers in the Brill Building at 1619 Broadway.

The Brill Building was the equivalent of Mecca for songwriters. It was named for the Brill Brothers, whose garment business originally occupied the corner of the block. On October 4, 1929, only twenty-five days before Wall Street crashed, the *New York Times* front page trumpeted:

Tallest Building to Rise in Times Square Area
Lefcourt Will Erect 1050-Foot Skyscraper

Lefcourt was real-estate mogul A. E. Lefcourt. He had subleased the land from the Brill Brothers. After Black Tuesday, financial setbacks forced Lefcourt to scale the building back from 105 floors to a mere 10. During construction, the Lefcourt empire collapsed. The Brills were forced to foreclose on the building and take over operations.

When construction was completed, the brothers hired the well-connected real-estate firm of Cushman & Wakefield to secure white-collar banking lessees. Their plans went sour. With the recent completion of the Empire State Building, blue-chip businesses were no longer looking for office space.

In 1931, the first tenants to lease in the Brill Building happened to be theater and nightclub owners. In 1932, when Southern Music Publishing moved in, hundreds of other publishers followed, and the building became an entertainment niche.

Don and Bobby set their sights on this Mecca. They felt sure they'd meet with success there. Darin had the talent and Kirshner had the nerve—a powerful combination. But it wasn't so easy.

Day after day, they went up and down the hallways of 1619 Broadway, knocking on doors. They were certain that if those music publishers behind those doors just heard their songs, that would be it—they'd be sold. But to their surprise, the publishers hadn't just been waiting for Don and Bobby to arrive on the scene. The young songwriting duo soon realized that no matter how great their songs were, getting to play them for the Brill Building's old-time publishers was a very difficult prospect.

One day in January 1956, though, the right door opened. It was George Scheck's door. Scheck was the host of a popular TV show with teenagers called *Star Time*. His office was at 1697 Broadway, next to the Ed Sullivan Theater. Pictures of Scheck arm in arm with celebrities adorned his wall. A young, Italian-looking, attractive nineteen-year-old woman was sitting alongside Scheck's desk when Don and Bobby were ushered in. She had long jet-black hair piled high on top of her curvy features. Scheck introduced them.

"Connie, these are the songwriters I was telling you about, Don Kirshner and Bobby Darin. Gentlemen, this is Concetta Franconero, otherwise known as Connie Francis."

At this point in her career, Connie Francis had not yet met with any success. Her first No. 1 record, "Who's Sorry Now," wouldn't be recorded until nearly two years later. I tried several contacts in an effort to interview Connie, who as of this writing is still performing, but I kept striking out. Then I struck gold.

I found an e-mail listing for Mike Church, her former manager, and sent him a friendly note explaining the book I planned to write and my eagerness to interview his one-time client. To my surprise, he wrote back swiftly and included her home and office numbers.

When I reached Connie by phone at her Florida home, there was no mistaking that voice: warm and sweet. She was happy to talk to me, and didn't hold back. She was so intent on getting the dialogue right from her first meeting with Don and Bobby that she read it out loud to me directly from her autobiography, Who's Sorry Now. *As she spoke about them, you could hear that she still held a soft spot in her heart for these two. It was the first of two conversations I enjoyed with her. Here's how she described it:*

Kirshner stepped forward and shook her hand. Darin just nodded coolly. Connie and Bobby immediately looked each other over. There was an instant attraction.

Scheck interceded: "They've got a song that might be right for you."

Don jumped right in. "Oh, Miss Francis, I loved your last record. Really wonderful! I loved that part about . . ."

Francis shot him a sarcastic look that read: *If you liked it, you must've been the only one.* Despite getting some airplay, it was another bomb; her third in a row. The look didn't deter Don, however.

"He complemented me profusely," she wrote in her 1984 autobiography, "and asked so many interested, ingratiating questions about my lackluster career that it became embarrassing."

Bobby seemed put off by the small talk. "Look, lady. Do you wanna listen to a hit, or not?"

"I'm dyin' for a hit," she shot back.

"Join the club. I dig."

"You do? For what company?"

"Is this lady a gas, Kirsh?" Bobby said, turning to Don. "What I meant is, like I'm hip, lady. Like I know where you're coming from."

"How?" she asked with a half smile. "I never met you before, have I? How'd you know I come from Belleville [New Jersey]?"

"Aw, this is too much, Kirsh. Tell me she's puttin' us on, will you?" said Bobby, frustrated. "Belleville, huh. Don't you mean Squaresville?"

Despite the back and forth antagonism, Connie squeezed next to Bobby on the piano bench and scanned the lead sheet of the song they brought her, "My First Real Love."

"I sing this one in A," she said to Bobby, in an effort to get on with the reason they were there. "Can you transpose?" This set Bobby off again.

"You want the key of A, lady," he said to her. "You've got A. You want H, you got that too."

There was something about Connie's no-nonsense attitude that immediately got to Bobby. At first she irritated him, but then the way she knew what she wanted and didn't back down awakened something in him. When she sang "My First Real Love" that morning, she found herself singing it to him. As he played the song for her, his expression went from rude and offensive to tender and adorable.

Connie instantly warmed and her face lit up as she sang the song. There was no doubt she was smitten too. She pretty much sang it flawlessly on her first try, then took the lead sheet and made a few notes on it.

"Now with these changes," she said, "it's not that bad. Let's try it again." The comment instantly set him off again.

"This is all I wrote, lady, " Bobby huffed. "Take it or leave it," He grabbed the lead sheet out of her hands and headed toward the door.

"Bobby, I think maybe you should apologize to Miss Francis," Don pleaded. Darin stopped and turned long enough to say, "No, *you* apologize to Miss Francis, Kirsh. I'm splittin'."

Kirshner turned to Scheck and Connie and said, "Don't worry, we'll make those changes," as he ran out the door after his partner.

Despite the friction between them—maybe because of it—Bobby and Connie had an undeniable spark between them. It didn't take long for them to patch things up and start dating. She fell instantly in love with Bobby, as just about everyone who knew him did, one way or another.

"My whole life revolved around Bobby," she wrote in her autobiography. "Everything he did, everything he said; every dream he dreamed for him and for me. I existed for those few magic moments when we could be together."

But "being together" wasn't that easy. They were forced to see each other secretly because Connie's overly protective father didn't want her dating a struggling songwriter. Often they'd sneak over to East Orange, New Jersey, to watch Kirshner lead the Upsala College basketball team. A superb athlete, Kirshner originally won a basketball scholarship to Seton Hall University, but felt out of place there.

"I think I was the only Jewish kid there," he told Darin. "I went there with my little cardboard suitcase, and everything was the Father, the Son, and the Holy Ghost. It wasn't a coed school—no girls—so I said, 'What am I doing here?'" It didn't take him long before he had a scholarship at Upsala and became captain of the team.

Bobby and Don often wrote together at Upsala College, where Don captained the basketball team. This was taken in the spring of 1956.

• • •

George Scheck, on the other hand, couldn't get Darin out of his mind. He was impressed with Darin's talent and performing skills and offered to manage his career too. Connie agreed to record Don and Bobby's song and invited Bobby to sit in on drums during the session and sing backup. They all had a good time and high hopes.

Unfortunately, "My First Real Love" failed to provide the breakthrough all three of them were looking for. MGM released it, but it failed to make the charts.

But Scheck (who is the father of Barry Scheck, one of the defense attorneys at the famous O. J. Simpson trial) hadn't lost faith in Bobby's talent. Within a month he sent Bobby to Decca Records, one of the biggest labels in the country at the time, for a tryout. Decca would sign him, which should have been thrilling news, but Bobby wasn't quite ready to celebrate. He had a bad feeling about the deal.

"They won't let me record our songs," he told Don. "And all they want me to sing are these jive numbers that make me sound like Perry Como." Still, although it wasn't exactly what he wanted, Bobby went through with the deal and stuck it out for a year.

During that year with Decca, Scheck kept pushing Don and Bobby's songs. Some of them included titles like "Keep-a-Movin' Momma," "Bubble Gum Pop," "Cute Little Ways," and "Love Me Right." He placed several with established recording artists like the Coasters and Laverne Baker, but none became hits. When you're a struggling songwriter and you're told that stars like Laverne Baker and the Coasters are going to be recording your songs, it's got to be a big high. But a few weeks later when the DJs aren't playing your tunes, you couldn't feel any more disappointed.

Don and Bobby kept making the rounds of everybody in the music scene. Most found them amusing, if not talented. Disc jockeys Bruce Morrow, known on the air as "Cousin Brucie," and Murray "The K" Kaufman at WINS were regular stops. As was Alan Freed at WABC, and Ira Howard, the man in charge of the pop charts at *Cashbox Magazine*. By this time, even though they hadn't broken through, they were so well liked around town everyone seemed to want to adopt them. And it appeared obvious to just about everyone that Darin's talent would eventually find the right home.

One night, while hanging out at Murray Kaufman's apartment, Bobby sat at the piano making up one quick comical tune after another. He excused himself to go to the bathroom just as Kaufman's mother telephoned.

"What are you doing?" she asked her son. When he told her about Bobby's silly songs, she said, "Why doesn't Bobby write something about taking a bath?"

• • •

In the '50s, *Cashbox Magazine* held more clout than *Billboard,* and for Ira Howard writing the pop music column for *Cashbox* gave him prominence and power. He suggested the red bullet that appeared next to records on the rise, leading to the phrase "going up with a bullet." He also was the first music writer to use the terms *rockabilly* and *bubble gum* to describe distinctive types of music. Yes, Ira Howard was big, and invitations to private parties honoring television and recording stars were always on his desk.

Songwriter Jack Keller influenced me to try and find Ira Howard, after describing how close a relationship Howard had with Don and Bobby for several years: "They were like three peas in a pod," Keller said. Using an online listing service called switchboard.com I was able to track Howard down in 2005.

"*Cashbox* in those days was like Grand Central Station for the music industry. Everybody used to come up there," Howard recalled. "I was sitting in the office one day in '57, when Don and Bobby came by for the first time. We started schmoozing and we sort of became quick friends. They were guys that you take to. They had electric personalities. People were drawn to them."

Of the three, Howard was the one with an income, so he didn't mind chauffeuring Don and Bobby around or paying the cab fare when they went out. Then one day he saw Bobby perform for the first time and he was stunned.

"We were at a poker game in a small office where Donnie was making $45 a week writing lyrics for publisher Al Lewis," said Howard. "At that game there was an upright piano against the wall. Every now and then Bobby would sit down and just make up new song after new song on the spot. I remember thinking to myself, *what a fantastic talent!*"

It wasn't meant to be for Darin at Decca. A big label, they had little interest in rock and roll, and when Bobby failed to get anything on the charts, they released him from his contract. But it turned out to have been a blessing. Almost immediately afterward, Herb Abramson from Atlantic Records decided to sign him. Atlantic was a label with nearly all black artists which specialized in R & B. In fact, that same year Jerry Wexler, originator of the term *rhythm and blues*, left *Billboard* to become a partner at Atlantic. They hoped Bobby would be the next Elvis—another white singer who sounded black. That combination held tremendous commercial appeal at a time when white kids were first beginning to listen to R & B.

It marked the launching of a career for Bobby, and a painful turning point for Don. If Bobby became a star, Don began to realize, he might be left out in the cold. He knew that for himself, publishing was where the money was. It was a good fit for him. He knew what he was great at—mostly having the chutzpah to sell himself—and he was aware of his limitations. "I knew Bobby was the one with the talent."

Certain that Bobby was now on his way, Don began to scramble. He cornered Jerry Leiber and Mike Stoller, the deans of rock and roll, coming out of Atlantic Records on West 57th Street. The two men were already famous songwriters. They had written "Hound Dog" as well as "Yakety Yak" and "Charlie Brown." Now they were producers and publishing their own songs.

Don introduced himself. He was so eager and spoke so fast, reciting nearly every song the pair had ever written or produced, that they agreed to give him a half-hour tutorial on the art of music publishing. The classroom? The Carnegie Deli, around the corner on 7th

Avenue. The delicatessen was legendary for its enormous sandwiches named after entertainment legends like Milton Berle and Jimmy Durante, but not for its décor or service.

Bare brick walls without decoration kept the place noisy, and the surly waiters always acted as if they were doing you a favor. But the corned beef and pastrami were another story.

Leiber and Stoller took to Don and were glad to show him the ropes. First the financials: when a record company records a song, it must pay the publisher and the songwriter one cent each for every copy sold. If your song sold a million copies both the songwriter and the song publisher would each receive a $10,000 royalty. In 1957, when $100 a week take home pay ($5,200 per year) was considered a "comfortable" living, writing a few hit songs wasn't a bad way to bring home the bacon. Multiply that by ten or twenty and a publisher can live quite nicely.

"We sat down and talked over a corned beef sandwich and a cup of coffee," recalled Leiber. "He asked some intelligent questions, like how do you copyright a song, and we told him about it. I said, 'Starting a song publishing firm isn't that difficult. Finding the right material to publish, is.' Don told me, 'Don't worry. I know where to find the material.'"

● ● ●

After several failed attempts with Bobby's recordings, Atlantic too was about to give him his release. Then one of the founders, Ahmet Ertegun, heard Bobby play a song in the hall outside his office.

I was a rollin' and a strollin', reelin' with the feelin',
Moving and a groovin', splishin' and a splashin', yeah!

"We knew Bobby was talented," Ertegun told me by phone in 2006, "but we just couldn't find the right thing for him. Then I heard him play this tune on a piano in the hallway."

Ertegun arranged for one last recording session. On April 10,

1958, Bobby Darin recorded "Splish Splash," with Ertegun producing the session.

In order to simulate the sound of dripping water, sound engineer Tom Dowd started the recording off by rapidly clicking his index finger against a Dixie cup. Dowd was maybe the most famous sound engineer in Atlantic's storied history and one of the first to ever use eight-track recording techniques. His little trick with the Dixie cup got Bobby's song started perfectly. When Darin finished, Wexler called down to Dowd.

"Master that baby," Wexler said.

"But it's not ready to be mastered," said Dowd.

"I don't care what it is. Get it out! It's a hit!"

After three years of pounding on doors, Bobby Darin had finally made it. Ironically, the song that made him a star was written without Kirshner. He had written it alone, after coming out of Murray "The K"'s bathroom, thanks to Murray's mother's suggestion.

Don began to worry, and with good reason. Soon after "Splish Splash" took off, Atlantic pressured Bobby to get more professional management than his pal Kirshner. Fortunately, Don saw it coming. After years of struggling with Darin, Kirshner knew that door was closing fast.

While that door was closing, Don created a new opportunity, enlisting the help of his friend Ira Howard from *Cashbox*. Don had casually met a producer for RCA named Al Nevins several times. He was thought to be one of the sharpest men in the music industry. They had first met at a *Billboard* party, and when Don realized that Nevins was the man who wrote "Twilight Time," a ballad that had been popular during the World War II years, he made sure to introduce himself.

At forty-one, Nevins had done it all. Fifteen years earlier, in 1943, he formed a trio called the Three Suns, which had met with tremendous success in the forties and fifties. At first Nevins only played the viola in the trio, but then he taught himself the guitar, which became an important part of their recordings. They became recording stars; they played nightclubs, and also had a national radio show on NBC.

The *New York Times* wrote a glowing feature on the boys. During their nightclub stints, soldiers returning from the war would often ask them to play their great World War II ballad "Twilight Time."

A weak heart had limited Al's performing, but he continued to produce the Three Suns' albums for RCA. Rumor had it that he was interested in song publishing too. That's what attracted Don.

Knowing he would need a powerful man to make an introduction if Nevins was to take him seriously, Don asked Ira Howard to meet him in the bar of a little Chinese restaurant at 54th and Broadway, next to the Ed Sullivan Theater.

It was four in the afternoon and the restaurant was very quiet.

"Ira," Don began, "Atlantic is trying to get between Bobby and me. And if that happens, I've got nothing." He wiped away a tear. Don was never afraid to show his emotions.

"I've never seen you look so sad! How can I help you?"

"I've got to get a meeting with Al Nevins," said Don. "I know he'll go for my idea of a rock-and-roll publishing firm. I've just got to get him to sit down and listen."

"Donnie, I don't know Nevins. I've never met him."

"You had enough juice to get somebody on the cover of *Cashbox*," Don said. "You must be influential enough to get Nevins's attention. Please. Call him for me. He'll take your call."

There was a long pause as Howard reflected.

"Please."

Howard called Nevins and told him that Don was well respected and that the best young songwriters on the street gravitated to him. He also said that Don had a brilliant approach to publishing rock and roll.

"He discovered Bobby Darin," Howard pointed out, "and helped to put him over."

On the strength of that recommendation, Nevins agreed to a meeting that would change the face of pop music forever.

2

On Broadway

Don was early for his meeting with Al Nevins as he got off the subway at Broadway and 50th Street. He climbed up the two flights of stairs to the street and was met with the sights of Times Square.

On one side of Broadway, the sign for the Hotel Astor caught his eye in the shape of a backward numeral 7, hanging from the top of the building. The word *Astor* dripped down along the side. On the other side he noticed that *Bridge on the River Kwai* was playing at the State Theater. A little farther down Broadway, smoke rings from the Camel cigarette billboard disappeared into the sky above the intersection where 47th Street meets Broadway and 7th Avenue.

He stopped for a moment on the west side of Broadway at 1619, between 49th and 50th, watching people going through the big brass doors of this Art Deco building. It was the Brill Building. A chill ran through his body as he remembered the many long days he and Bobby spent trying to sell their songs there.

Walking a little farther up Broadway, he stopped at 1650, on the corner of 51st Street. Al Nevins had a small office there. A huge billboard on the side of the 1650 building read: *The Best Known Address in the Entertainment World.*

Don knew there was merit to that claim. During the forties and fifties, Irving Berlin, one of the greatest songwriters who ever lived, had once occupied the corner offices on the second floor at 1650. It had floor-to-ceiling windows overlooking the Winter Garden Theatre, which was right next door.

Presently occupying Berlin's old office was Mitch Miller, the head of A & R—Artists and Repertoire—for Columbia Records. Current public opinion held that Miller was the most powerful man in the record industry. Oh, how Don wished he could meet Mr. Miller and pitch some ideas to him.

The marquis at the Winter Garden trumpeted that *West Side Story* was playing. In the preceding years, the *Ziegfeld Follies,* featuring stars like Al Jolson and Gypsy Rose Lee, played there.

Now Don stepped inside 1650 and took the elevator up to one of the top floors. Being in that familiar environment would help calm him down for his meeting with Nevins. Cigar smoke hung in the hallways. He could hear songwriters pitching their new tunes through the air vents above the frosted doors. *Ah, the good old days,* he thought, or bad, as the case may be.

In either 1650 or the Brill Building at 1619 Broadway, you could write a song, hawk it to a publisher, cut a demo, and sell it to a record company without ever leaving the building. Both buildings were music industry anchors. Anyone who was anyone in the music business had an address at either 1619 or 1650 Broadway. In the thirties and forties, some fly-by-night publishers would even make up business cards with one of those addresses, even though they didn't actually rent space there. They'd simply use the lobby as their office.

If you were a teenage songwriter, there was some hope for you at these two buildings, but not much. Since all sorts of riffraff circulated through the building, both legitimately and not, the security guards never stopped the teenagers from trolling from floor to floor trying to sell their songs. Getting someone to hear them was their next hurdle, and if some publisher or kind assistant was generous enough to do that, there was an even bigger hurdle ahead: getting them to actually buy the song, then have it recorded by an artist and actually played on the radio. These seemed like insurmountable steps to these kids.

Rock and roll was making inroads, however, at both places.

The new songs couldn't be stopped—songs like the Everly Brothers' "Wake Up Little Susie," fourteen-year-old Paul Anka's blockbuster "Diana," and the Penguins' classic teenage anthem "Earth Angel." But the old Tin Pan Alley songwriters were still hanging in strong.

The Tin Pan Alley period originated around 1885, when a group of songwriters and music publishers set up shop on West 28th Street in Manhattan. Legend has it that the group got its name from neighbors complaining that the constant banging on pianos sounded more like the banging of tin pans. In the '30s, the core group moved to the Brill Building and hung on into the '50s, when rock and roll would eventually take over.

When he thought about the recent hits put out by those Tin Pan Alley songwriters, Don shook his head and cringed. They were songs like "How Much Is That Doggie in the Window," "The Ballad of Davy Crockett," "Dance with Me Henry" . . . they were corny enough to make a teenager sick.

Don looked at his watch. Almost time for his all-important meeting. He took the elevator down. Going through the lobby, he glanced at the tenant list and found three record labels that catered to teenagers. George Goldner owned two of them: End Records and Gone Records. Also there was Florence Greenberg's Tiara Records. Don knew that Goldner, who'd discovered Frankie Lyman and the Teenagers, had a new group under contract—Little Anthony and the Imperials. Now Florence Greenberg was putting together a group of all girls and calling it the Shirelles. Rock and roll was in the door, and Don smiled at that thought.

● ● ●

"This is one of my favorite lunch spots," Al Nevins said. "It's quiet, and the food is very good."

It's also very expensive, Don thought, looking at the House of Chan's menu. He hoped Nevins planned to pay. He glanced around the room at the starched white linen tablecloths. On the tables were decorated plates.

Nevins ordered for both of them, and then looked up as the waiter poured tea. "So, Don, your friend Ira Howard tells me you're interested in starting a song publishing firm with me."

Don felt the need to clear his throat. He took a sip of water. "Yes, that's what I've been thinking."

Nevins looked vaguely amused. "Why do you think we should do this together?"

Don took a deep breath and then began. "Because you've got the know-how, and I've got the feel." Now that he was talking, he relaxed. This was the most important meeting of his life, and he had to come across as confident, maybe even a little brash.

He leaned forward. "Listen, Al, when I was younger I thought I'd be hitting cleanup for the Dodgers. I was good but not good enough."

Nevins' mouth twitched at the word _younger_.

"Then I found Darin. I thought we'd be the greatest songwriting team in history. In the last three years I've knocked on every door in town, trying to sell our songs. I know every secretary in the Brill Building by her first name and how she likes her coffee. I also know there are some great young songwriters walking the halls of that building who aren't being heard."

"Why is that?" Nevins seemed intrigued. Kirshner hardly missed a beat in answering.

"The hall on each floor of the Brill Building was our office. We would bring our brown bags, eat lunch on the ground hunched up against the wall, and talk about our songs. No matter how good you were—the odds were a hundred to one against you. If you were an aspiring songwriter, you couldn't sell a song to a record company unless it was published. You couldn't get it published unless you got in to see the publisher and you couldn't get in without an appointment. For the most part, publishers only gave appointments to established songwriters, so for the kids writing rock and roll, it's one big frustrating vicious circle."

Don took a couple of deep breaths and quickly downed a glass of water. He saw Nevins' expression change. He looked interested and nodded encouragement. Now he was ready to fire another shot.

"I've got the pulse on the teen idols, and I know what teen romance is all about. I've got the instinct for what kids want. Music is changing, and I think you know it. Rock and roll is coming in and it's coming in big, and no one has a strictly rock-and-roll publishing firm. All the good young writers would flock to us. The middle-aged songwriters from Tin Pan Alley can't give the kids what they want."

Don looked at Nevins closely, hoping his remark about "middle-aged" hadn't put him off. He seemed okay, though.

"They're writing stuff like 'The Yellow Rose of Texas,'" Don said. "Give me a break." Don knew the days were numbered for the established publishers. He saw the window of opportunity and was about to throw it wide open.

The waiter came with a tray. While he set out the bowl of steaming white rice and the food in metal dishes that Nevins had ordered, Don took a deep breath. They couldn't have been more opposite. Don knew he was brusque and to the point. Nevins seemed cool and reminded him of Cary Grant. At about five foot ten, Nevins had the appearance of someone who visited the gym regularly, and his dark eyes and perfectly groomed short dark hair won over many a lady during his performing days. He was dressed elegantly and had an expensive haircut. Dressed in a button-down white shirt and his best slacks from Sears, Don didn't want to think about his own appearance.

He'd heard that Al lived on Sutton Place—a ritzy address far from the streets of the Bronx where Don grew up. And the man looked like he'd just come back from Vegas or Florida, with a deep, healthy tan. It was April, for God's sakes. Don looked down at the pasty white hands in his lap.

The waiter removed the metal covers from the serving platters with a flourish, and Nevins nodded his go-ahead to the man to serve lunch: lo mein with chicken and cashews. Don waited politely until Nevins had taken his first bite before digging into the chicken. He hoped he would be able to eat.

"I like your determination," Nevins said. "And your passion for rock and roll."

"Thanks."

"I'm really not too interested in rock and roll," he continued.

Don's heart sank, and he put down his fork.

"It's not my world," Nevins said, and shrugged.

"Well, I—"

"I come from the nightclub scene, you understand." He twirled the lo mein on his fork. "But I'm smart enough to know that rock and roll is an art form that is beginning to take hold in our industry."

Our industry? Don thought, and took a sip of hot tea. He worked to keep his expression neutral.

"Of course I'm aware of artists like Elvis, Little Richard, and Chuck Berry," Nevins went on. "I think they represent where the business is headed."

"Right! And just think of the potential audience out there—"

"Yes, and I'm confident, from what I hear that you can do what you say and deliver the talent," Nevins said.

He reached across the table and offered his hand for a shake. "What do you think about putting our first names together and calling our company Aldon Music? It will only cost $50 each to take out a license."

Don felt a flush of happiness redden his face. "I like it very much. And I promise you'll never regret this."

In truth, Nevins didn't have a lot to lose. He was intrigued with the idea of publishing and more intrigued with the niche of rock and roll that Kirshner knew so well. What could it cost him to do this—the $50 a week he'd pay Don until it worked out or didn't? If it worked, he'd be a player on a much bigger scale in the business. If it didn't, he was owed a very big favor from Ira Howard, one of the most influential people in the record business. So on the first week of April 1958, Aldon Music was born.

● ● ●

Don wiped the barbecue sauce off his hands and wrists. He and Bobby Darin and their friend Dick Lord were gnawing on spareribs at Duffy's on 47th Street, in a booth in the back of the restaurant. A red and white checkerboard tablecloth covered every tabletop.

"You must be really hungry," Don told Bobby. "You've hardly said a word since the food arrived."

Bobby pushed his plate aside. He glanced at Dick, and then looked back at Don. "Listen. I . . . Atlantic . . ."

"What?"

"They're pressuring me to get a new manager," Bobby said at last.

Don couldn't believe what he was hearing, even though deep down he'd known this was coming. "But I'm your manager! We've been in this together since that day at Natalie's house!"

Things got very quiet.

"They want me to get with someone who's full-time, who's been in the business a long time." Bobby spread his greasy hands, palms up. "I'm sorry."

Don got emotional. A tear trickled down his face. "Have I ever let you down?"

"No, Donnie, of course not. This isn't what I want. Believe me."

After a few awkward, silent moments, Don pulled himself together. "Okay. If that's how it has to be, then you have to do it."

"Kirsh, I promise, I'll find a way to make up for all the years we wrote together." He shook his head. "Our friendship is a forever thing. I hope this won't—"

"No, it's cool, Bobby."

Don wasn't hungry anymore, but he picked up a rib and ripped into it as a way to quell the awkwardness. *This is awful,* he thought. He and Bobby had been fighting battles together from the beginning. *Now Bobby has finally won the war and look what happens. He fires me.*

Almost as bad was the threat it posed to his brand-new arrangement with Al Nevins. Don had used the management deal he had with Bobby as leverage when the Aldon partnership was formed. Al even arranged for the "business" to pay Don $50 a week until some royalties started coming in. Now Don had nothing to bring to the table but predictions and promises. How would Al take the news? Would he say their deal was off?

A few weeks later Bobby showed up at the Aldon office unexpectedly. He was going to fix the problem by making them an offer they couldn't refuse. As he walked in he found Don rearranging some chairs. Bobby instinctively sat down at the piano and started tinkering.

"Hey, Kirsh, where's your new partner?"

"Over at RCA working on the next Three Suns' album."

"Hey," said Darin, "did you see in the paper that the First Lady, Mamie Eisenhower, said the Three Suns were her favorite group." With that they both shared a laugh. It was a good way to break the ice.

"Yeah, I saw it in the *Post*," Don shot back. "Can you imagine what she'd think if she heard Little Richard sing 'Tutti Frutti'?"

After another laugh, Bobby paused then got down to business.

"You guys are in the song publishing business, right? Well, Atlantic says you can't be my managers, but they could never object to you publishing my songs. So I've decided to give Aldon Music fifty percent of the publishing rights to my next three hits."

Don's eyes lit up. "That's unbelievable, Bobby," he said, and thought about how pleased Al would be when he found out. "Got anything in the hopper ready to record?"

"There's a couple that are pretty groovy coming up. They're called 'Queen of the Hop' and 'Dream Lover.'" Then Bobby spun around and sang "Dream Lover" for his buddy Kirsh as if he were performing at the Copacabana nightclub.

> *Every night I hope and pray*
> *A dream lover will come my way*
> *A girl to hold in my arms*
> *And know the magic of her charms*
> *'Cause I want (yeah, yeah)*
> *A girl (yeah, yeah)*
> *To call (yeah, yeah)*
> *My own,*
> *I want a dream lover so I don't have to dream alone.*

Kirshner was truly blown away. He slumped down in his chair, wiped the sweat off of his forehead and said, "Wow, wait till Al hears this."

In the dozens of times I interviewed Don Kirshner for this book, he was never more emotional than when discussing his close relationship with Bobby Darin. Their friendship lasted into infinity. Bobby was the best man at Don's wedding in 1959, and vice versa a year later. And several years after Darin's unexpected death from heart failure, Kirshner named his only daughter Daryn after him.

"Queen of the Hop" and "Dream Lover" put Aldon on the publishing map. They were giant hits. "Queen of the Hop" was first, and reached No. 9. Then Darin struck with "Dream Lover," which hit the top spot in England and reached No. 2 in the States. Now all of a sudden Aldon Music was a name people in the business were associating with hit songs.

● ● ●

On April 7, 1958, the same week Al and Don became partners, Nevins' standard from his nightclub days, "Twilight Time," hit the charts again. This time it was a recording by the Platters, a group managed by Buck Ram, who had originally written the lyrics to go with Nevins' melody. Two weeks later, "Twilight Time" was No. 1 on both *Cashbox* and *Billboard.*

But it almost never happened. The label wanted to push the other side, a forgettable gospel number, and had booked the group to sing it on *American Bandstand.* When Buck Ram got wind of it, he had his assistant, Jean Bennett, call Dick Clark at his home on City Line Ave. in Philly. She begged Clark to let them do "Twilight Time" instead and got him to listen to a minute of the song over the phone. "Okay," said Clark. "'Twilight Time' it is."

Don still remembers the impact this milestone had on him. One evening that April, while getting a quick bite at Hansen's Drug Store, he was listening to his transistor radio while waiting for his food to arrive. He was at his usual spot, all the way down the long, long row of counter seats. He had the radio tuned to 1010 on the AM dial. It was WINS, the station that lured Alan Freed from Cleveland, the man who coined the phrase *rock and roll.*

At that particular moment at Hansen's, Don was listening to Cousin Brucie's early evening show, when Morrow made an announcement that sent chills down his spine:

"Okay, cousins," Morrow began. "It's now time for, yes, the No. 1 song in the land! Get ready to snuggle and hug, because this is one of the ultimate make-out songs of all time. Remember I warned you. Here are the Platters."

Then he whispered, "Shhhh, it's 'Twilight Time.'"

"Twilight Time" was one of Don's favorite songs, and as a kid growing up, acts like the Platters were gods to him. He also loved their previous No. 1 hit, "Smoke Gets in Your Eyes."

"I was so proud of Al that night," Don remembered. "The Platters' success with 'Twilight Time' was a great omen for us. I would call around and say, 'My partner, Al Nevins—he wrote 'Twilight Time,' No. 1 for the Platters . . . ,' and then I would go into my pitch."

Don was right—it was a great omen for them. Now all they needed was a talented unknown kid like Neil Sedaka to knock on their door.

The Hungry Years

"Neee-illl, Fat Howie from upstairs wants to see you." Ronnie Sedaka giggled as she passed her brother on his way to the front door.

Howard Greenfield did not want to be paying this call in 1952, but his mother had insisted. She'd heard little Neil Sedaka playing the piano at a Catskill resort over the summer, and she thought Howie and he should meet.

Now, he looked down at Neil, who was five feet three inches and three years his junior. Howie, sixteen, towered over him by nine inches. "My mother says you're a pianist," Howie began. "I'm a poet. Maybe we should write songs together."

In 2005, I caught up with Neil Sedaka and got him to tell me this story and many others. It wasn't easy getting to him. My first lead came from a woman named Laura Pinto, who managed the websites for songwriter Jeff Barry and several other performers from the '60s. Barry put me in touch with Laura, who in turn put me in touch with Sarah Goldstein, who helped manage Neil's publishing business.

I sent Sarah an e-mail introducing myself and requesting help obtaining an interview with Neil. She wrote back quickly and explained that he was in Australia on tour, and it would be difficult to find time due to his busy schedule when he returned to the States. At that point I picked up the phone and called her. I explained how important it was and how central Neil was to the story.

"I'll ask," she said, "but I certainly can't promise anything."

Two months later, I was starting to get worried that I might never get the Sedaka interview. By then I had been able to interview many of the key players. There'd be a big hole, though, without Neil. So I wrote Sarah Goldstein another note:

Dear Sarah:

Yesterday I spoke with Don Kirshner. I've also interviewed Gerry Goffin, Jack Keller, Ron Dante, Artie Kaplan, and others who shared those early days at Aldon Music. It's all coming together, but I need to talk to Neil. If I can talk to Neil—for even the briefest time—it would be a tremendous help.

Yours Truly,
Rich Podolsky

I was discouraged when I didn't hear back from her for a while. Then one afternoon, about a week later, the phone rang. The voice was unmistakable. My heart nearly jumped out of my chest. "This is Neil Sedaka," he said. "Is this Rich?" I took a deep breath and tried hard to tone down my excitement.

Fortunately for me, Neil was in a great mood and wanted to talk about the old days. He remembered everything as if it had just happened yesterday: details, conversations, everything. I felt enormously lucky to have been sitting in my office when the phone rang. Even though he started out the conversation telling me he only had fifteen minutes, we wound up speaking for over an hour and covered a lot of ground. One of the stories he told me was about that fateful day when Greenfield first knocked on his door.

Neil did not invite Howie inside the Brighton Beach, Brooklyn, apartment. "I don't want to write songs," he told him. "I don't know how. I'm going to be a concert pianist."

Howie already knew that Neil taught piano for $2.50 an hour and was on scholarship for Juilliard's Saturday classes. Howie had heard strains of Bach and Chopin filter into the building's hallways from the apartment. Although he had shed his baby fat, Howie was painfully reminded that he was fat when he was younger, and that other kids in the building, including Neil's sister, had made fun of him.

"Yeah, well, songwriting is kind of fun. Why don't I come inside, and we can try it. Then you can decide."

The thirteen-year-old reluctantly opened the door, and they went to the Sedakas' upright piano. By the end of that day in October 1952, they had written a horrible song called "My Life's Devotion" and recorded it on a wire recorder Howie had brought with him. Neil called their efforts "a ruptured rumba" but was thrilled to have been able to create something out of nothing. He was hooked.

The boys' friendship blossomed, and they went on to write a song a day for five hundred days, mostly when Mrs. Sedaka went shopping, because she was horrified that her little boy wasn't practicing his Juilliard assignments.

Neil welcomed the friendship at a time when he was having difficulty socially at school. Neil was a perfect bull's-eye for the older boys at school who combed their hair greased back in ducktails and wore black leather jackets. They hung out in the backroom of a sweet shop across from Lincoln High School and blocked Neil, who was short and skinny, from playing the jukebox. Neil was a gentle kid who would rather practice his piano than play stickball with the other kids, which made him an easy target for the bullies.

After more than two years of writing songs with Howie, in 1955 he worked up the nerve to audition for the Lincoln High School Ballyhoo Variety Show. He played the piano, and a drummer and saxophone player backed him up. He sang an original song he and Howie had written called "Mr. Moon"—bump-and-grind rock and roll.

Rock and roll was in its infancy on the radio, just catching on with teenagers, and when he sang it in the Lincoln High School auditorium, the audience went wild. It was a huge turning point for Neil. Having been somewhat shy his whole life, he suddenly felt as if he had won the state football championship.

The triumph was short-lived. Principal Abraham Lass called Neil into his office. "I cannot have you play that outrageous song in the second show," Lass told him. "I will not tolerate that kind of reaction among the students here."

But word of Neil's performance had already spread through the hallways, and Lass' decision did not sit well with the student body. The teenagers were incensed, and their hunger for rock and roll couldn't be abated. They signed a petition that insisted Neil play "Mr. Moon" again. It worked, and he played the talent show to a second enthralled audience.

Now that he was a big shot at Lincoln High, Neil had the confidence to start his own group. He invited a classmate he had met in chorus, Jay Siegel, and his friend Hank Meddress to be part of his group. He also invited Cynthia Zolotin, a girl with a great voice. They became the Linc-Tones, and they practiced after school. Neil played the old upright piano and recorded everything they sang. There were a lot of singing groups around at the time, but no one else's repertoire included originals.

"We're going to sing our own songs," Neil told them. "Someday we'll hear them on the radio."

Neil Sedaka's Linc-Tones had played a few gigs. They sang at high school dances and even appeared on the local television show *Dance Time* to perform a few of Neil's and Howie Greenfield's original songs after one of the producers had heard them perform at the Brighton Beach Jewish Community Center.

Jay Siegel, didn't share Neil's optimism about their future.

"I never seriously thought that anything would come of it," said Siegel, who a few years later with Meddress and two others recorded "The Lion Sleeps Tonight."

"We came from a middle-class neighborhood. Neil's father was a taxi driver. My dad worked in a sweatshop as a furrier in New York City. Nobody I knew had a job they enjoyed. Everybody looked forward to Fridays and hated Mondays. For us to say that making music could earn us a living was way beyond our comprehension, because that was too much of a joy to do."

But Neil did not share his doubts. He knew that he and his pals were in the right place at the right time. When Elvis' two-sided monster "Don't Be Cruel" and "Hound Dog" each rose to No. 1, rock and roll's future was solidified.

His Linc-Tones were sounding better than ever, thanks to a new friend, Carol Klein, who went to nearby Madison High School. She was so passionate about making music her profession, she'd already picked out her stage name—Carole King. Neil and Howie and Jay and Hank would go to Carole's house sometimes after school and rehearse in her basement.

Fifteen-year-old Carole taught them very sophisticated harmonies. She'd teach them one part at a time, and then they'd put it all together. Her musical skills were much more advanced than most of theirs, and she was a great piano player. Neil was not easily impressed, but he was with Carole.

They talked about starting a group together, but Neil, Howie, Jay, and Hank had to take a bus to get to the Klein house, which was fifteen minutes away from where they lived in Brighton Beach. It was just too far away to make that kind of commitment.

The distance didn't bother Neil, though. From time to time, he and Carole would meet on the street corners and at the beach to sing the hits of the day. Once, they were sharing a pie at Andrea's Pizza Parlor and singing "Earth Angel" between slices. While they did become close friends for a while, it is unlikely that they actually dated as Neil has suggested.

He knew Carole would make it. He thought his group would make it too. Then one day it seemed like it was going to happen in a flash. Someone knew a manager who knew the guy who owned a local Brooklyn record label, Melba Records. They had heard Neil's group sing on the local TV show *Startime* and wanted them to record three of Neil and Howie's songs, but the manager, a guy named Happy Goday, insisted that they change their name from the Linc-Tones to the Tokens, which they agreed to. Neil wasn't too excited about the deal, partly because it didn't come through him and partly because he had barely heard of Melba Records.

Nevertheless, they recorded "While I Dream," "Right or Wrong," and "Everybody Knows." The songs got some local play but not much beyond that. With the deal depending on record sales for the group to get compensated, Neil barely received a stipend for the use of his material.

Meanwhile, Neil and Howie and Carole continued writing. Then one day Sedaka found out that the Clovers, one of their favorite groups, were recording a new album for Atlantic Records. The Clovers, in 1956, were one of the most successful doo-wop groups under contract. Between '51 and '59, they would have twenty-one of their records hit the charts, including "Devil or Angel" and their most famous, "Love Potion No. 9."

Without thinking twice, Neil and Howie took the A train into Manhattan. They got off at Columbus Circle and walked to 57th Street and 8th Avenue, where Atlantic was located. They knocked on the front door. It was locked. No one was in sight.

Neil wouldn't give up. He banged on the door. Finally someone opened it.

"Can I help you?" the man asked, looking down at Neil.

"Yes. Are the Clovers recording here today?"

"Why do you want to know?"

"Because we wrote a song for them."

The man laughed. "Come on in, boys. You've got chutzpah."

He opened the door wide and let Neil and Howie inside. "My name's Jerry Wexler. So you've written a song for the Clovers, huh? Okay, let's hear what you've got."

After they played a few of their original compositions, Wexler was intrigued. "You have a feel for what I want," he said, "but your talent is still pretty raw. You show promise, though." He looked at Neil. "I like you, but you'll never make it as a singer. Your voice is too high."

The chutzpah paid off. A few weeks later, the connection they made with Wexler that day yielded Neil and Howie's first sales to a major label. Wexler bought some of their rhythm and blues numbers for Clyde McPhatter, Laverne Baker, the Clovers and the Cardinals. Neil and Howie couldn't have been more thrilled. They celebrated by going home and writing some more songs specifically written for Atlantic's artists.

Within a month, while still riding high on their sales to Atlantic, Neil and Howie decided to try the Brill Building and to 1650 Broadway. They went from door to door and from floor to floor, hitting up more than thirty publishers that day. But they couldn't interest any of them in their songs. The decision-makers were still from the old Tin Pan Alley days and didn't recognize the power of the new music.

These publishers lunched at Jack Dempsey's restaurant, on the ground floor of the Brill Building, and reminisced about vaudeville.

That was fun for them. Meeting with some snot-nosed songwriters was not.

The boys were not easily discouraged, though. They decided to see if they could get an appointment at Hill and Range, famous for being Elvis' publishers, located on one of the top floors of the Brill Building.

At both 1619 and 1650 Broadway, Neil and Howie and other teenage songwriters trolled the halls, hoping some publisher would let them present their songs. Running into other young songwriters in the corridors was commonplace. They listened to each other's songs and bucked each other up. Sometimes that wasn't easy. They all knew the facts: publishers gave appointments only to established songwriters, so for the kids writing rock and roll, with rare exceptions, it was practically a no-win situation.

When the teenagers entered the Brill Building, they walked the length of a very long corridor to get to the elevators. The way back to the lobby door was always tough after an afternoon of rejections. They'd be stopped by their friends outside and asked, "Is anyone buying?"

But this time was different. Neil was thrilled. He managed to get an appointment with Paul Case at Hill and Range, when the secretary was impressed with their recent sales to Atlantic. As they walked down Broadway before the meeting, they passed by Lindy's, world famous for its cheesecake, and saw Jimmy the Greek's photo in the window. New York's best bookmakers hung out at Lindy's, forever immortalized by Frank Loesser's musical *Guys and Dolls*. Ten years earlier, the Greek was simply known as Jimmy Synodinos, a twenty-nine-year-old gambler from Steubenville. Then he placed a $10,000 bet with a bookmaker at Lindy's, predicting that Harry Truman would get re-elected. At 17-1 odds he won $170,000 and became forever known as Jimmy the Greek.

An hour later, though, neither Neil nor Howie was in the mood for cheesecake. Case had turned down all five songs they played for him, including "Stupid Cupid." They were devastated.

As they left the Hill and Range offices, they ran into a couple of other songwriters they knew, Mort Shuman and Doc Pomus, sitting on the floor with their lunch bags. Pomus' crutches were on the floor next to him—he had been stricken with polio as a kid. Ironically, for a man who couldn't walk, he would soon write the lyrics to the rock-and-roll classic "Save the Last Dance for Me."

Neil and Mort had gone to Lincoln High together. He told Mort and Doc what happened with Paul Case.

"Too bad, buddy," Mort said. "But if you're not in a hurry, a new publishing firm is opening just down the block at 1650."

The chill of being rejected by Hill and Range still stung but Neil and Howie were desperate for a chance, and so they headed right down to Aldon Music. When they opened the door, they saw a closet-size office with boxes all over the floor and two desks pushed together in the middle of the room. Shoved against the wall was an upright piano. To Neil, Aldon looked to have been in business only a couple of days, and the office wasn't ready yet for walk-ins.

"We'd like to see the publisher," Neil asked a young guy with his sleeves rolled up. He was sweeping the floor.

The guy leaned on his broom. "We're in conference. Come back in an hour."

They agreed, and as they walked down the hallway Neil muttered to Howie, "I think the conference is, "How are we going to pay for this office.""

Don put the broom in a small closet and rolled down his sleeves. "They should be back soon," he told Al, and buttoned his cuffs. A little while later there was a knock at the door.

"It's open," Don called, and the two kids came inside.

Words rushed from the short one's mouth as if he were a door-to-door salesman who might get the boot any second.

"I'm Neil Sedaka and this is Howard Greenfield. I study at Juilliard. We've been writing together for five years and have had several songs published and recorded."

"Like what?" Al wanted to know.

"Well, we've sold several R & B songs to Atlantic for Clyde McPhatter, Laverne Baker, and the Clovers," Neil replied.

"And just recently Dinah Washington came out with our song 'Never Again,'" Howie added.

Al shot a look at Don that said, *I find that hard to believe.* "Really?" he asked.

Don jumped in. They'd find out in a minute whether the boys had something to offer. He pointed to the upright in the corner. "Okay, let's hear what you've got."

Neil took his place behind the piano and positioned the chair so he was half sitting, half standing. It reminded Don of how Bobby had played the first time they were at Natalie's place.

Neil played a few songs, which Don thought were good. When the kid was a few bars into the next one, "Stupid Cupid," the bell went off in Don's head. Neil banged out the notes in a rousing rendition of a song Don instantly knew teenagers would love. And he knew just the person to record it.

Stupid Cupid you're a real mean guy,
I'd like to clip your wings so you can't fly . . .

Hey, hey, set me free,
Stupid Cupid stop pickin' on me.

Don looked at Al to see his reaction, but his partner did not look happy.

"Where'd you get those songs?" Al demanded.

"What do you mean?" Neil asked. He looked shocked as he turned to face the challenge. "We wrote them, that's where. We've written over five hundred songs in the last three years. If you don't believe me, you can ask Ahmet Ertegun and Jerry Wexler."

"Excuse us for a moment," Don said. He was totally blown away. Ertegun was a founder of Atlantic Records and Wexler was one of his partners.

While Neil and Howie waited by the piano, Don pulled Al aside. "Did you hear that song, Al?" Don whispered. "That song's a hit! This is exactly the kind of talent I knew was out there. Did you ever see such talent? I can't believe nobody's signed them."

"Even if they did write those songs," Nevins said, then paused and glanced over. "Just look at them. They look like *pishers.*"

"I don't care what they look like," Don whispered urgently. "We need to sign them."

Al's eyes narrowed for a moment. He was silent. "Okay," he said at last, "but this is your deal, not mine."

"Fine. This is what I told you I'd do for you. You won't be sorry."

They strolled back to the boys standing beside the piano.

"We think you've really got something," Don said, "and we want to sign you to write exclusively for Aldon Music. We'll give you each fifty dollars a week against future royalties. We'll publish your songs and help get them placed."

Howie was about to say something, but Neil put a hand on his friend's arm and looked around at the boxes and the dust. Don could see the kid was skeptical.

"You get us a hit and then we'll sign."

"I'll get you that hit," Don promised. "Come back here in a couple of days. I want to introduce you to an old friend of mine. Her name is Connie Francis."

Stupid Cupid

Maybe it's something in the stars or perhaps the alignment of the planets. On the twelfth day of any given December, the forces seem to come together to birth remarkable singers. Frank Sinatra was born on December 12, 1915. Joe Williams on the same day in 1918. Dionne Warwick in 1940. Tim Hasse of Manhattan Transfer in 1941, Mike Pinder of the Moody Blues in 1942, and Dickey Betts of the Allman Brothers in 1943.

And on December 12, 1938, Concetta Franconero was born. The daughter of George and Ida Franconero, she was four years old when her parents gave her an accordion as a birthday gift. Her first success was on George Scheck's *Star Time*, a local New York talent show, in 1947. It was Scheck who later became her manager.

At the tender age of ten, still singing and playing her accordion, she won the *Arthur Godfrey Talent Scouts* competition on national TV. At Godfrey's urging, she changed her last name to Francis. Despite this dazzling start, for the next ten years her career seemed to be going nowhere.

George Franconero, though, was a very persuasive man. A roofing contractor by trade in the tough town of Newark, New Jersey, Franconero somehow persuaded MGM Records to sign his daughter. Her contract included creative control, which was unheard of for an unknown. Maybe George Franconero made MGM an offer they couldn't refuse. A few years later, with the aid of a shotgun, he made Connie's lover, Bobby Darin, an offer he also couldn't refuse.

For two years, Connie Francis recorded one failure after another. She even recorded the song Don and Bobby brought her, "My First

Real Love," without success. When they met in January 1956, she told them she was "dying for a hit." She wasn't just kidding.

By late '57, she was about to give up and take a job as a secretary in her aunt's steno pool, when her father persuaded her to record an old favorite of his from 1923. It was "Who's Sorry Now," a song she hated and was very reluctant to sing—especially on what was to be her final recording session. She was so reluctant she saved it for last in the session, hoping time would run out. When twenty minutes of the session remained unused, Francis recorded the song in just one take.

That was October 1957. MGM released the song, but Connie disliked it so much she refused to travel to Philadelphia to promote it. And like her eight previous releases, it died on the vine. But MGM's Philly distributor had a different idea. He sent it to Dick Clark, host of every teenager's favorite show, *American Bandstand*.

Connie was celebrating New Year's Day 1958 at home with her family in Belleville, New Jersey. At 4 p.m. she went into another room and turned on *Bandstand* on their sixteen-inch black-and-white Motorola TV. Dick Clark was introducing a new number.

"This song is by a new girl singer who's headed straight for the No. 1 spot," Clark proclaimed. Much to her shock, it was "Who's Sorry Now." Connie Francis became a star overnight. The success and publicity drew a call from the *Jackie Gleason Show*.

George Franconero thought he had broken up the romance between Bobby and Connie, but they continued to see each other secretly. Finding that it became too difficult to continue a secret relationship, they finally threw in the towel, but when Bobby found out Connie would be performing on the Gleason show, he rushed down to the theater during rehearsals to see her one more time.

Once together it was like they were never apart. Suddenly, from the back of the theater, Connie's father came running up the aisle, shotgun in hand. Bobby quickly jumped out of her arms and down the opposite side of the theater. In one row and out the other, Franconero chased Bobby, shouting at him and flailing his rifle the entire time. When Bobby made it to the hall, he couldn't find an exit, so he ran into the men's room. To his good fortune, the bathroom had a large, wide window, which Darin lifted open and jumped out of. Since they were on the first floor, the fall was only a few feet. But the experience was enough to keep Bobby away from Connie. For Connie, it was a traumatic event. She later would refer to Bobby as "my one and only true love."

Bobby and Connie together (with Ed Sullivan) during happier times. Notice Sullivan's dangling cigarette ash. Years later he died from lung cancer.

From the time they first met, Don and Connie remained close. He may have been Darin's partner, but he was able to maintain his own relationship with Connie, albeit as friends. Connie would come to Don's basketball games when he captained the team at Upsala College, and when Connie's fan mail became overwhelming, Don got her an assistant she could count on.

In early May 1958, with her secretarial career on hold thanks to "Who's Sorry Now" and just before Neil and Howie walked into Aldon Music, Francis released her next song. It was another ballad, chosen by her father, even older than "Who's Sorry Now." This one, a No. 1 hit in 1918, was called "I'm Sorry I Made You Cry." Connie's version, however, barely cracked the Top 40, and died at No. 36. After that she was determined to pick her next song. That's when Don called to tell her about these two amazing kids he had just met.

"I want you to meet these two young songwriters," Don told her. "I think you'll love them."

"I haven't got time. I have to go to the hairdresser."

"We'll meet you there," he quickly replied. She agreed, and when he hung up the phone, he turned to Sedaka, who was sitting next to him. Kirshner lit up with a big smile and said, "Bub, we've got a date to meet a lady."

It didn't matter if you were male or female, teenage or senior, a delivery boy or a cleaning lady; Kirshner called everybody "Bub." It would be, "Bub, you got a second? Bub, tell me if you like this song." Or, "Bub, let's meet for lunch at the Turf."

For a guy in the music business, Kirshner was a straight arrow. He not only didn't smoke or drink, he didn't drive either. So he ordered a car to take him, Sedaka, and Greenfield to meet Connie in New Jersey.

After a traffic-snarled trip from Manhattan through the Lincoln Tunnel into New Jersey, Kirshner's limo arrived outside of Bamberger's in Newark at the corner of Broad and Halsey. It was one of those scorching hot July days and the boys were glad the driver kept the engine running with the air-conditioner on.

After waiting fifteen minutes, Don decided to investigate. He tiptoed into the front door of the hairdresser's, half embarrassed because he had never set foot in a beauty parlor before. When he returned he informed Neil and Howie of the news. "Connie's appointment is running a little late. She'll be at least another half hour."

Sedaka and Greenfield groaned in unison, then decided to get out of the car despite the heat and sit on a nearby stoop in the shade. With temperatures into the 90s, they were soon back inside the car, which was forced to circle the block several times because of the parking regulations.

After another half hour, Don decided to check on Connie again. This time when he came out she was only a step behind and kept pace despite her six-inch heels. Without asking, she ducked into the front seat, carefully making sure her hair was not disturbed, while Don squeezed into the backseat with the boys.

Concetta Franconero had classic Italian features, including long, beautiful pitch-black hair. If you didn't know she was from Jersey, you'd probably guess South Philly. She just had that Italian South Philly look.

After losing nearly all his money on a rotten business venture, George Franconero was forced to move the family to a run-down rented house on Brookdale Avenue in Newark. And even though Connie had had a big hit, royalties weren't coming in yet.

As they walked into Connie's house, the boys couldn't help but notice that there weren't any rugs and that the radiators were exposed. The place looked depressing. Connie saw Neil shoot a look over at Howie, and thought to herself: *What did you expect? Tara?*

After a while, Kirshner had to return to his office, leaving Sedaka and Greenfield behind to play their songs for Francis, whose mom kept nagging them to eat. "Are you hungry, are you hungry? You look like you're starving. Eat something!" she begged them.

Kirshner wanted them to play "Stupid Cupid" for her, but the boys were set on trying to find a match for her big hit "Who's Sorry Now," so Neil started playing one slow song after another.

"You must have played me every ballad you ever wrote," Connie told them after an hour had gone by. "Look, fellas, I don't know how to tell you this, but I don't think you're going to make it in this business."

She was bored and began writing in her diary. The encounter was depressing Sedaka. While he played and tried to engage her, she spent time on the phone and made various trips to the bathroom.

Turning to Howie he said, "Maybe we should play 'Stupid Cupid.'"

Greenfield adamantly disagreed. "'Stupid Cupid,' that's not her style. You can't do that. Besides, it's not ethical. We promised it to the Kalin Twins."

The Kalin Twins were no run-of-the-mill recording act. They had recently recorded a catchy tune called "When," which in fact had reached No. 5 on the charts that very week.

"Well, we're with Connie Francis now," Sedaka said, "and we're losing her. I'm going to play it."

When she returned, he sat down and banged out the first eight bars, starting with a jazzy, upbeat riff. She lit up with excitement and stopped him in mid-song.

"'Stupid Cupid'! What a smash!" Francis excitedly declared. "You guys have my next record!"

Before she agreed to record "Stupid Cupid," her father talked Kirshner and Nevins into splitting the publishing fees on any Aldon Music song she recorded for a period of one year. Although it was an unusual arrangement, for Al and Don the deal made sense. Aldon was a fledgling publisher and Francis was an established star.

By the time they left Connie's house that day, she and Howie had bonded like girlfriends. He started kidding her about the diary she was writing in so secretly, and he tried to get a peek at it.

Connie Francis gives an alluring look as she glances back over her shoulder while getting ready to record "Stupid Cupid."

"No, that's why I have a lock and key," Connie told him. "No one looks into my diary!"

When he left that night, he left with two things: a care package of sandwiches from Mrs. Franconero and an idea for a new song. As the car made its way back to Brooklyn, Greenfield wrote down these words:

How I'd like to look, into that little book,
The one that has the lock and key.
And know the boy that you care for,
The boy who's in your di-a-ry . . .

Sedaka, Greenfield, Nevins, and Kirshner were all confident that "The Diary" would be a hit. Don had the perfect group to place it with, Little Anthony and the Imperials. In September 1958, the group's "Tears on My Pillow" reached No. 4 on *Billboard*. It was a slow, haunting story song, much like "The Diary."

The Imperials recorded for George Goldner's End label, located a few floors above Aldon at 1650 Broadway. Goldner had a reputation for picking hits, then gambling his profits away. When he had a big loss, it usually meant handing over his record company to the bookies. Each time he lost big, he simply started a new label.

In 1948, at the age of twenty, Goldner started the Tico record label and discovered Latin sensation Tito Puente. In 1953, he began an R & B label he called Rama and struck gold with the Crows and the early rock-and-roll doo-wop classic "Gee." In early '56 after losing Rama, he hit again. On his new Gee label, named for the hit song, Frankie Lymon and the Teenagers recorded "Why Do Fools Fall in Love." When forced to sell both Rama and Gee, Goldner rebounded by starting two more recording labels, End and Gone.

Jerry Leiber had tremendous respect for both Kirshner and Goldner because of something they had in common. "Don Kirshner and George Goldner had the two best commercial ears in the business," said Leiber, "because they both had the mind and the heart of a fourteen-year-old girl. That's why they could pick hits, especially romantic ones. They were pretty much infallible."

Leiber clearly remembers a time when Goldner's talent bailed out Leiber's own Redbird Records, which had hit a very bad business streak. At the time Redbird had ample record stock—eighteen master recordings—but Leiber knew the next one chosen for release would be critical to his company's survival, and didn't know which one to choose.

"We were in trouble," Leiber recalled. "We knew how to write songs and how to produce records, but we didn't know how to promote them. We were just about out of gas and I went to this spot we used to hang out at, Al and Dick's on 55th Street, and ran into Goldner at the bar." Goldner was out of a job. He had already lost four record labels at the track, and had just lost his fifth and last when he ran into Leiber.

Leiber told Goldner how confused they were at Redbird about which record to release next, and how crucial that decision was. If Leiber agreed to give him a piece of the business, Goldner said he would listen all night in their office and give them the winner in the morning.

"So I give him the keys and I go over the next morning at 11 o'clock," said Leiber. "He's sitting upright at my desk and he's holding up this acetate [record] in his hand, and he says, 'On my mother's grave. This is the one.'"

And then he played it. It was an unknown group called the Dixie Cups, singing, *"Goin' to chapel and we're gonna get married."*

"GEORGE!" Leiber pleaded. "Take it off! I HATE that fucking record!"

"Who's picking the record, you or me?" Goldner asked.

"I guess you are," Leiber said.

"Then you better let me do it," said Goldner. "I don't give a shit what it is. But I'll tell you this. It's a fuckin' hit!"

Leiber and Stoller released it on the Redbird label, and within a month it was No. 1.

• • •

While running End and Gone in 1958, Goldner was headquartered at 1650 Broadway. He loved Kirshner's enthusiasm and thought Sedaka and Greenfield had great promise. After hearing Neil's demo, he agreed that "The Diary" was a perfect follow-up for Little Anthony and the Imperials.

Busy trying to sign new talent, Goldner had someone else produce Little Anthony's version of Neil's song. But when Goldner played it for him, Neil cringed.

"It's awful, you can't release this," Neil said, not realizing he might be insulting Goldner. "Why didn't they just do it the way I laid it out on the demo?"

"Yes, I have to agree," said Goldner. "It's not in the right tempo. Your demo is much better. Why don't you record it yourself?"

Goldner's golden ear told him that Little Anthony's recording of the song was dead on arrival. So, armed with the success of "Stupid Cupid," Neil went back to Nevins and Kirshner.

"All they had to do was record it just like I sang it on the demo," Sedaka complained. "I'm tired of giving these songs to people who screw them up," he told them. "I'd like to sing them myself. Can you get me a record deal?"

They agreed and thought it was worth taking a chance. Nevins then arranged an audition with RCA. Al had a great relationship with RCA's A & R man, Steve Sholes, from Al's days producing the Three Suns' albums for the label. Neil was more nervous than ever as he prepared to meet Sholes. *This guy just signed Elvis,* he thought to himself, *and now I'm auditioning for him!*

They walked down Broadway to Sholes' office. Neil could feel goose pimples all over as they strolled down the street. He hadn't felt an energy run through his body like this since he first sang before the entire student body at the Lincoln High Ballyhoo. When they arrived Neil was stunned by Sholes' appearance. He weighed about 300 pounds. After introductions Neil finally sat down, took a deep breath, and played "The Diary" for him. And then he waited. It was only about ten seconds before Sholes responded, but it seemed like ten hours.

Sholes leaned forward as Neil, Al, and Don anxiously waited for his answer. "Yes, we'll sign you," Sholes finally said, and then he cracked a huge smile and shook everyone's hand. "It's a great love song that every teen can identify with."

Before recording "The Diary," Neil was helping Connie rehearse for her recording of "Stupid Cupid," when arranger Chuck Sagle overheard him.

"Hey, you sing pretty good," Sagle told him. "You ought to record yourself." Sagle's opinion held merit because he had been the producer of an already classic rock-and-roll song, "Little Darlin,'" by the Diamonds.

Neil told him that he indeed was about to record, and asked Sagle if he'd also arrange for him. Sagle agreed and worked with Neil through his first few hits—until he was named head of A & R for Epic Records, which was owned by CBS.

Neil's first recording session for "The Diary" sounded a little too polished, so Nevins booked another session the next day, and that did the trick. And when RCA pulled some strings and had Neil introduce the song on *Bandstand,* he became an instant celebrity.

> *When it's late at night,*
> *What is the name you write,*
> *Oh, what I'd give if I could see.*
> *Am I the boy that you care for?*
> *The boy who's in your diary.*

"'The Diary' went to No. 14 on *Billboard* and the Top 10 on *Cashbox* and I was over the moon," said Sedaka. It sold over 600,000 records, sending Neil out to buy his first car, a white-on-white Chevy Impala convertible. In 1958 a Chevy Impala convertible was *the* car. It was the epitome of cool.

"I'd drive down Kings Highway (in Brooklyn) and I'd set every button on the radio to a rock-and-roll station," Neil recalled. "I could switch stations with the press of a button and sometimes I'd hear my record on three different stations, one after the other. Hearing my songs on the radio—what else was there to life?"

If Neil was over the moon, Don and Al certainly were too. Not only did they have a Top 15 song with Connie Francis, but they also had a Top 15 song with their own artist, Neil Sedaka, who *they* were producing for RCA.

As 1959 approached, things couldn't have looked any better. It was a special New Year's Eve for nineteen-year-old Neil and his girlfriend, Leba Strasberg. They celebrated at Nevins' penthouse apartment on the corner of East 57th Street and Sutton Place.

Kirshner (left) and Nevins celebrate Neil's success with "The Diary."

Nevins' penthouse apartment was straight out of the movies. Built within a Chinese pagoda that he had constructed on the roof, it was lavishly decorated in an ornate Oriental motif, with the walls and ceilings painted black. Chinese dividers separated the spaces, and each piece of the black ebonized lacquer furniture was finished in Chinoiserie detail. In the kitchen, rows of polished copper pots and utensils hung from custom racks—all complimenting the spotless serving areas from where Nevins' Asian houseboy prepared and served the drinks. Outside the pagoda apartment, on the private terrace, was a large fishpond that complemented the Asian design. From there, guests could relax near the water while enjoying breathtaking views over the East River and the 59th Street Bridge, which connects the borough of Queens to Manhattan.

In the living room, Don introduced his girlfriend, Sheila Grod, to Howie and the other guests. Neil was serenading Leba from the piano—a job he had grown accustomed to. He had met Leba while singing at the Esther Manor Hotel in the Catskills, which was owned by Leba's parents.

While the guests enjoyed the upbeat mood of New Year's Eve, in the kitchen only Nevin's houseboy heard the radio news broadcast: "Fidel Castro and armed Cuban rebels have taken over Havana. Dictator Juan Batista has fled the country."

Sedaka didn't realize it, but like Batista, his career was about to take a dramatic turn.

Twilight Time

Some would say Al Nevins was put on earth for two reasons: first, to write the beloved World War II standard "Twilight Time," and second, to give Don Kirshner the platform to change the face of pop music.

But there was a lot more to Al Nevins than that. He conceived, managed, and played with the Three Suns, an incredibly successful trio that starred on radio, records, in films, and nightclubs throughout the '40s and '50s. He also helped propel the careers of arrangers Buck Ram and Sid Ramin, among others. And he was generous to a fault. If Al Nevins was your friend, you didn't need any others.

Nevins was born on September 1, 1916, the son of immigrant Russian Jewish parents, Samuel and Celia Tepper. Albert and his younger brother, Morty, were born in Washington, D.C., before the family moved to Brooklyn in 1920. As a child, Al had to fight two enemies: rheumatic fever and a stuttering problem. He worked hard and beat his battle with stuttering, but never overcame the limitations of a weak rheumatic heart.

As children, both Al and Morty learned the piano. Later Al moved to the violin and viola while Morty learned the accordion. To support himself, Al played in the pit for several Broadway shows.

In 1938, at the age of twenty-two, Al, Morty, and cousin Artie Dunn formed a group they called the Three Suns. Al and Morty borrowed another cousin's last name, Nevins, to replace their given name, Tepper. Knowing a viola wasn't going to work in a trio, Al started taking guitar lessons from Charlie Macey, the best guitar man in New York. Their sound was a unique one for a trio, combining a guitar with an accordion and an organ.

They began with appearances in Buffalo, Albany, and Pittsburgh, followed by a stint at the Adelphia Hotel in Philadelphia. It was at the Adelphia, in 1944, that Al got the telegram he had been waiting six years for; they were finally going back to New York. They were booked for two months at the Circus Bar of the Hotel Piccadilly on 45th Street. Two months turned into a seven-year stay. It was during their run at the Piccadilly that the Three Suns became famous. A large sign in the hotel's window announced them:

After seven years on the road, the Three Suns returned to New York as headliners.

The Circus Bar became one of New York's most popular night-clubs. In the mid-'40s, they started doing a late-night (12:30 a.m.) radio show three nights a week for WNBC Radio that was broadcast nationally. Because of their popularity, a recording career ensued.

In 1944, they wrote and recorded "Twilight Time," one of only six songs the trio had ever published. Al and Morty wrote the music, but neither bothered with a lyric. Enter Buck Ram.

Born in Chicago in 1907, Samuel "Buck" Ram grew up listening to the choirs and gospel music at a local black church. Always wanting to write music, Ram was sidetracked when his parents insisted he study law. While away at college, he wrote his mother a poem, which Bing Crosby later turned into one of the most popular songs of the era, "I'll Be Home for Christmas."

After getting his degree, Ram moved to New York and started writing and arranging music for the big bands. He felt very comfortable around the clubs in Harlem, and in the 1930s and 1940s he scored shows at the Savoy and arranged music for some of the greats, including Duke Ellington, Glen Miller, Cab Calloway, Benny Goodman, and Count Basie. He also did some arranging for the Three Suns, and when he came across their haunting melody, he started to scratch out these words:

Heavenly shades of night are falling
It's twilight time
Out of the mist your voice is calling
It's twilight time . . .

"Twilight Time" became the Three Suns' first big hit in 1944. It rose to No. 14 on the charts and has never stopped being played or recorded by other bands and singers, including Doris Day. In 1946, songs by the Three Suns reached the Top 10 twice. In 1947, they signed with RCA Victor, their first major record label. RCA had them cover the Harmonicats' version of the 1918 hit "Peg o' My Heart." It became their only No. 1 song.

On March 2, 1947, the *New York Times* did a lengthy feature on the group, noting that they would be mobbed during breaks in their nightclub show by out-of-towners who had stayed up to listen to them on the radio. One fan was a marine from Toledo, Ohio, the article said, "who first heard the Suns on V-disk during the campaign in Iwo Jima. Now he wanted to see them—and would they please play 'Twilight Time.'"

The group became so popular that their album *Soft and Sweet* carried this line it its advertising: "The Three Suns have remained a part of us like Hot Dogs, Baseball and Grandma's treasured recipe for apple pie." It's no wonder they were First Lady Mamie Eisenhower's favorite group.

Arranger Sid Ramin said Al Nevins was meticulous about sound quality, especially when the Three Suns recorded for RCA. "On many of the recordings, Al did not play, he just sang," Ramin told me after I located him in Manhattan. "He hired George Barnes to play guitar for him in the studio," Ramin recalled. "George was a wonderful guitarist. The unfortunate part was George would do things on

A 1946 menu from the Three Suns' stint at the Hotel Piccadilly; clockwise from top: Morty, Al, and Artie.

the recording, and when the boys were playing live, the audience had expected to hear the things George had done, and Al was not that good. We used to have a good laugh about that."

They also shared the special burden of a speech impediment. Nevins had learned to control his own stuttering, and he helped his friend do the same. "He stuttered a little bit and I stuttered a lot," said Ramin. "He was very simpatico for me. He would try to tell me how to control my stuttering. We'd talk about it all the time. He was a great, great friend."

At five foot ten inches with dark hair and eyes, Nevins was unmistakably handsome. He dressed impeccably. Said Jerry Leiber: "He was the best-looking, best-dressed bass player I ever saw. He looked like he just stepped out of *Gentleman's Quarterly*."

In 1954, Nevins was thirty-eight years old and his rheumatic heart started to worry him. He had already had a minor heart attack. Doctors told him to take it easy and limit his traveling. He would have to stop performing. He started to think about his next move. He would produce.

By 1956, Al Nevins was already well off. "Twilight Time" had been good to him. He was able to put his money away, and being single, he was able to save it. He had a magnificent apartment on the East Side at 57th Street and Sutton Place, with a Japanese houseboy, and by 1957, he had taken a very small office at 1650 Broadway, which he used as his production headquarters.

It was at this tiny little one-room office that Nevins would bring Kirshner in, and together they'd begin to change the future of pop music.

6

Oh! Carol/Oh, Neil

After that magical New Year's Eve at Nevins' place in 1958, Sedaka lost his touch as fast as Batista lost Havana. Just like that, he could no longer write a hit.

A sweet ballad that didn't sell called "I'm Crying My Heart Out for You" followed his debut hit, "The Diary." The next was a Jerry Lee Lewis–type rousing number called "I Go Ape." It was a semi-hit in England but a failure in the United States. With one flop after another, Sedaka's stock was sinking fast with RCA. They discussed dropping him. Dreading that fate, Sedaka ran to Nevins for help.

"Can you help me?" Sedaka pleaded. "Please see what you can do."

Nevins intervened, talking to the executives at RCA, and managed to get Sedaka a reprieve. But Kirshner was concerned about Neil's future beyond the temporary Band-Aid. For the first time, he offered Sedaka advice on what to write.

"Write a song with a girl's name in the title," Don suggested, "and talk in the middle like the Diamonds did in 'Little Darlin'."

In 1957, before Sedaka's arranger, Chuck Sagle, came to New York, Sagle had arranged and produced "Little Darlin'" in Chicago for Mercury Records. It was a spine-tingling, doo-wop version of Maurice Williams' original R & B recording. The song began with the driving beat of castanets followed by lead singer Dave Somerville's pleading voice.

Oh, little darlin'
Oh, little darlin'

Oh-oh-oh, where ar-are you
My love-ah
I was wrong-ah
To-oo try
To lo-ove two . . .

It became an instant rock-and-roll classic and an "oldies but goodies" standard. At Aldon, it was a running gag that every time Don would give someone advice, he inadvertently would wind up telling them to "Write something like 'Little Darlin'.'"

I caught up with Sagle on the phone one summer afternoon in 2005. Jack Keller mentioned that he thought Sagle still lived in Nashville and I was able to find his listed number there.

"Neil said, 'Let's do one like that,'" Sagle recalled. "So it turned out that the song that saved Neil's career, he wrote as a takeoff on 'Little Darlin'.'"

Sedaka doesn't quite recall it that way. He listened to Kirshner and Sagle, and then studied a page in *Billboard* magazine called The Hits of the World.

"I looked at the No. 1 record in every country of the world and analyzed it," Sedaka remembered. "And that's how Howie and I wrote "Oh! Carol." I took the beat, I took the drum licks, I took the guitar licks, I took the harmony changes, and I went to school on them. Howie wrote the lyric in twenty minutes but was embarrassed. He thought it was terrible. But it was exactly what I wanted."

What Greenfield thought that was "terrible" was his rhyming *fool* with *cruel* at the start of the song.

Oh, Carol, I am but a fool,
Darling, I love you, though you treat me cruel

"I know it's a shitty line," Greenfield cracked when asked about it, "but I can't change it, and I won't."

Following Kirshner's suggestion, Sedaka did arrange for a section in the middle of the song in which he talked, a la "Little Darlin'."

On cue Sedaka recited the words with the music behind him. Something felt off, so he did it again. He did take after take, but something about that part of the song just wasn't right. Everyone in the room realized it wasn't working. Fortunately Nevins, who was producing, was thinking fast that day.

He noticed a teacher and three high school chorus girls off to the side who were watching the session. The girls were actually a group called the Kittens, whom Sagle had invited that day. A light bulb went off in Nevins' head. He quickly turned to the girls and invited them to sing a falsetto background behind Neil's talking segment.

It turned out to have been a stroke of genius. The unplanned background vocals worked beautifully. "Oh! Carol" was an international hit, sold over four million copies, and became Neil's first Top 10 song. Kirshner celebrated by buying himself a new sport coat at Phil Kronfeld's men's store around the corner at 52nd and Broadway, next to Lindy's. Shopping at Kronfeld's would become a celebratory habit for Don in the coming years.

"Oh! Carol" debuted on October 12, 1959. The B side was called "One Way Ticket to the Blues," a song written by Jack Keller, an old friend and rival of Sedaka's from Brooklyn.

The two had known each other since 1956, when they played at the same dance at the Ocean Avenue Jewish Community Center in Brighton Beach, Brooklyn. At the time, they wagered on who would breakthrough first.

Keller won. His first hit song, "Just Between You and Me," by the Chordettes, reached No. 8 in September 1957. Neil didn't strike with a Top 20 song until "Stupid Cupid" debuted in August 1958. But Keller kept up with Sedaka's career, and when he bought a copy of "The Diary," he saw something new. A caricature of Sedaka's face was on the record label, an idea Kirshner suggested to RCA. He looked closer and read: *Produced by Nevins-Kirshner.*

"I figured if they could get Neil's picture on the label," said Keller, "that they were pretty powerful, and someone that I needed to meet."

It didn't take him long to find them. He inquired around through his Brill Building contacts and found out that Nevins and Kirshner's firm, Aldon Music, was located just down the block at 1650 Broadway. He walked in cold one day and asked the receptionist if he could meet with either Nevins or Kirshner.

"And who should I say is calling," she asked.

"Please tell them Jack Keller, the composer of 'Just Between You and Me.'" She asked him to wait while she disappeared. When she returned, she asked if he could meet with Mr. Kirshner and Mr. Nevins later that afternoon.

At that meeting Keller brought them a demo he had made of "One Way Ticket to the Blues"—a very catchy tune that cleverly weaved the titles of half a dozen former hits into its lyrics. Both Kirshner and Nevins flipped over the song and offered Keller a contract immediately.

When the single with "Oh! Carol" on one side and "One Way Ticket to the Blues" on the other was released, neither the publisher nor the record company could decide which side was the hit. "Donnie came to me and wanted to know which side to push," recalled *Cashbox Magazine*'s Ira Howard.

"RCA wanted to push 'One Way Ticket.' I told him 'Oh! Carol' was best for our market. It's funny, because "One Way Ticket to the Blues" turned out to be a huge record everywhere else in the world, and was No. 1 in Japan for months."

Howard's instinct was right on the money, though. "Oh! Carol" was a huge hit in this country and around the world. It stayed on the *Billboard* charts for eighteen weeks, peaking at No. 9. It not only saved Sedaka's recording career, it set everything in motion for Aldon's success. It also marked the beginning of a winning streak for Sedaka and Greenfield, who followed that international success with ten successive hits, an incredible run. They were:

"Stairway to Heaven"	No. 9	April 1960
"You Mean Everything to Me"	No. 17	August 1960
"Run Samson Run"	No. 28	August 1960
"Calendar Girl"	No. 4	January 1961
"Little Devil"	No. 11	May 1961
"Happy Birthday Sweet Sixteen"	No. 6	November 1961
"Breaking Up Is Hard to Do"	No. 1	July 1962
"Next Door to an Angel"	No. 5	October 1962
"Alice in Wonderland"	No. 17	February 1963
"Let's Go Steady Again"	No. 26	May 1963

For years rumors circulated that Sedaka wrote "Oh! Carol" about his friend Carole King—and that they had also dated. When I had the opportunity to interview him, I couldn't wait to ask if he had really written the song for her.

"Yes, I did," Sedaka insisted, although he was vague about whether they were ever officially an item. "It was a popular name, and we were so close. And Howie and I were the first to bring her up to meet Don at Aldon Music."

Chuck Sagle, who was both complimentary and critical of Sedaka, didn't remember it that way. In his recollection, he was the one who brought King to Aldon's attention. Shortly after "Oh! Carol" hit the charts, Kirshner got a call from Sagle, who had just been hired as the head of A & R for Epic Records.

He was calling about "Oh, Neil," an "answer song," literally responding to "Oh! Carol," written by Goffin and King, and performed by King. Sagle needed permission from the publisher of the original to put it out.

"Don, I've got this young singer-songwriter here you should meet," Sagle began. "She's written an answer record to 'Oh! Carol' called 'Oh, Neil.' Don, she's seventeen and her energy is amazing. And there's one other thing—she's seven months pregnant!"

● ● ●

One person who could certainly settle the score on who introduced Carole King to Aldon would be King herself. However, like many a writer before me, I was unable to land an interview with her. It wasn't for lack of trying.

When I began researching this book in 2004, I couldn't imagine that these legendary songwriters would object at all to having their stories told. I assumed they might in fact welcome the opportunity to have a part in telling them through my interviews. It seemed to me that for artists with such adoring audiences, whose lives had been written about so many times before, it wouldn't be a big deal to share some of their history with their fans, especially in their own words.

Most of the people I spoke to were in fact happy to open up. Others needed a little coaxing, and obliged, as if they were doing me a favor. One in particular, though, remained perfectly elusive. That would be Carole King.

I first tried to contact King by writing a formal letter to Christine Russell, who was listed as "manager" of CK Productions on the Carole King website. I requested an interview and I was willing to meet anywhere at any time. Phone would do too, although in person was preferred. A few weeks later, I received an e-mail from Russell instructing me: "If you want to interview Carole, contact Lorna Guess," whom she identified as King's road manager.

I was overjoyed by Russell's response. Since she made no bones about sharing the name of King's road manager, I took it that Russell had preapproved it. Of course, at that point, early in my research, I was completely unaware that as a general practice, Carole didn't do interviews, and that she had a long history of turning down such requests.

At the same time, I was still trying to nail down an interview time with Barry Mann and Cynthia Weil. I had been exchanging e-mails with Cynthia, who had given me some hope that eventually she and Barry would talk to me. I kept writing and asking if we could discuss a possible meeting over the phone, but she preferred to keep me at a distance. I felt that if she could hear my voice and how much I cared about their music, it would be hard to turn me down. But Cynthia only would correspond via e-mail.

From the very beginning Cynthia wanted to know which other Aldon song-writers I had interviewed. This seemed to be a prerequisite for her speaking with me. After nearly six months of day-to-day research and networking, I responded to Cynthia's original question with this bubbly, enthusiastic response:

"Since we last corresponded, I have interviewed Don Kirshner, Neil Sedaka, Gerry Goffin, Jack Keller, Jeff Barry, Connie Francis, and Tony Orlando, among others, and I plan to meet with Carole King when she comes to New York this July."

At that point, I honestly did expect to meet with King, especially after the success I was having getting in touch with everyone else. Many of them seemed so eager to have their stories told. I felt like I was on top of the world. So when Christine Russell wrote and instructed me to contact Lorna Guess, that's exactly what I did, expecting my efforts to result in an interview.

What I didn't know was that Cynthia Weil and Lorna Guess were close, through Cynthia's lifelong relationship with Carole. Cynthia apparently forwarded to Lorna a copy of my e-mail that said I was expecting to meet with Carole when she came to New York. A few days later, my phone rang and it was Lorna Guess.

Lorna immediately told me that there would be no interview with Carole, period.

"What do you mean?" I asked, totally stunned. She said that my e-mail suggesting Cynthia do an interview with me because I had one lined up with Carole was not true. I tried to explain the circumstances, that I thought I had reason to assume an interview was forthcoming, and that I meant no harm—certainly that I did not intend to pull a fast one on anyone. Lorna Guess was having none of it. There was nothing I could say to reverse the decision.

I immediately wrote Cynthia trying to explain the situation:

"I sincerely apologize if I misrepresented Carole's position. I expected to meet her this summer after getting Christine Russell's note. I meant no harm. I beg you to call anyone else on that list of people I've interviewed to confirm this, or I'll be glad to have them all write or call you to confirm that I've worked with them. Please, please call Jeff Barry or Neil or Jack Keller or Artie Kaplan or Artie Butler or Gerry Goffin and ask them about me. Unfortunately you contacted the one person where nothing was set yet."

I felt all along that if Cynthia had been willing to discuss the matter on the phone, the entire misunderstanding could have been avoided. Unfortunately she didn't call any of the songwriters I suggested to check me out. But she did send me back this short, cold note:

> *Barry and I are not available for an interview. If that should change*
> *I will contact you.*
>   *—Cynthia*

I wrote Lorna a similar letter of apology, trying for a Hail Mary to reverse her decision. Here is her e-mail response:

> *I am afraid that I still must decline the interview request. As you may know Carole seldom does interviews, and she has been earnestly writing her own book over the past year [2004, still unpublished as of 2011]. She does not feel an interview for your book is appropriate for her. I hope you will accept this reply as the final word, and know that we do not harbor any hard feelings with regard to our phone conversation.*
>   *Kind regards,*
>   *Lorna Guess*
>   *Artist Manager*
>   *CK Productions*

I'll admit I still harbored a hard feeling or two, after having been accused of misrepresenting myself. I'd been a working writer with a solid reputation throughout a thirty-year career. Being disparaged and discredited in that way hurt.

But while the incident shook me, I wasn't about to give up. The interviews with everyone else were going so well, that I decided to try to get to Carole another way. A good friend of mine in the entertainment business, Alan Frank, heard about my plight and offered to help. He told me he was a friend of Carole's daughter Sherry, who lived near him in Bedford, New York. He called and extolled my virtues to her, and she agreed to a phone conversation with me in February 2005.

Sherry couldn't have been any nicer. Sherry understood my plight and said she'd be glad to pass on a note to her mother. But she also cautioned me against holding out any hope. We agreed that I'd send the letter to Carole via e-mail through Sherry, who would forward it. In it I explained to Carole that Aldon Music—its founders, artists, and many hit songs—was the focus of the book.

I assured her that anything we talked about would relate to that. I also told her how much her music meant to me through the years.

On March 1, 2005, I hit "send." Sadly, I still haven't heard back.

While I didn't ever get to talk to Carole, I was fortunate to have been able to track down Goffin, her ex-husband and songwriting partner. Although the two divorced in 1970 after ten years of marriage, two daughters, and dozens of hit songs together, they remain fairly close. He was able to provide loads of interesting information about their life and work together.

I first tracked Goffin down through the Internet, actually finding his Beverly Hills address. I immediately wrote him a letter outlining my project and asking if we could speak. About a week later the phone rang and it was Gerry. He was happy to cooperate and especially wanted to talk about the great songs he and Carole had written together.

Although he was nearly seventy, he was still writing songs on a daily basis at the private studio in his Beverly Hills home. He spoke slowly and deliberately, always careful to state his facts correctly. Sometimes there were long pauses while he contemplated an answer. I appreciated that thoughtfulness.

Goffin revealed that he and Carole were working to put a show together featuring all the great songs they had written, both together and individually. He said he was especially proud of this. The show's tentative title was Some Kind of Wonderful. *The idea was to showcase their songs through the years, and string them together through a vehicle similar in structure to* Mamma Mia, *where the story takes you from one great song to another.*

Being unsuccessful in their attempt to reach Broadway with that show, Carole's team switched to a more personal story line. New York backers' auditions in May and November of 2011 were well received, according to the New York Post. *"Will You Love Me Tomorrow," Carole and Gerry's first No. 1 song, the* Post *reported, was the number that brought down the house. That song, however, was conspicuously missing from the 2011 Broadway show* Baby It's You, *highlighting the career of the Shirelles. The producers of that show stated that they were denied the right to use "Will You Love Me Tomorrow," which was the Shirelles' first huge success.*

In 2008, producers who tried to mount a Broadway musical based on Don Kirshner's life were also unable to secure the rights to early King and Goffin tunes written under Kirshner's guidance. On one hand, it's hard to believe that King would deny Kirshner—the man who discovered her, believed in her, carried her financially, and stuck with her through two years of flops before her first success. On the other hand, King had been planning her own show for years, and it's not difficult to understand that she would want control over how her songs were to be used.

• • •

I very much enjoyed talking with Goffin. He was very forthcoming and eager to chat. The first time we spoke, we started talking and two hours later we had only scratched the surface. I excused myself to attend our family dinner and promised to call him back. An hour later, the phone rang again and it was Gerry, wanting to talk some more. He was just as inquisitive as I was about how Don Kirshner, Jack Keller, and some others were doing, and thrilled by every detail I had to share with him.

We covered a lot of ground when we spoke. He went on and on, not only about the hit songs he wrote with Carole, but also several he wrote with Keller ("Run to Him," "Venus in Blue Jeans"). While reminiscing, Goffin blurted out, "I wish I could write with Jack [Keller] again. We wrote some great songs together."

I had spoken to Keller many times at that point, and was only too glad to pass along Gerry's wish. Within a week, Goffin and Keller were back on the phone. After thirty years apart, they renewed their songwriting partnership long distance. Jack would write a melody and then send it to Gerry by e-mail or FedEx and Goffin would work on the lyrics. I was thrilled to play a part in it.

And so it went with Gerry. He'd reminisce effortlessly, out loud, about certain times, both with and without Carole. He'd pick up the phone and call me as frequently as I would call him. Through it all he never had a bad word to say about Carole. The closest he ever came was when I relayed a story to him that Neil Sedaka's and Carole's high school friend Jay Siegel told me. Siegel said he had run into Carole at a Rock and Roll Hall of Fame event. Although they were old friends and had sung together in her basement in high school, she seemed distant. "Carole didn't want to talk about the sixties," Siegel told me.

When I told the story to Goffin, he said, "Carole doesn't want to talk about the sixties because she has Tapestry," *recorded in 1971, which has sold more than 25 million albums. But he left it at that. It should be noted that when Carole performed some of her early hits in concert recently, she was very generous about sharing credit with Goffin on those early songs.*

Gerry also tried, though unsuccessfully, to help me get an interview with Carole. He was, however, invaluable in helping me learn the story behind their writing partnership, how they met and married, and the story behind some of the greatest rock-and-roll songs ever written. And for that, I thank him.

● ● ●

Carole King was only fifteen when record executives began taking notice, but she'd been grooming herself for years, playing piano since she was four years old, and beginning to write songs not too long after that. As a teenager, after school she'd take the long subway ride from Brooklyn into Manhattan and knock on the doors of the record companies. It wasn't long before they fell for this little fireball and started buying her songs. Her talent was so infectious that not only did they want to own her songs for others to record—they wanted her to record them.

"I loved Carole's voice. You could pick it out instantly," said former Atlantic Records partner Jerry Wexler. Eager to sell her songs, she was professional and earnest, especially for a teen. "I remember when Carole first started coming around, she brought me a record she made for me to listen to. It was a 45 [rpm]. When I put it on my 45 turntable, it didn't track. She got so upset she started to cry."

In 1958, one of the doors Carole knocked on belonged to ABC-Paramount's Don Costa. After he met Carole, he fell in love with almost everything about her. Costa had been arranging and producing for Steve Lawrence and Eydie Gorme and also was working with Paul Anka, the big teenage star of the day whose song "Diana" topped the charts when he was just fourteen years old. When King played her songs for him, Costa thought he just might have found the female version of Anka. Carole and Gerry had written a song called "Goin' Wild," which Costa produced with Carole singing, and released it shortly thereafter. But once again, it didn't get the needed airplay and failed to hit the charts.

It was earlier in 1958 that she first met Gerry Goffin at the Queens

College lounge, where he was studying chemistry and she was studying to be a teacher. A mutual friend introduced them and Gerry liked what he saw right away.

Just sixteen years old at the time, Carole was five feet two inches and weighed about a hundred pounds. She was both tough and sweet, with medium-length, dirty blonde hair and blue eyes. Gerry was immediately attracted to her. She had a way of arching her eyebrow and smiling, without actually smiling. Even though she always dressed conservatively in a blouse and long skirt with bobby sox, there was definitely something sexy about her.

At age nineteen, Goffin was a very handsome kid—a slender five feet ten inches, with dark eyes, jet-black wavy hair, and a fiery temper. The attraction between him and Carole was mutual, but King initially wanted to keep things cool.

"I was a young horny kid and all I wanted to do was make love and write songs," Goffin said with a laugh. "When I first met Carole I told her, 'I'm going to make you within two weeks.' She said, 'You'll never do it.' It turned out that I won that bet.

"I wrote this little Broadway show called *Babes in Woods* and gave it to Carole so she would write the music to it. After she did, she said to me, 'Okay, now we have to write some rock and roll.'"

A sensitive, emotional kid, Goffin was naturally drawn to music. His parents had separated when he was five. "When they divorced it just about killed me," Goffin recalled, sighing deeply. Music eased the pain. He liked to listen to the classic pop singers of the day, like Perry Como and Eddie Fisher, and dreamed of someday making his own music.

"I wanted to be a songwriter since I was eight years old. A few years later I wrote my first song: 'Tell Me You're Mine Again,' which I wrote with Eddie Fisher in mind. I showed the lyrics to my father, and he said, 'You make me very proud.' That made my head swell."

Besides his good looks, there was another thing King liked about him—he showed immediate promise as a lyricist even though he didn't listen to much rock and roll. Although one of her former writing partners—namely Paul Simon—didn't seem to be as impressed with Goffin.

"Paul Simon went to the same school," Gerry said, "and they did a little writing together. Carole took me up to see Paul and he didn't like me too much." In his mind, it had to do with the fact that Gerry only wrote lyrics. "Some musicians are snobby about guys who just write lyrics." (Although down the line, Simon may have broadened his perspective). "I met him again years later and he was much nicer," Gerry recalled.

They began writing together almost immediately. Between writing songs and making out, they were nearly inseparable. One of the first songs they wrote together was "Short Mort," a parody of former Mousketeer Annette Funicello's hit "Tall Paul." RCA took a chance with it, recording Carole singing "Short Mort." But it wasn't a hit either.

In '59, Atlantic Records paid Goffin and King $25 for a tune called "The Kid Brother," which was recorded by Mickey Baker and Kitty Noble of the singing duo Mickey and Kitty.

"Carole's brother, Richard, used to torment us when we were trying to make out," Goffin remembered. "I'd have to give him a quarter to get him to go away. 'The Kid Brother' was a problem a lot of teenagers had. But I don't think the record was very good." "The Kid Brother" also failed to chart.

In fact, Carole's brother, Richard, was more than just your typical kid brother annoying his teenage sister. He was mentally challenged and only lived at home with the family on weekends, spending weekdays in a special home, Sheila Weller wrote in her 2008 book, *Girls Like Us*. It was a sensitive topic for the very private King. She rarely spoke of her brother. But it was obvious to Gerry that she loved him, and maybe writing a light little song about a kid brother helped ease the pain.

By the time Sedaka had a hit with "Oh! Carol" in the fall of '59, Goffin and King had begun to hone their writing skills. When they wrote "Oh, Neil," it led to a chance meeting with Kirshner that would change their lives.

● ● ●

Carole King was born Carol Klein on February 9, 1942, in Brooklyn.

She exhibited natural musical talent so young that she was practically a toddler when her parents let her take piano lessons. Writing songs naturally came next. By the time she was thirteen, she was staying up late every night listening to Alan Freed's *Moondog* show on 1010 WINS radio. Freed and his show were so popular that if teenagers could vote he would have been mayor. Before she turned fourteen, Carole had become an audience regular at Freed's rock-and-roll shows at the Brooklyn Paramount, which featured acts like Chuck Berry, Little Richard, and the Everly Brothers.

She knew what she wanted and it wasn't taking her long to get there. She began by changing her name, adding an *e* to Carol, giving her more individuality, and swapping her last name, Klein, for King. She chose it from the Brooklyn phonebook. She may have felt King was a more professional and less Jewish name to begin her career with—a name that blended more easily into the American fabric of the '50s. According to Goffin, her parents, who were divorced, weren't too crazy about this career she had planned. Her father, Sid Klein, was a retired fireman, and her mother, Eugenia, was a schoolteacher. Eugenia introduced Carole to both classical music and Broadway musicals, and composer Richard Rodgers became an early favorite. Although money was tight, her mom took Carole to Broadway whenever she could get tickets and played the cast albums of some of the great shows at home, like those of Rodgers and Hammerstein.

Goffin made himself at home in the Klein house. Maybe too much at home. He was there all the time and often slept over. Although her parents were divorced, Sid Klein was often there—he and Eugenia eventually remarried—and he wasn't that crazy about Gerry.

"We thought it was safe to make love when Carole had her period," Goffin said. "I didn't use any protection and she got pregnant." That didn't go over well with Carole's parents. "When she got pregnant, her father wanted to throw me out. In fact he threw Carole out. It was tough on her. She was just seventeen."

Now homeless and expecting, the young couple had to scramble to find a place to live. They found a little apartment and tried to carry on with their lives. But even though they were now on their own, they weren't completely free of her father and his expressed desire to split them up. Sid Klein was not only determined to pull them apart as a couple but as a songwriting team as well. He went to great lengths to keep his daughter and her boyfriend from succeeding, even reaching out to people in the industry and attempting to forbid them from doing business with King and Goffin.

"Carole's father did not dig it," recalled Jerry Wexler." He sent out letters to stop anybody from doing anything that had to do with the combined work of Goffin and King. He had a great distaste for Gerry Goffin and wanted to break them up, and he put us on notice not to accept their songs."

"Her father accused me of trying to use her," Goffin recalled. Things got very heated between the two men. There was tremendous animosity there. Eventually things reached a boiling point. "I wound up getting in a fight with him and punched him in the mouth at his house in Rosewood [Queens]," Goffin remembered. Ironically the fisticuffs were the first step toward patching things up. "He ran upstairs, then came down and shook my hand and said, 'if you're man enough to fight for my daughter, you're okay.'"

That détente made it easier for the couple to ease into their adult life together, first by getting married—something Goffin said was in the cards anyway. "If Carole didn't become pregnant, we would have still gotten married," he said. "We really loved each other."

It was a big wedding on Long Island, and yes, despite her condition, Carole did wear white. Goffin's mother gave them a little money and Gerry got a job as an assistant chemist. Their first apartment was a tiny, run-down studio on Ocean Parkway in Brooklyn. Over the Labor Day weekend, Goffin painted the whole apartment black and yellow and cleaned the floors and got the place in the best shape he could.

"It wasn't even two rooms," said Goffin. "It was one room and the bathroom was in that one room. We slept on a foldout couch. It was really the pits."

To say they struggled that first year is putting it mildly. Money was incredibly tight. They ate at her mother's as often as possible. With

Gerry's small assistant chemist's salary, and Carole not working so she could continue songwriting full-time, they barely scraped by.

They dreamed one day of making it big—and of money, literally. One day Carole woke Gerry up in the middle of the night.

"Gerry," she said, "there's ten thousand dollars in the watermelon."

"She was so cute when she did that," Goffin recalled. "So I went to check the watermelon and there was no ten thousand dollars. It was just a dream."

Eventually Goffin joined the Marine Corps Reserves to ease their financial struggle. The extra money he brought in made it possible for them to move to a bigger apartment. Their next place was a basement apartment at 2635 Brown Street in Sheepshead Bay, Brooklyn—three rooms for $125 a month with their own little carport. The extra cash also allowed Carole—still pregnant—to keep writing her music without worry about getting a job. She was determined to break through.

When Carole's high school friend Neil Sedaka started enjoying success at Aldon, she knew she needed to meet Al Nevins and Don Kirshner. Her path toward them began at Chuck Sagle's new office as head of A & R for Epic Records. Sagle had an open-door policy and would see any singer or songwriter who was willing to wait until he was available.

"Usually it was a waste of time," Sagle said. "Then all of a sudden one day, Carole turns up. She's about sixteen or seventeen from Brooklyn and she knocked me out of my chair. She pounded away and sang three songs and I remember thinking, 'This is terrific.' So I signed her to Epic as a singer and sent her over to Don and Al as a writer."

Before he sent her over, he recorded her on CBS' Alpine label doing "Oh, Neil," Carole and Gerry's comical answer to "Oh! Carol."

The session was recorded January 4, 1960, with King Curtis on sax and Sticks Evans on drums. The most amazing detail: Carole, still just seventeen, was seven months pregnant with Louise. And she sounded amazing.

In an attempt to settle the matter of whether it was Sedaka or

Sagle who first brought Carole to Aldon, I asked both Goffin and Kirshner about it. Unfortunately, neither could recall the exact details.

Neither Goffin nor Kirshner recalled exactly how Carole got to Aldon, but Sedaka thought that he brought her in. Goffin doubts Sedaka's claim.

"I don't really think Neil wanted her in the office," Goffin said, sort of as a matter of record, without any noticeable animosity in his voice. "He didn't want the competition."

"Neil was somebody to reckon with in those days," Sagle recalled, "and Carole was just a kid. It's quite possible that Neil didn't want her there. Neil was kind of a jealous guy. When I took the job with CBS [Epic] I was exclusive to them. Neil became quite upset that I couldn't arrange for him anymore."

Sagle was adamant that it was his call, and not Neil's, that brought Carole to Kirshner's office. "And when I called Don," recalled Sagle, "he responded with three words that improved his career immensely: 'Send her over.'"

Carole and Neil pose with producer Chuck Sagle during a promotion shot for both "Oh! Carol" and "Oh, Neil."

Will You Love Me Tomorrow

Regardless of whether it was Sedaka or Sagle who made the introduction, it didn't take much to persuade Kirshner to meet with Carole King. Just the idea that she would write a song in response to another—one that was presumably written about her—made her seem very clever.

"I just loved the feel of an answer record," said Kirshner, "so I wanted to meet her." Kirshner is unclear about the exact circumstances under which they met. "I wasn't sure if she was a writer or a singer," he said. "So I either went to a studio to meet her or she came to my office, it's a little cloudy." But in any case, he was immediately taken with King.

"There was a certain magic about her." All she had to do was perform one song and Kirshner was impressed. When Carole sat behind a piano, she turned into a performer who commanded your attention. "What you need to understand," said Kirshner, "is that she played every song as if it already was a hit."

"What do you do?" Kirshner asked her, meaning write or sing.

"I'm writing," she said.

"What's your husband do?" he asked. She explained Goffin's role as a lyricist. "Those are great lyrics," he said.

Kirshner knew he was on to something good, but he wasn't sure exactly what. "I schlepped over to Brooklyn [Queens actually] where Gerry was working at Argus Chemical," Kirshner recalled. "I think I took two subways because I didn't drive in those days or have a car." Kirshner sat down with Goffin at the chemistry lab and then rolled out the big sell.

"Whatever you guys are doing, I'll give you $1,000 now [for the year against future royalties]," Don promised. "I'll do like I did with Bobby [Darin] and with Neil and make you guys the biggest writers in the country."

Goffin stopped what he was doing when he heard "biggest writers in the country." Then his eyes lit up on Kirshner's next proposition.

"If I get you a big record, will you sign with me for five years?"

Goffin couldn't say yes fast enough. He couldn't think of a better alternative to being a chemist. His dream—their dream—was coming true.

Although King's and Goffin's talent were clearly apparent, that first hit record was very elusive. The songs Carole recorded in '58 and '59 for RCA and ABC-Paramount had one thing in common: they didn't have the hook to reel in the teen audience. That missing hook continued to elude them in Carole and Gerry's first year and a half writing for Aldon. And it wasn't as if Kirshner wasn't going all out for them. He placed their "Show Me the Way" with Atlantic for Ben E. King, the soul singer best known for writing and recording "Stand by Me." And he got his good friend Eydie Gorme to record King and Goffin's "The Dance Is Over," in 1960 for ABC-Paramount. Disappointingly, though, neither record went anywhere.

Kirshner even had them write a song for someone he thought was a can't-miss young demo singer he signed named Kenny Karen—the son of an orthodox Jewish rabbi, who ultimately never quite made it. The song Carole and Gerry had written for Karen was a beautiful ballad called "The Light in Your Window." RCA had Karen record it, but again there was no outcry for the record.

The failure to break through was hard on a young couple already struggling, and whose lives were now changing in a big way. Carole was barely eighteen in March 1960 when their daughter Louise was born. Ironically, it was that same month the FDA approved the new Envoid birth control pill—nine months too late for Carole and Gerry.

Each weekday Carole would bring the baby to the Aldon office, along with a collapsible playpen. She'd open it up in the secretaries' bullpen and plop Louise down. While the secretaries watched the baby, Carole went to the piano in her cubicle and wrote most of the day. At the same time, Gerry continued to work at his chem lab. But even with his job and the salary from Aldon, King and Goffin could no longer make their money last the month now that they were parents. The combination of tight finances and a sense of failure were heartbreaking, especially for Carole. After "The Light in Your Window" failed, Kirshner found her slumped over her piano crying, with the door to her cubicle closed.

"It can't be that bad," Don consoled her, after nudging the door open a little. "Believe me. You and Gerry have what it takes. You'll have a hit before you know it."

"It's just," she said, with her voice trailing off.

"It's just what?" he prompted.

"It's just that we're a month behind on the rent and we have to get things for Louise," she said, bursting into tears again. She turned to him with a face that was beet flush, but couldn't meet his eyes.

"Wait here," Don said. "I'll be right back."

Kirshner walked down the hall with purpose right into Nevins' office. He didn't ask but told him that Aldon was going to pay a month's rent for Goffin and King and also buy them a new crib for the baby. Kirshner didn't have to insist, though, because Al would have never turned them down.

Nevins was a wonderful man. He was a father figure in the office. There wasn't a problem there he couldn't solve. He was a very giving guy. Artie Kaplan, who wore many hats at Aldon including songwriter, summed up the relationship Nevins and Kirshner had with their young disciples.

"Neither Nevins nor Kirshner ever really said no to any of us," Kaplan explained. "If we brought a song to either of them that wasn't up to snuff yet—it wasn't as professionally crafted as it would have been a year or two later in our careers—they would never say, 'Don't make a demonstration record,' although they were paying for it. They would say, 'Are you happy with this song? Are you happy with this work?' And when you're young, you tend to think everything you write is a gem. And if we were convinced, they'd allow us to go in and [they'd] pay for the demonstration record. We made a lot of bad ones, believe me."

Carole and Gerry struck out forty-five times over that eighteen-month period, according to Kaplan. But thanks to Kirshner's nurturing and Nevins' problem solving, they never felt discouraged enough to give up. Then one night everything changed.

"Carole was out playing mah-jongg at her mother's," recalled Goffin, "and I was at a Marine Corps Reserves meeting. When I came home, there was a note that said, 'Donnie needs a lyric for the Shirelles.' She wrote the melody and left it for me on a huge Norelco two-track tape recorder. I heard it and I thought, *This is something different,* and I was inspired by it."

Goffin sat down briefly to write the lyrics. "It just came out of me," he said. "We were struggling so; it was like God was watching over us. And I wrote the opening lyrics in about five minutes."

> *Tonight you're mine completely.*
> *You give your love so sweetly.*
> *Tonight the light of love is in your eyes;*
> *But will you love me tomorrow?*

Before writing "Will You Love Me Tomorrow," King and Goffin listened to the Shirelles' previous hit, "Tonight's the Night," to try and capture a similar energy. This wasn't unusual. Incorporating a chord or a phrase from an artist's previous hit was a common practice by most good songwriters during that period. It was known as writing a song "sideways."

But Goffin's lyrics were like none other. While other songs casually referred to sex, Goffin's lines were explicit. There was no mistaking what that teenage girl wanted to know when she cried, "Will you still love me tomorrow?"

When it was completed, Carole went into Kirshner's office and played it for him on his red piano, singing her heart out as usual. Kirshner was floored.

"It's a smash!" he bellowed out so that the entire floor could hear. "It's a fucking smash."

Even though Kirshner asked them to write the song for the Shirelles, when he heard how beautiful it was, another singer came to mind—Johnny Mathis. He was the king of the love songs in 1960.

If you wanted Mathis to record a song, you had to get it approved by Mitch Miller, the chief of Columbia Records and the most powerful A & R man in the business. For months Kirshner tried to get an appointment with Miller, to sell him the songs of his bright new writers. But Miller wasn't interested. But now, with "Will You Love Me Tomorrow" proudly in his briefcase, Kirshner felt confident to pull every string he could. Finally Miller agreed to see him.

For Kirshner, this was huge. "I was thrilled to meet him," he said. "It was like meeting Babe Ruth."

Miller didn't waste any time. He heard Kirshner's thirty-second pitch about Aldon, then cut to the chase and asked him to play Carole's demo. During the next two minutes Miller hardly reacted. Then he turned to Don and gave him an opinion he wasn't expecting: "I don't think it's a song for Johnny Mathis," Miller said. "It's more a song that a woman would sing instead."

When I reached Miller, who was in his late nineties, by phone at his New York City apartment in 2007, he barely recalled the meeting.

"We had our own writers for Johnny Mathis," he said. "Besides, we didn't like doing business with new outfits [like Aldon] with everyone talking about payola at that time. We had to be very careful."

Kirshner was devastated. For six months he'd tried to get an audience with Miller, and when he finally did, he got shot down. Fortunately, though, as he walked back to the office, he stopped feeling sorry for himself and started to realize the wisdom of what Miller had just told him. He realized that his quest for a Mathis song had blinded him, and that Miller was in fact correct: "Will You Love Me Tomorrow" was a woman's song. When he returned to 1650 Broadway, he ran into a familiar face in the lobby, that of legendary house-wife-turned-record producer Florence Greenberg.

"She had just started Tiara and then Scepter Records and she had the Shirelles," said Kirshner. "Florence was like a *tanta*," an aunt, he remembered. "I had a nice relationship with her, and she had a pretty good producer named Luther Dixon."

The Shirelles were something of a hot commodity. Already in 1960 the Shirelles had three songs hit the charts, with their most recent, "Tonight's the Night," reaching No. 39. Kirshner went back to plan A and played Carole's demo for Greenberg and Dixon. They both felt it was perfect for the Shirelles. But they hit a major snag: Shirley Owens, the group's lead singer, didn't like it.

I tried for years to reach Shirley through her manager, who kept promising he'd have her call me, but never did. I finally caught up with her outside the stage door of an oldies concert in Manhattan in 2009. Here's what she told me about what almost became the biggest mistake of her career:

"When I first heard Carole play it on the piano," Shirley said, "it sounded like a country-western song to me. So I told everyone I didn't think it was a Shirelles song. It just sounded too country."

For Shirley, the song just didn't have enough soul to it. Kirshner, King, and Goffin could have given up, demoralized. But Carole promised to rework the arrangement to Shirley's liking. And she did. Her changes coupled with Dixon's prodding convinced Shirley, and she finally agreed to record it.

Carole desperately wanted a string arrangement for the song and lobbied Dixon for the chance to do it. Though she was barely eighteen and not experienced at arranging, he agreed to give her a shot. If the melody and the lyrics are the real estate of a song, the arranger and the producer are the song's architect and builder. The arranger usually decides the instruments required for the recording of the song and writes the parts for each musician to play.

Carole was influenced by Leiber and Stoller's classical string arrangement of "There Goes My Baby" and by the 1959 ballad "Since

I Don't Have You" by the Skyliners. The only problem was, as strictly a pianist, she had no idea how to write for strings.

"She didn't know squat about arranging," said Artie Kaplan, "so I told her to go to Terminal Music on 48th Street. It was a famous music store in those days, and she bought a little book, a little blue folder that was maybe twenty-five or thirty pages on how to write for a string section, because she had never written for a violin section before.

"And she read the book—I was at her house that night—and she came up with the arrangement that eventually became the arrangement of that record," Kaplan said. "You know, people go to Juilliard for years to try and learn how to write for strings, and she picked it up almost by instinct."

Kaplan handpicked the musicians of that string section for the recording session. He selected guys that that he knew would be helpful. And they were.

"Carole originally wanted violas but she couldn't get them," Goffin remembered, "so she wrote for two cellos and four violins and she made it sound like a string quartet. I was so proud of her."

He wasn't the only one who was impressed. When the Shirelles heard Carole's new string arrangement, they were blown away.

They recorded the song in December 1960, less than a month after Jack Kennedy was elected president. By January it was No. 1. The song spoke directly to teenagers in love. It made perfect sense that Goffin would create lyrics and a story the kids could truly relate to; in effect, those lyrics reflected his and Carole's lives after he got her pregnant.

"On the radio it doesn't get much realer than that," wrote Mitchell Cohen in *Phonograph Magazine*. The song shows that "passionate embraces and emotional commitment are not necessarily flip sides of the coin," making it "one of those magical connections between art and life."

"Will You Love Me Tomorrow" was more than just the first No. 1 hit for Goffin and King. That song had so much power it became the first No. 1 song of any girl group— black or white—in the modern rock-and-roll era.

Through his buddy Ira Howard at *Cashbox*, Don had found out a few days ahead of time that the song would be No. 1 on the following week's charts. He decided to surprise Goffin with the news. He realized he could no longer afford to have Goffin working in a chemistry lab all day. At least not after he wrote lyrics the whole industry was talking about. He needed Goffin to produce more of that songwriting gold.

"At that point they were family, they were my kids," said Kirshner. "I was their father figure. But if you realize it, I was only six or seven years older than them at the time. But you've got to understand, the secretaries were diapering Carole's baby. This was a family unit. So when Gerry says I paid their rent several times, you don't think twice about those things. You're family."

Kirshner has fond memories of the day they told Goffin in person. "I grabbed Carole and we got a limo, and we drove up to Queens where Gerry was working," he recalled. "When we went inside he was mixing up all these potions. I told him, 'Gerry, you don't have to do this anymore.'" That got Goffin's attention. "'Your song is No. 1,'" Kirshner continued. "'You're going to be one of the greatest song-writing teams in history.'"

"When Don said that, I felt like a big load was lifted off of us," Goffin recalled, picking up the story from there. "He told us we'd each earn ten grand on the song—enough for us to get credit cards."

That was big money for a young couple with a baby living in a three-room basement apartment in 1961. This was big news. "I shut down my work station and followed Don out to his car," Goffin said. "And I can honestly say that I haven't done an honest day's work since."

• • •

That very week, President Kennedy made one of the most famous inaugural addresses in our history. In it he said, "Let the word go forth from this time and place, to friend and foe alike, that the torch has been passed to a new generation of Americans . . ."

The speech moved Kirshner greatly, and he thought about how it was now his time and how he had opened the door for the teenagers who couldn't outfox the connections of the old Tin Pan Alley writers. Kirshner was passing his own torch to a new breed of songwriters, and Goffin and King were among the first who took that torch and ran with it.

A few days after Kirshner surprised Goffin at his job, Kirshner and Nevins invited Carole and Gerry to join them at the annual BMI industry awards dinner being held in the Grand Ballroom of the Hotel Pierre in New York. For eighteen-year-old Carole and her husband, this would be their first black-tie affair. They were probably the only teenagers in the room and they looked it. Little did it matter. They had just written a No. 1 song and were about to have another.

Carole (seated, far right) and Gerry (above her) look oh, so young at this January 1961 BMI Awards dinner. Al Nevins (standing, far left), Jack Keller (next to Nevins), and Howie Greenfield (standing next to Goffin) are also in the photo.

Mack the Knife

On September 20, 1959, Soviet Premier Nikita Khrushchev was meeting President Dwight Eisenhower at Camp David discussing the Cold War, Rod Serling's *Twilight Zone* was about to debut on ABC, and Bobby Darin's "Mack the Knife" was No. 1 on the charts.

The charts! That's all Don Kirshner ever thought about. He never thought about money, only the charts. If he had a hit song on the charts, life was good. If he didn't, he kept working until he did.

On this day in September, life was good for Kirshner; two songs by Aldon songwriters were on the charts, his best friend, Darin, had the No. 1 hit, and it just happened to be Kirshner's wedding day. He and Sheila Grod were getting married at her uncle's home in the posh New York suburb of Englewood Cliffs, New Jersey.

In addition to Darin, who was the best man, the guests included Neil Sedaka and Howie Greenfield, early rock-and-roll stars Jimmy Bowen and Buddy Knox (his big hit was "Party Doll"), Atlantic Records' partner Jerry Wexler, country-rock singer Billy "Crash" Craddock, local TV singer Tina Robin, and Kirshner's business partner, Al Nevins.

Sheila Grod was a sweet girl from the small town of Hillside, New Jersey. Two years earlier, she'd met Don at a fund-raiser he was hosting. She was designated as his assistant. It's a job she held for the next fifty years.

"Persistent is what I'd call him," Sheila recalled. "He kept asking me out and I kept turning him down."

She finally agreed to go out with him after Kirshner told her he had no intention of getting serious because he was focused on mak-

ing it in the music business. And on their first date he took her bowl-
ing at the Port Authority bus depot at 42nd Street and Seventh Ave.
Not exactly a romantic setting.

He did, however, find time to get serious once before.

"Donnie dated a rich girl named Linda for about a year," recalled
Dick Lord, who was pals with Darin and Kirshner in those early
days. "Her father asked him what he was going to do with his life.
When Donnie said he wanted to be a songwriter, her father told him
if he wanted to marry Linda, he had to sell suits in his men's store.
Donnie tried it once and he hated it. Good-bye, Linda."

Darin and Lord didn't know Sheila as well as they knew Linda.
"While Bobby and I were driving to Donnie's wedding," Lord ex-
plained, "we kept saying to each other, 'Whatever you do, *don't* say
Linda.'"

Linda lived in a spectacular house on the right side of the tracks.
Until he was twenty-one, Kirshner, who grew up in the Bronx and
Washington Heights, had never gone out with a girl who didn't live
in an apartment building. But that all changed with Linda. Her home
felt more like a mansion to Kirshner, who was struck by the beauty of
its big winding staircase.

"Believe it or not," said Kirshner, "I had never been to a home
with a staircase before. I looked at it and I said to myself, 'Oh my
God, it's right out of *Gone with the Wind.*'"

But Sheila's father, who worked as a butcher in Newark, wasn't
rich, and there certainly wasn't any winding staircase. The Grods
lived on the ground floor of a two-family house. Sheila's romance
with Kirshner was whirlwind. He'd bring around friends like Darin,
and Steve Lawrence and Eydie Gorme.

Sometimes they'd all meet Sunday nights at the long soda foun-
tain, or in one of the booths at Hanson's Drug Store at 50th and
Broadway, and wait for the trade papers to come out. Hanson's was
a little bit like Schwab's in L.A., where Lana Turner was discovered
twenty years earlier. Hopeful actors, singers, and songwriters made
Hanson's their headquarters.

When *Cashbox* and *Billboard* were dropped off, Kirshner and the

Best man Bobby Darin poses for a photo with the bride, Sheila Kirshner, at Sheila's uncle's house in posh Englewood Cliffs, New Jersey.

gang could hardly wait for the bundles to be opened before they'd grab a copy to see if any of their songs made the Hot 100.

Kirshner and Nevins modeled their publishing firm after what the great Max Dreyfus accomplished with his company in the '20s. Dreyfus might have been either the smartest or the luckiest song publisher in history. In 1917, he started by hiring Jerome Kern as a song-plugger to hawk sheet music. Realizing Kern's promise, Dreyfus signed him to a long-term contract. He soon did the same with George and Ira Gershwin, Cole Porter, and Rodgers and Hart. They were all under contract to Dreyfus, writing songs at his company's downtown office.

In 1929, after the talkies came in, movie studios were desperate for musical material. Dreyfus wisely sold his little company to Warner Bros. for an incredible $11 million just before Black Friday on Wall Street and the onset of the Depression.

On this his wedding day, Kirshner's dream of being a publisher was now a reality, but because royalties trailed by at least six months, it had not yet made him rich, or even comfortable, for that matter. "We had to wait for the wedding presents to come in to pay for the wedding," Kirshner recalled with a laugh.

After the wedding ceremony and all the congratulations had died down, Kirshner and Darin sat on the front steps of Sheila's uncle's house. They loosened their ties and Darin lit a cigarette. Kirshner recalls the irony of the moment: "'Mack the Knife' was No. 1 and we were both broke."

● ● ●

Despite the slow stream of royalties, Darin kept getting bigger with each recording. "Splish, Splash," "Queen of the Hop," "Dream Lover," and "Mack the Knife" were all Top 10 songs and it seemed like Bobby could do no wrong. He was opening for George Burns in Las Vegas and Sammy Davis Jr. spoke openly of what a tremendous talent he thought Bobby was.

Right before Thanksgiving, Don got a call from a TV producer in Hollywood. "Bobby is going to be the surprise guest on *This Is Your Life* in a few weeks, and we'd like you to be there to surprise him. Can you come to Hollywood to be part of the show?"

For Kirshner the answer was easy, plus the publicity it would generate for him would be great. "You bet. When do you need me?" he asked.

This Is Your Life, one of TV's first reality shows, was one of the most popular television programs in the '50s. Each week, host Ralph Edwards surprised someone—usually famous—to the delight of the audience.

Don flew out to Los Angeles along with Bobby's childhood friend Dick Lord, and they stayed at the Roosevelt Hotel, just down the street from the broadcast.

Then on December 2, the big night arrived. Dick and Don were smuggled backstage at the El Capitan Theatre in Hollywood, alongside George Burns and Sammy Davis Jr., among others. About halfway through the show, Ralph Edwards asked Bobby if he knew this voice:

"Do you remember when we couldn't sell a song and had to scrape together thirty-five cents for a bowl of spaghetti?"

"Yes, Bobby," Ralph Edwards said, jumping in, with his voice building to a crescendo, "you were the best man at his wedding—your former songwriting partner and now the president of Nevins-Kirshner Music Publishing—Donnie Kirshner."

Said Kirshner: "I think I was twenty-something years old [actually twenty-five] and I'm on *This Is Your Life*. It was unbelievable! It was such a thrill for me. It was one of the first times I was in California and they paid for my hotel, and it was a big deal. What a heady experience. I'm a kid and I'm in the [green] room with Sammy Davis Jr. and George Burns. Can you imagine?"

By June 1960, Aldon Music was humming on all cylinders. After "Oh! Carol," Sedaka and Greenfield were back on track. Their next release, "Stairway to Heaven," reached No. 9 on *Billboard*.

Steve Lawrence and Eydie Gorme, who became close friends of the Kirshners', were celebrities in their own right by 1960. A few years earlier, they had been regulars on NBC's late-night TV show hosted by comedian Steve Allen. It was called *Broadway Open House* and was the forerunner to *The Tonight Show*. Their appearances made Steve and Eydie instant celebrities.

I tried to reach Steve and Eydie through their son, David, a very successful song-writer in his own right. A friend at Disney Theatricals gave me a number for David, but he wasn't home. I left a voice mail on his machine and hoped for the best. A few nights later, the phone rang and the call reader showed a Las Vegas area code. I picked up the phone. "Is this Rich?" the voice asked. "This is Steve Lawrence returning your call." My heart jumped but I tried to remain calm.

"Donnie was an enigma," Lawrence told me. "He had no musical training and didn't play an instrument. If you ever heard him sing, you'd ask him what he did for a living. But he had that wonderful ability to hear the great potential in those writers and those songs. It really was his great gift. He saw the boom that was happening. He was sitting right on the cusp of it and he was smart enough to take advantage. Al Nevins should be commended for letting Donnie run with the ball. And it turned out to be one very big ball."

While Steve and Eydie had both enjoyed modest recording success, Kirshner was determined to help them cross over onto the pop charts. In the first six months of 1960, Kirshner accomplished this feat twice, handing Lawrence "Pretty Blue Eyes" and "Footsteps." Both made the Top 10 on *Cashbox* and *Billboard*.

"We were a couple of Jewish kids together, starting from nothing," Kirshner remembered fondly. "His dad was a rabbi. Mine was a tailor. We just had the same likes. We would go every other weekend to the Concord [hotel in the Catskills] together. We'd diaper their kids; they'd diaper ours. And we just became kind of inseparable. Sheila and Eydie and me and Stevie. We had a great groove together. And as we grew up together I didn't realize they were stars. They were just Steve and Eydie."

Goffin and King's "Go Away Little Girl" later became Lawrence's only No. 1 song and "Blame It on the Bossa Nova," written by Barry Mann, was the biggest hit Gorme ever enjoyed, peaking at No. 7.

Steve and Eydie were also close friends with Bobby Darin and followed his career closely. When "Mack the Knife" reached No. 1, it stayed there for nine weeks, an amazing record that remained intact for the next twenty years. The song not only made Darin a huge star but allowed him to crossover and win wide-ranging audiences. Besides the teenagers who bought "Splish Splash" and "Dream Lover," adults were now clamoring to see him. Bobby's dream had always been to play the Copacabana nightclub in New York. On June 15, 1960, that dream came true.

Along with Steve and Eydie, at Kirshner's table that opening night were Sheila's parents and also Dick and Arlene Gersh. The Gershes had a very successful public relations business and had become close with the Kirshners. Dick Gersh was the first to call Kirshner "the Man with the Golden Ear," which *Time* magazine later used. *Time* outlined how Kirshner's unique talent of finding young songwriters and songs that no one else wanted had propelled him to the top.

Darin's dressing room at the Copa was actually a suite in the tiny Hotel 14, adjacent to the nightclub, on East 60th Street. Darin would leave his dressing room, walk down the hall, and take the freight elevator down to the basement. From there he could access the Copa's kitchen and weave through it, as they did in the film *Goodfellas,* to a point where he was just a few feet from the audience behind a curtain.

In actuality the Copa had no stage, which was one reason performers loved playing there. Table after table was squeezed into the small showroom that night, until about 750 people were packed in.

"There were about one hundred over the legal limit," Steve Blauner, Darin's longtime manager, told me. "When Bobby entered the room, he actually jumped down a few steps and was on the exact same level as the customers. Some customers were even eye to eye with his crotch. And Bobby loved being right there with the people."

When Darin performed, it reminded Kirshner of the thrill he got the first time he heard him sing. "I lived vicariously through Bobby," said Kirshner. "When he was onstage, I was onstage."

Although a third of the audience were high school kids on their prom dates, Darin sang standard after standard, concluding with "Won't You Come Home Bill Bailey," the same song he sang for Kirshner the first day they had met. Chills went down Don's spine. He couldn't believe how great Bobby was and couldn't help but feel a part of it.

The reviews couldn't have been any better. Famed gossip columnist Walter Winchell attended every night of the two-week run and called Darin "the greatest performer since Jolson."

And the *New York–Journal American*'s Gene Knight described Darin's performance this way: "He has a knowing glance, a syncopated style from head to toe, a large charge of self-assurance, a finger-snapping, shoulder-shrugging beat, and a show-wide projection that belies his brief four years as a performer."

After his run at the Copa, Darin was recognized as the fastest rising star in the country. Hollywood came calling and Darin landed a part in a film opposite the hottest young female box-office star in the country, Sandra Dee. Yes, the same Sandra Dee immortalized in the Broadway show *Grease*. The film, *Come September*, was shot on location in Italy, and before it was over, the two of them were engaged. Upon his return to New York, on December 1, 1960, Darin phoned his old friend.

"Kirsh," he said. "We're gonna get married tonight."

"Great!" Kirshner responded. "Where?"

"Your place, 11 o'clock."

"M-my place?" stuttered Kirshner.

"Yeah, you gotta help me out, Kirsh," said Darin. "Can you get a rabbi or somebody?"

"Your place" was Don and Sheila's tiny Elizabeth, New Jersey, apartment. The ceremony, before a select few friends, took place well after midnight. One of those friends was Joyce Becker, who first met Darin while interviewing him for her high school newspaper in 1958. She soon found herself in the unpaid but highly sought after job of answering Darin's fan mail.

"I would sit in the vestibule at Donnie's office, and Bobby would sit on the floor and sing to me with his head in my lap," said Becker. "I hated to leave, but I needed a real job when I graduated. Donnie called Connie Francis, and the next thing I knew I was her assistant for $50 a week. When Connie was dating Bobby behind her father's back, I was the foil. She would stay over my house in the Bronx instead of going home to New Jersey."

Becker and Francis drove to Darin's wedding that night, along with Neil Sedaka and Howie Greenfield in Neil's new white Chevy convertible. She remembered Sheila Kirshner's frantic call to her earlier that day.

"Sheila called me hysterical," said Becker. "'They want to get married and use my living room,' Sheila screamed to me. They lived in a very plain, little garden apartment in Jersey. It was teeny."

The Kirshners were living in a one-bedroom apartment on North Broad Street in Elizabeth. After entering, you walked through a small vestibule. There was a baby carriage in the doorway, along with a playpen and some toys in the living room, all for the Kirshner's baby boy, Ricky. Somehow they had to make those baby things disappear.

"We scrambled and got everybody together," Sheila Kirshner recalled. "We happened to know somebody that knew a judge. In three to four hours we had everything going. And then Bobby and Sandy came. She was just a kid, barely eighteen. Everyone crowded into our tiny kitchen. That's where they got married, in that tiny kitchen. We're not talking Trump Tower."

When Darin and Dee headed out of Kirshner's apartment, it was two in the morning. Someone must have leaked it to the press because flash bulbs went off everywhere. The next day, Kirshner's name was in every paper across the country that carried news of the wedding. Don Kirshner was only twenty-six years old and felt like he was on top of the world.

Everybody's Somebody's Fool

Everybody's somebody's fool
Everybody's somebody's plaything
And there are no exceptions to the ru-u-ule
Yes, everybody's somebody's fool

Fifteen dollars a week, plus room and board and all you could eat. That's what Jack Keller earned on his first summer gig as a musician in the Catskill mountains. And when the band's drummer dropped out just a week before their reporting date, Keller talked his best friend, Paul Kaufman, into taking a drum lesson and joining him.

"The first day we arrived at the hotel, Paul asked me to look at a lyric he had written. Up to that time, the thought of writing a song never really entered my mind," said Keller. "When I sat down at the piano and tried to write the music, I felt a feeling that took over my whole being. I knew this was a big deal, because I couldn't make myself stop—even though I knew I was missing lunch."

Keller continued to write songs, and when a friend told him he could get him an appointment with Frank Sinatra's publisher, he quickly followed up. On January 3, 1955, he walked into the Brill Building for the very first time. At five feet eleven inches with dark hair and horned-rim glasses, Keller looked like a very suave Clark Kent and made a good impression on Jack Benanti, the general manager of Barton Music. Benanti was the first person in the music business that took Keller under his wing.

"I started hanging around Benanti's office," Keller recalled. "Back then, songwriters brought their music sheets in, and I would play and sing their song for Benanti, who didn't read music and was tone deaf.

Now get this—based on my performance, he would decide whether or not to send the song to Sinatra."

While hanging out at Barton Music, Keller started meeting some influential people in the business, like ABC-Paramount's famous producer Don Costa, and Roulette Records' famed producing duo Hugo and Luigi. Early in '57, Keller's big break came when a Mafioso type introduced him to a lyricist named Cathy Lee, instructing Keller to write with her. It was an offer Keller dare not refuse.

"She gave me three lyrics and I went home and wrote my first hit song, 'Just Between You and Me.' We played it for Jack Benanti, but he didn't want to give us an advance on it. Cathy then insisted we take the song to other publishers she knew. One of them, George Paxton, said he'd give us an advance of $50 each and another $50 after a recording was released." Never guessing anything would happen with the song, Keller pocketed the $50 and then forgot about it.

In the early '50s, Keller's father, Mal, a local bandleader, had built up a nice business and became known as the king of the wedding and Bar Mitzvah bands in New York. In order to learn the hits of the day, Mal bought something called a Tunedeck, a rudimentary record player, which came with the short forms of thirty hit songs each month. From listening to the Tunedeck over and over, young Jack learned the basics of songwriting without realizing it. He also learned to like country music.

"Mitch Miller was a great A & R man at Columbia," said Keller. "Being the label's top executive, he would take all of Hank Williams' country songs and have popular artists cover them. Tunedeck always sent a few covers each month, and it was Hank Williams' great melodies that stayed with me all through the years."

Keller's father would book as many parties as he could each weekend, and on some Saturday nights he would shuffle between seven different catering halls.

"He'd come in and get everybody crazy with his patented accordion sing-along, collect the check, then be off to the next catering hall," said Keller, laughing.

It was his father who insisted Jack practice the piano after school, when he wanted to play stickball. And when his father suddenly passed away, Jack just as suddenly became the man of the house. Heart disease ran in the Keller bloodlines. In the previous four generations, no Keller man had lived long enough to see his grandchildren being born. In the back of his mind Jack always worried that his own time might be short.

He took a job at a bank in Manhattan to ensure some money went home, but his mother encouraged him to keep writing. After work he would call home right before he got on the subway to let his mother know he was on his way.

One day she asked him, "Did you hear your song on the radio today?"

"Don't kid me about that," Jack said, annoyed.

"No, really," she replied. "That song you wrote—'Just Between You and Me'— was on WINS. They said it was going to be another hit for the Chordettes, just like 'Mr. Sandman,'" which was a huge No. 1 song for the Chordettes a few years earlier.

Keller rushed home, quickly had dinner, and then turned on the radio, hoping to hear the song. Impatient, he met some friends and drove around for hours listening to the car radio.

"It wasn't until 11 p.m. that night, listening to Murray the K, that I heard the recording of 'Just Between You and Me' for the first time," said Keller. "That was a great moment. You've got to realize that when you're that young and you write a song, you only dream about hearing it on the radio some day. You don't think about money. At least I didn't until the next morning. That's when I called the publisher, George Paxton, and asked for my other $50."

That was July 8, 1957. From that day forward for the next five months, all he thought about was where the song was on the charts as it climbed to No. 8 on both *Cashbox* and *Billboard*. It wasn't until November when the song started to drop that Keller realized, *I have to write another song!*

Soon after, Keller hooked up with established lyricist Noel Sherman, who had written hit songs for Perry Como and Nat "King" Cole. Sherman had been writing with his brother, who became too ill to work. He taught Keller how to be a professional songwriter. He taught him how to dress, how to talk to publishers, and he taught him good work habits.

In the next eighteen months, the team of Keller and Sherman had twenty-three of their songs recorded by such established artists as Peggy Lee, Nat "King" Cole, the Kalin Twins, Perry Como, the Four Lads, and the Chordettes. A couple of those were on the B side of Top 10 hits, which made for a pretty nice payday for young Mr. Keller, because the writers of the B side got paid the same amount as the songwriters of the A (the hit) side of a record. When Noel Sherman himself became ill in 1959, Keller was fully prepared to go off on his own.

The first time Keller walked into Aldon Music in October '59, it was still that original one-room office—with a desk and a phone, and a phonograph on the floor—that Nevins had seventeen months earlier. Kirshner wasn't in, but Al Nevins was there and was impressed by Keller and asked him to come back. When Keller returned a few weeks later, Aldon had moved to a much larger space on the sixth floor.

Said Keller: "I had just finished making a demo of 'One Way Ticket (to the Blues)' that I had written with a friend, Hank Hunter. When I played it for Donnie, he went crazy."

Kirshner marched Keller into Nevins' office and said he wanted to sign him, publish his song, and pay him immediately for the cost of the demo.

"Sit down and relax," Nevins told Keller. At that moment he seemed to be the opposite of Kirshner's over-the-top enthusiasm. Nevins was cool and under control. Then he surprised Keller with his next question.

"Do you need any money?"

"Do I need any money!?" Keller repeated. "Mr. Nevins," said Keller, "in the four years I have been demonstrating my songs for publishers, nobody has ever asked me that question."

Before Jack could answer, Nevins interceded.

"Faith," Nevins said over his intercom to his secretary, "make out a $60 advance check to Jack Keller for demo expenses, and another for $200 against future royalties." It was Nevins' way of trying to purchase the publishing rights to the song, no matter what happened.

Three days later, they signed him to a six-year exclusive songwriting and production contract, largely because they wanted Sedaka to record "One Way Ticket (to the Blues)" on the other side of "Oh! Carol."

"When they asked me how much I wanted to sign, all I could think of was what I made the year before, which was $10,000," Keller recalled. "They said, 'That's no problem,' and I signed."

Then they asked him to play "One Way Ticket" for Sedaka. "A few days later, when I walked into that little office, with only a piano and a desk, Neil and I laughed."

Jack Keller, looking a little like Clark Kent, always looked professional.

They laughed because they had met several times before. They first bumped into each other in 1956. They were each part of the listed entertainment at a dance at the Ocean Avenue Jewish Community Center in Brighton Beach, Brooklyn.

"When Neil finished playing his number at that dance, I introduced myself and told him that I was going to write a hit song someday. Neil smiled, and then said, 'You might, but I'm going to write one first.'"

The next time they met, it was 1958, outside the offices of publishers Hill and Range at the Brill Building. Keller had won the bet and Sedaka congratulated him for striking first with "Just Between You and Me."

"A short time later, when I saw Neil's picture on the RCA label and heard his record, 'The Diary,' I knew he had done it too."

A further inspection of the record label told Keller that "The Diary" was a Nevins-Kirshner production. He quickly found out who they were, got an appointment, and soon thereafter would join Sedaka and Greenfield as part of the Aldon Music team.

"Jack was very together, unlike all my other kids, who were just free spirits," Kirshner remembered. "I always felt every time he walked out of my office that he had taken notes. And he had the kind of personality and persona I gravitated to. He always delivered."

As one of the first writers signed at Aldon, Keller watched the company become a dynasty overnight.

"When you had a hit, the doors were open to you," he said. "After 'Stupid Cupid' and 'The Diary' it started to build and build, and when 'Oh! Carol' hit, Aldon pretty much took off like a rocket.

"I remember hearing Donnie on the phone in that first office, saying, 'Yeah, we're hit publishers. We just put out 'Stupid Cupid.' Then a few weeks later I heard him saying, 'We've got a big hit. We just published 'Dream Lover.'" That was Darin's payback for all the years Don struggled with him."

Keller was also being groomed to produce the young singers and songwriters Kirshner would sign. One time Nevins brought Keller along to observe the recording of an album by the Three Suns, Nevins' old group. On one take Keller noticed something that didn't sound quite right.

"I told Al that if the guitar player does it this way, instead of that way, we'll get the sound Al was looking for," recalled Keller. "Well, the guitar player was George Barnes, one of the best in the country. What I didn't know was that he was also one of the surliest. So Al says to me, 'Go out there and tell him how to play it.'"

From behind the control room, Nevins announced to the musicians they were taking a short break and he sent Keller out to talk to Barnes. "When I told Barnes my suggestion, he started mumbling something under his breath and then he stood up, took off his guitar, and handed it to me. 'Here, you play it,' he barked. When I looked back at Al, he was laughing hysterically at the two of us. He had set us both up."

When "Oh! Carol" took off for Sedaka, Keller was also collecting the same amount on the 1.8 million copies sold. But Keller felt he could only write B sides for so long.

Kirshner, who didn't want to lose him, had the perfect solution. Sedaka was going on an eighteen-city promotional tour with "Oh! Carol." Not wanting to waste a great talent in Howie Greenfield, Kirshner asked Keller and Greenfield to write together. The results were amazing, as if they had been writing together for years.

"Howie, he was a fabulous guy and a talented guy and a workaholic," Keller said. "It was great chemistry with us. I liked to create and he was a pusher. He had no qualm about initiating a conversation with an artist to make appointments to listen to our songs. I had no problem sitting down and playing them our songs, but I wasn't comfortable initiating the calls."

By this time Greenfield had grown into a tall and very handsome young man with neatly combed dark brown hair and dark eyes. He no longer was "Fat Howie." He usually wore a V-neck striped sweater to the office with a turtleneck underneath it. When he wrote he never sat. He paced and smoked. He constantly had a cigarette smoldering.

"Everybody's Somebody's Fool" was the first song Keller and Greenfield ever wrote together, and they didn't have Connie Francis in mind when they wrote it. It was the great rhythm and blues singer, Laverne Baker, they wanted to record it when they sat down to write. After finishing the song, Greenfield told Keller that he was going to the movies with Connie that night and that he might show her the lyric.

During a recent European tour, Francis' father had her tour Germany to see what its market was like. While there she discovered they liked country-and-western music. That night at the movies, she told Howie to write her an up-tempo country song. When he asked why, she responded, "Because I'm going to record it in German."

"Deutschland uber alles!" Greenfield said, snapping to attention and saluting.

Connie and Howie had become very close friends since that first afternoon when he and Sedaka gave her "Stupid Cupid." After the movies, they went out for a bite and he showed her the lyrics to "Everybody's Somebody's Fool." Then, leaving Connie in the booth at the coffee shop, he ran to a telephone to call Keller with the news.

"She loves it," said Greenfield, before turning his back to Francis and whispering, "Can it be done like 'Heartaches by the Number'?"

"Are you kidding me?" Keller asked.

"No, I'm dead serious," said Greenfield. "She wants a country hit."

Keller quickly went to the piano and played it. "Yeah," I guess so," he said. "I'll just change the tempo."

Keller even added an organ in the demo, emphasizing a country feel. After Francis completed recording all the cuts for her upcoming album, she was trying to decide which song to release to the radio stations. With her were Keller, Greenfield, and Arnold Maxim, the president of MGM Records. Here's how Keller recalled the debate.

Arnold said, "If you put out that country song, I think your career is finished." "Arnold, I don't know if you saw my contract," Francis responded sarcastically, "but I have creative control. So watch me!"

"Everybody's Somebody's Fool" was introduced in May 1960 and was No. 1 by July. After it became the biggest record she ever had worldwide, she sent Arnold Maxim the record in a shoebox with a salt-and-pepper shaker inside.

Keller and Greenfield followed up with another No. 1 record for Francis three months later. When Connie asked Howie and Jack to write the follow-up to "Everybody's Somebody's Fool," they went out and bought three Hank Williams albums and listened to them over and over, then sat down and wrote "My Heart Has a Mind of Its Own."

Said Francis, "I didn't know if I wanted to record it, because I thought it was too much like 'Everybody's Somebody's Fool.' It was up-tempo and it was country. But my father, who picked all my songs, said, 'You're going to have another No. 1 hit with this one.' And he was right again."

"My Heart Has a Mind of Its Own" was already the fourth Top 10 song Greenfield had written for Connie Francis. He would give her six altogether, three with Sedaka and three more with Keller.

He had written "Stupid Cupid" and "Frankie" with Sedaka, and the two No. 1 country songs with Keller. In April 1961, Howie's follow-up with Keller, "Breakin' in a Brand New Broken Heart," rose to No. 7 on the charts. It would have gone much higher if Francis had released it sooner, but a dispute she and her father had with Nevins and Kirshner over publishing percentages kept the record under wraps for months.

Greenfield and Keller would also later team up to write one of television's most famous theme songs, "Bewitched."

The relationship Howie Greenfield shared with Connie Francis was a special one. "We were very close," she remembered. "When Howie was writing songs, he would call me every eight or sixteen bars to see how I felt about it. I have an eight-by-ten picture of Howie that he inscribed, 'Every love song I've ever written, I wrote with you in mind.'"

Not realizing her son was gay, Howie's mother frequently tormented him, saying, "Why don't you marry Connie?"

Once, when Connie was out of town, Greenfield sent her a telegram to cheer her up. It read:

There once was a girl named Concetta,
Whose friend tried in vain just to get her,
He tried 90 times,
Spent all of his dimes,
Should he take out a loan or forget her?

"What a talent he was!" she raved. "He had such a great feel for lyrics. He would have been a great songwriter in any generation. He was tall and good-looking. Brown hair and brown eyes. Very sweet and very funny. And most of all, he was a great friend." There was love in her voice as she spoke those words.

The back-to-back No. 1 songs that Keller and Greenfield wrote for Francis made her the premiere female recording star in the country. When MGM decided to make a film about teenagers on spring break, Francis was their first choice. The picture was called *Where the Boys Are*, and when they asked her if she'd sing the title song, she told MGM she knew exactly who should write it. Then she put in a call to Howie Greenfield.

Where the Boys Are

Till he holds me, I wait impatiently
Where the boys are, where the boys are,
Where the boys are, someone waits for me

Hungarian-born Joseph Pasternak came to America as a teenager during Woodrow Wilson's presidency. He got a job in 1923 as a waiter in the Universal Pictures commissary. Three years later, he was one of their key European directors.

In 1936, Joe Pasternak took an untried teenage soprano named Deanna Durbin and turned her into the darling of a nation. His production of *Three Smart Girls* not only saved Universal Pictures from bankruptcy but earned Pasternak a Best Picture Oscar nomination as well.

Pasternak rapidly built a reputation as a producer who could work with young actresses. In 1939, it was Marlene Dietrich in *Destry Rides Again*. In 1943, it was a young Judy Garland in *Presenting Lily Mars*. And in 1948, it was an even younger Elizabeth Taylor in *A Date with Judy*.

By the time Pasternak approached Connie Francis in 1960 to star in *Where the Boys Are*, three of his films had already been nominated for Best Picture and he certainly had a track record Connie's father, George Franconero, could respect.

Pasternak met with Francis and gave her the script and the book *Where the Boys Are*, and told her she had the potential to be another Judy Garland. Connie was particularly impressed with Pasternak's production of *Love Me or Leave Me* a few years earlier, with Doris Day portraying Ruth Etting, and decided that she wanted to work with him.

George Franconero objected, not to Pasternak's track record but to the script about three Midwestern coeds who go to Fort Lauderdale on spring break.

"They've got a scene near the end of this movie where a girl is leaving a motel with a guy," he told his daughter. The girl he was referring to wasn't even Connie's character, Angie.

"Nobody will see anything," she said.

"That's beside the point. You're not doing this movie!"

Francis was turning twenty-one that year, and this was one of the rare times in her life that she decided to go against her father.

"That's it. I'm doing the movie!" she said with assuredness, then ended the discussion.

The real conflict came up when Pasternak told her he had the best songwriters in Hollywood working furiously to write the title song for her.

"I have to have it written by my two friends from Brooklyn," she told him.

"Who are they?" he asked.

"Neil Sedaka and Howie Greenfield. They write all my hits. Neil just won an award for 'The Diary.'"

"Never heard of them," said Pasternak. "Besides, I've got Sammy Cahn and Jimmy Van Heusen, the best in Hollywood, writing this song on consignment, and that's never happened before."

"You've never heard of them because you don't pay any attention to the pop charts," she told Pasternak, getting a little upset. "You've got to give them a chance."

"All right," said Pasternak. "They've got a week, but it's got to be here by Wednesday. That's when we're picking the song."

After getting a one-week reprieve, she rushed to the phone and excitedly called Greenfield, who wasn't quite as excited when she broke the news to him.

"Where the Boys Are? What kind of stupid title is that?" he barked back at her. "Who can write a song with a title like 'Where the Boys Are'?"

She not only convinced him that he and Sedaka could, but that they could do it fast.

"In those days there was no Federal Express or anything like that," said Francis. "But I knew a stewardess from Eastern Airlines who would take it from Neil and Howie in New York and bring it to me in Fort Lauderdale."

Sedaka and Greenfield actually wrote two different songs entitled "Where the Boys Are" for Pasternak's MGM team to consider, with Sedaka singing the demo on each. They rushed it to the stewardess, who brought it to Francis in time for the meeting.

"Neil and Howie and I all agreed," recalled Francis. "One of the versions we loved and the other one we all hated. Joe Pasternak came to me after their meeting with the decision."

"'You're right, Connie,'" he told me. 'This is the song.' And it was the version the three of us hated. I guess it didn't matter, because it became a hit all around the world."

Having two of their songwriters compose the title song of a Joe Pasternak–MGM film was another big step forward for Don Kirshner and Al Nevins' two-year-old company, Aldon Music. But Kirshner wasn't content with just getting the company's name in the end credits. He wanted his own name up there as well. When Kirshner approached his partner on the subject, Nevins wasn't nearly as anxious to upset the applecart.

"Al, I'm going to call Joe Pasternak and tell him our names need to be on the credits too."

Nevins sat at his desk stoically, looking like an ad for *Gentleman's Quarterly,* and motioned Kirshner over to a chair in front of his desk. "Relax, sit down. Let's talk about this," he said. "Don, you know that Joe Pasternak is one of Hollywood's biggest producers. Three Oscar nominations."

"Yes, of course I know," said Don, who started to get a little edgy.

"Well, this man isn't going to listen to us," Nevins offered with a fatherly tone. "He doesn't care two cents about Nevins, Kirshner, or Aldon Music. All he cares about is his movie. And besides getting the title song in this picture, we have a chance for them to use another Sedaka–Greenfield number. Why not let well enough alone?"

"Because we deserve it, Al, that's why," Kirshner said as he got up and headed toward the door. "It's not like they're independent song-writers. They're under contract to us."

As Kirshner walked out, he heard Nevins uncharacteristically holler, "I'm begging you, Don. Don't make that call." This was one time when Kirshner's ego got the best of him. He marched into his office and picked up the phone.

"Mr. Pasternak, this is Don Kirshner. I'm really nobody," he began. "I know you've got this film and you're putting the songwriters' names on the credits. But we've worked very hard on this. And of course you know that Sedaka and Greenfield are under contract to us. So, if you can, I'd like you to put 'Nevins-Kirshner' on the credits, too."

"Who are you again?" was Pasternak's reply.

"We've worked very hard and we're building a business," said Kirshner very calmly. "And we'd like our names on it too."

"Are you telling me how to . . . ," Pasternak squawked, before Kirshner interrupted.

"Why don't you think about it and call me back."

Two weeks later, Kirshner got a call directing him to where he could see a private screening of the film. Even before an actor spoke a single word, Connie's voiceover came up and filled the theater as the camera panned the beautiful beaches of Fort Lauderdale. With his wife, Sheila, by his side, chills ran down his spine when he saw the opening credits. There it was on the screen as big as life:

> "Where the Boys Are"
> Words by Howard Greenfield
> Music by Neil Sedaka
> Courtesy Nevins–Kirshner

Only five years earlier, Don Kirshner was an usher in a movie theater and now his name was on the screen. It was a moment he'd never forget.

"I never dreamed the film would be a huge smash and I never dreamed it would start the whole spring break thing," said Kirshner. "I would have been happy even if it was a bomb."

Where the Boys Are was far from a bomb. It was the biggest grossing low-budget film in MGM's history. Besides Francis, it starred playboy types George Hamilton and Jim Hutton and introduced sexy Paula Prentiss to movie audiences. Yvette Mimieux and Barbara Nichols were co-stars. It opened to big box-office numbers at Radio City Music Hall in New York and around the country.

Time magazine may have captured the film's unusual appeal when it described it as: "One of those pictures every intelligent moviegoer will loathe himself for liking— a corny, phony, raucous outburst of fraternity humor, sorority sex talk and house-mother homilies that nevertheless warms two hours of winter with a travel-poster panorama of fresh young faces, firm young bodies and good old Florida sunshine."

Pasternak was smart enough to have the screenplay based solely on the first half of Glendon Swarthout's novel. In the second half of the book, the so-called innocent kids decide to smuggle guns to Fidel Castro's revolutionaries in Cuba. By the time the picture was released, Castro had already taken over Cuba, and shortly thereafter he dissolved all relationships with the United States and its corporations.

In the picture, Connie wore either a long pink or blue dress in all of her scenes. No jeans, no shorts, just dresses. In fact, it seemed like all the girls wore dresses below the knee line in this film. And oddly enough, the main source of music was jazz, not rock and roll. They did use another Sedaka–Greenfield song (performed by Connie) called "Turn on the Sunshine"—a harmless silly song. Although it was her first film, Francis did more than hold her own with the veteran actors—she in fact seemed the most believable.

Connie Francis teamed up with Joe Pasternak four years later, making a less successful film, *Looking for Love*. She would go on to make a few other pictures of a similar ilk before her film career ended.

Francis never attended the premiere of *Where the Boys Are* because "I didn't like the way I looked, acted, or sang." But while attending the Provincetown International Film Festival in 2001 to screen a new 35-mm print of the film, Francis quipped about her film career, "I've got some nerve being at a film festival."

Halfway to Paradise

Ritchie Valens was only seventeen years old when he became the first Latin rock-and-roll sensation. His love song "Donna" rose to No. 2 on *Billboard* and landed Valens a tour with the great Buddy Holly. When Holly's plane went down with the Big Bopper and Valens aboard, it assured immortality for all three. The date was February 3, 1959, which Don McLean's "American Pie" later identified as "the day the music died."

Michael Anthony Orlando Cassavitis was fourteen when Valens died and it crushed him. Like Valens, Cassavitis had Latin blood, being half Greek and half Puerto Rican. He called himself "Greek-a-Rican." And like Valens, he was short, a little overweight, and had a case of teenage acne. And like Valens, Cassavitis could sing better than anyone he knew.

He decided that if Ritchie Valens could make it, he could make it. So he bought a little secondhand guitar and started auditioning for anyone who would listen. His audition song was Valens' Spanish anthem "La Bamba."

"My father was Greek," he said, "which gave me the courage to knock on doors. For two years, I knocked on almost every door on every floor of the Brill Building and 1650 Broadway, hoping to get discovered, without an ounce of encouragement from anyone."

One day in the summer of 1960, he had just finished another fruitless trip in the Brill Building and decided to try the Turf restaurant on the ground floor for his impromptu auditions. The Turf was a favorite hangout of musicians coming from the demo studios a block away on Broadway. Sheet music with the artists' photos was plastered all over the walls. The Turf had an inexpensive clam bar and you could get a great burger there.

Artie Kaplan was an old high-school friend of Jack Keller's. When he got out of the army in 1960, Keller introduced him to everyone at Aldon Music, where he settled in, wearing many hats. On this particular summer day, he and his songwriting partner, Brooks Arthur, were having lunch at the Turf when Cassavitis walked by singing a few bars of "La Bamba." "Hey, hey," they said, and called him over. After introductions, they walked outside and right there on the sidewalk on Broadway, between 49th and 50th streets, he sang the entire song for them. They were so taken with the kid that they urged Kirshner to meet him.

"I walked into Donnie's office the next day," Cassavitis explained, "and I'm sitting there playing my little guitar and singing 'La Bamba.' I was a fifteen-year-old, fat, pimple-faced kid, coming in as a kid who wanted to be the next Frankie Avalon and get a record deal."

Kirshner's office must have looked amazing to a teenager from Union City, New Jersey. On one wall was a scroll of the hits that Kirshner's company had recently published. It was like a *Who's Who* of the songs he'd been hearing on the radio. There was also a beautiful red piano that had liquor in a neat compartment on one side and candy on the other. Kirshner was a young twenty-six-year-old executive, but to a fifteen-year-old kid from the mean streets, he must have looked forty-six. As the young man played and sang his song, Kirshner stretched back in his chair, put up his feet, and closed his eyes.

"When you played a chord that he liked, it was orgasmic for him," Cassavitis recalled. "And he'd have this look, like 'Oh my god, that chord!' If you sang a melody right or if you hit the right sweet spot in your voice, he had an amazing ability to respond to it, then discuss it, to break it down and then cast it. I mean, he was genius!"

When the kid finished his song he waited, it seemed, forever. Kirshner opened his eyes, sat up, and leaned forward in his chair.

"Kid," Kirshner said with certainty, "you're going to be a big star."

And then he changed the kid's name.

"You can't be Michael Cassavitis," said Kirshner. "It sounds like an actor. Do you have a middle name?"

"Yes, Orlando," said the kid.

"Orlando, I love that," said Kirshner. "We'll just go with one name, like Fabian."

"I don't think I can handle that. What if we use my confirmation name, Anthony?"

"Tony Orlando?" Kirshner said. "I love Tony Orlando! It sounds like you're Bobby Rydell from South Philly. It's perfect!"

So Michael Anthony Orlando Cassavitis became Tony Orlando that day, but he didn't really believe Kirshner's prediction that he was going to be a big star.

"I remember when I left that office, I laughed and said to myself, 'This guy's lying to me.' I had gone to every record company in this town. They tell me nothing and kick me out. But *he* tells me I'm going to be a big star. And I never went back."

For months I tried to track down Tony Orlando. Jack Keller and Artie Kaplan had convinced me that Orlando was an intricate part of the Aldon story. Thanks to Keller's help, I was able to locate Tony's manager, who gave me a number to reach him in between a busy road schedule. When I finally got him on the phone, I couldn't get him to stop talking about Don Kirshner and the magic that was Aldon Music. We literally spoke for hours.

Kirshner couldn't believe the kid didn't come back. After two weeks went by, Don started asking around about him. There was something about the kid's voice he couldn't get out of his head. Finally he found his phone number and called.

"There's a Don Kirshner on the phone. He's looking for you," Tony's mother told him.

"Hello," said Orlando.

"Where are you?" demanded Kirshner. "I told you I'm going to make you a star."

"You gotta be kidding," said the kid.

"No. Now you tell your mother and your stepfather to bring you down here. We're going to put you under contract. I have a great idea. Now get in here!"

Kirshner knew exactly what he was doing. He was going to groom Orlando like he and Nevins had groomed Sedaka. He made a deal to produce Orlando's debut album for Epic Records, a CBS-owned label, which wanted rock-and-roll exposure.

Nevins and Kirshner were the first independent producers to bring master recordings and produced records to the major labels.

"By producing artists themselves, Don and Al opened the door for an entire industry change," said Orlando. "It opened the door for every great entrepreneurial producer thereafter, starting with Burt Bacharach and Phil Spector to name a few. They opened the door to an industry that wasn't there before."

After signing, Orlando was never a stranger again. The first day he showed up for work, Kirshner laid out the game plan. Then he introduced him to Jack Keller.

"Jack is a great writer and producer," Kirshner told him, "and he's going to teach you the studio and how to get comfortable there."

Keller had also worked with Carole King and Gerry Goffin when they first came to Aldon, as he later would with Barry Mann and Cynthia Weil. If Nevins and Kirshner were the father figures to these young kids, then Keller was the uncle they all loved.

"Jack was my first producer, my professor, and my great friend," said Orlando. "All of us at Aldon Music—Barry, Cynthia, Neil (Sedaka), Carole, myself—have him to thank. He was the office's musical shepherd. We all owe him a great deal. I know I do."

Then Kirshner introduced King and Goffin, who still hadn't written a hit song at this point. "Tony's just signed with us," Kirshner told them. "I want you to work on his rhythm-and-blues side, so listen to Ben E. King because I want him to sound like that. I want this Latin–Greek white boy to sound black."

Orlando was surprised that Kirshner did not address his appearance.

"He never said to me, 'Tony, lose weight.' And he never said to me, 'Tony get rid of the pimples.' I lost the weight and lost the pimples that year. I just did, it just happened."

For months Orlando would work with Keller, King, and Goffin. Keller would take him to the studio and teach him how to use a mike. Gerry and Carole would drive him to their Brown Street apartment in Brooklyn, work together for hours, then drive him home.

King and Goffin had a three-room garden apartment. You walked into the living room and to the immediate right was the kitchen. There was no dining room. The piano was an upright pushed against the wall that separated the living room from the kitchen. Around that wall was the bedroom.

"I was there when they wrote 'Halfway to Paradise,' and 'Up on the Roof' and 'Will You Love Me Tomorrow,'" Orlando recalled. "I loved those songs and wanted to record them so badly."

Orlando, who dropped out of school after the eighth grade, says he got his education at Aldon Music. "I never finished high school, but being at Aldon was like going to Harvard. My classroom was Jack Keller's living room in Riverdale and Carole and Gerry's living room in Brooklyn."

Keller, Goffin, and King were his singing professors. Coaching him on the phrasing on "Halfway to Paradise," his debut song, Carole and Gerry told him to pronounce "paradise" as a "pair of dice" you're going to throw on the table.

"Pair of dice" had a more commercial sound to it. It was more soulful. Orlando said that most singers then wanted to sound black. It was a very important part of making hit records. Lasting records. Orlando studied Sam Cooke's, Jackie Wilson's, and Ben E. King's singing styles. And guiding him every step of the way was Carole King.

"She had this great laugh and a beautiful innocence about her," Orlando recalled. "I have this image of Carole in a ponytail with freckles. There was something sexy about her, yet she never put out a sexual-ness. The longer you got to know her, the sexier she became. And at the same time she was this amazingly strong woman, who at the tender age of eighteen was a mother, yet commanding the respect of a full orchestra. I never saw her get upset. She always found the humor in something, or tried to find the good in people or the good in a performance."

Orlando paints a slightly different picture of Gerry Goffin.

"Gerry was complicated. He was a genius," Orlando recalled. "Gerry Goffin was quiet and respectful of people's feelings. I often saw Gerry pull the ivory right off the piano. I mean he would literally lift the ivory up out of frustration because he wasn't happy with the line he had written. He was harder on himself than he ever was on anybody else."

All through the winter of 1960 Orlando worked with King and Goffin and Jack Keller, singing their demos and learning how to get comfortable in a studio. Then one day, soon after Jack Kennedy edged Richard Nixon to become the 35th U.S. president, Kirshner called with the news of a deal with Epic.

"It's going to be the first big independent deal," he told Orlando. "You'll be the first pop singer on Epic's label. They've got Roy Hamilton and Lester Lannon and society orchestra leaders like that, but nobody like you."

What Kirshner had pulled off for Orlando was unheard of in the business at that time. He convinced a major record label to allow his little company, Aldon Music, to package an entire album for them. Aldon would provide the talent (Tony Orlando) and the songs (written by Goffin and King) and produce the album. Epic would supply the promotion and distribution. Their success opened an entirely new industry called independent production.

Kirshner had decided that "Halfway to Paradise" would be Tony's debut song for Epic, but Orlando begged to do another song by Goffin and King, "Will You Love Me Tomorrow." When they all arrived at the studio on 23rd Street, Kirshner broke the news to Tony.

"You won't be recording that song because we gave it to the Shirelles."

"But I love that song," Orlando said, protesting.

Said Kirshner: "Listen to the words," remembering what Mitch Miller had told him. "No teenage boy says that to a teenage girl. Only a teenage girl has that concern."

Orlando understood and eventually agreed. "When you look back, he was dead right. Donnie's instinct to read a lyric and to give it rea-

Tony Orlando, surrounded by (from left to right) producer Jack Keller, Don Kirshner, and Al Nevins. In less than a year, Tony turned from a frog into a prince.

son and purpose was always overlooked by the people in the industry. They saw Donnie as this flamboyant entrepreneur—maybe egocentric type of guy—who had these hit records. No! Donnie nurtured those records. He gave lessons. Donnie would say to Carole, 'Oooh, I loved the bridge. Make it a little bit warmer' like that record or this record. And they would go back and transform a song into a hit."

Epic decided to both introduce Orlando and release "Halfway to Paradise" on March 21, 1961. The introduction would occur on *American Bandstand.* Leading up to the big day, Epic ran an unusual ad campaign in all the trades. For four consecutive weeks, full-page ads ran in *Cashbox, Variety,* and *Billboard* that said:

> On March 21st Epic will introduce
> A Name You Will Always Remember
> A Voice You Will Never Forget:
> Tony Orlando.

And with the ad they ran a silhouette of Orlando next to the ad copy. In the fourth week, his debut record was introduced and the silhouette was filled in with Tony's picture.

As exciting as it was to go on with Dick Clark the day his first record was released, all Tony wanted to do was meet *Bandstand* regulars Carol Scaldafarri and Janet Hamil. To Orlando, one looked like Sophia Loren, the other Doris Day. Clark arranged for him to meet them, and sure enough, they paid no attention to him at all.

"And then on live television, during a commercial," said Orlando, "Dick Clark hands me a piece of paper that says, 'Your drug store is open.' And I didn't know what he meant by 'drug store.' I wondered what the hell is he talking about. I looked at his face."

"Your zipper's open," Clark whispered. "Hurry up; we're coming back from commercial!"

"Are you telling me that all of my family and everybody back in New York that's watching this show, and they saw me with my zipper open?"

"Yes, but don't worry about it," said Clark. "It's no big thing anyway!"

• • •

"Halfway to Paradise" peaked at No. 16 on *Cashbox*, not bad for a complete unknown to the pop music world. Kirshner had another young songwriting team in mind to write Orlando's second hit, "Bless You." Their names were Barry Mann and Cynthia Weil.

But it wasn't until the early '70s that Orlando became a huge star, when he was accidentally coupled with a pair of female voiceover singers called Dawn.

If he didn't know he was a star after "Knock Three Times" and

"Tie a Yellow Ribbon" reached No. 1, he certainly knew it after he was immortalized in the 1976 Academy Award–winning film *Network*.

In the film, newscaster Howard Beale tells everyone that he's "mad as hell" and he's "not going to take it anymore." When the ratings jump, Beale gets his own show. Inspired by Beale's high ratings, the network executives give the hour following Beale to the Symbionese Liberation Army, a black militant group, in what amounts to TV's first reality show.

When Beale's ratings eventually slump, an SLA leader (who describes herself as a "black, commie bitch") complains bitterly about Beale, her lead-in:

"He's plague, he's smallpox, he's typhoid," she bitches to the network suits. "I don't want to follow his goddamn show. I want out of that eight o'clock spot. I've got enough troubles without Howard Beale as a lead-in—you guys scheduled me up against *Tony Orlando and Dawn*."

Who Put the Bomp

Who was that man?
I'd like to shake his hand
He made my baby fall in love with me

The summer of '56 was Jack Keller's fourth playing a hotel in the Catskill mountains. The Catskills then were known as the "Borscht Belt," because of the predominance of both Jewish clientele and performers. It also was a great training ground for comedians, with such greats as Dean Martin and Jerry Lewis, Buddy Hackett and Alan King working there regularly.

The big hotels, like Kutcher's and Grossinger's and the Concord, had the big-name talent and drew the most well-heeled customers. But smaller hotels, like Esther Manor, where Neil Sedaka played the lounge as a teenager, and Zalkin's Birchwood Lodge, also filled up during the summer months with guests who wanted to be entertained in the evening.

Keller spent this particular summer at Zalkin's, in Ellenville, New York. The hotel happened to be located next to a settlement of Hasidic Jews, who got upset each Friday night when the noise from the band disturbed the beginning of their Sabbath.

"They would go out on the road near the entrance to Zalkin's and yell and scream at the cars to go back where they came from," said Steve Wallach, whose grandfather owned the hotel. "It was quite a Keystone Cops scene. We were chasing them away while they were chasing the customers away. It seemed like every weekend we had to call the real cops."

At this point in his career, Keller had been writing songs and taking them to prospective publishers at the Brill Building for more than a year. He was unaware that another prospective songwriter was working at Zalkin's that summer. Barry Imberman, who was seventeen, had taken a job as a busboy and spent every free moment he had at the piano.

One afternoon, Keller was walking back toward the kitchen when he saw a crowd of busboys and waiters around a piano. "I looked in and I saw Barry," Keller recalled, "and he's playing a song called 'Eileen,' which was a takeoff on Paul Anka's hit at that time, 'Diana.' So I walked up to Barry and I introduced myself, told him I thought he was very good, and found out we we're from the same neighborhood in Brooklyn."

The musicians playing the hotel would take off after their show Saturday night and didn't have to be back until 9 p.m. Monday night. That gave Keller all day Monday to push his songs at the Brill Building. Because busboys didn't have a day off, Keller offered Mann a proposition.

"If you want, I'll take your songs down to the Brill Building with mine, and see if anybody'd like 'em," Keller offered.

The young busboy behind the piano practically froze. He was dying to get a song published, but he didn't know if he could trust Keller. Finally he spoke.

"I—I gotta . . ." he stuttered. "I gotta ask my mother," he finally said. Keller paused for moment, then burst out laughing. It was the beginning of a beautiful friendship.

● ● ●

They were just four kids with a dream: Carol Klein, Neil Sedaka, Jack Keller, and Barry Imberman; four Jewish kids from Brooklyn, still in their teens, with just this in common: (1) they lived less than twenty square blocks apart and (2) they all learned piano on uprights their families could barely afford. All they ever wanted out of life was to write a rock-and-roll song and hear it on the radio. That pulling desire led them all to the guiding hand of Don Kirshner under the Aldon Music roof.

Barry Imberman was born February 9, 1939. Ironically, he shares the same birthday as Carole King, who was born in '42. And like King, he shortened his name to something more suitable for rock and roll. He changed it to Barry Mann. By 1960, they'd both be writing songs, practically side by side on upright pianos with only a paper-thin wall separating their cubicles at Aldon Music.

Mann grew up on East 13th Street near Avenue U in Brooklyn. He was about five feet seven inches tall, with dark hair and eyes. Despite being short, he had a very confident swagger. His mother, Emma, was determined that Barry and his brother, Norman, get a musical education and had them both take piano and elocution lessons.

"Their mother made them toe the line and their father, Sidney, scared the hell out of me," said Mann's former neighbor and long-time friend Artie Resnick, when I reached him by phone in 2005. "I remember sitting in their house listening to the two brothers sing and play ukuleles like it was natural as life."

Resnick and Mann both attended P.S. 153 before moving on to Madison High School. Resnick, who later became a successful lyri-cist ("Under the Boardwalk," among others), recalls when Mann told him about his secret ambition. It was at a beach club where Resnick was a cabana boy.

"He started telling me about his dreams to be a singing star," Resnick recalled. "He was going to have some strange name like Fa-bian and wear a zebra-skinned coat. It sounded crazy but you could see he was determined. I didn't see him again until a few years later, when he was at Aldon in one of those tiny little cubicles. He closed the door and played a couple of his songs for me. He was amazing. I was in awe of his talent."

After high school, Mann began studying architecture at Pratt In-stitute in New York. But he couldn't dismiss the thrill he got from writing and singing a song. So he dropped out, much to his mother's chagrin, and started knocking on doors on Broadway. One belonged to a publisher at Lowell Music whose card he had saved from the Catskills. Mann played him several songs he had written, and the guy told him to make a demo of one called "The Ecstasy of Love." Showing just how green he was, he asked the man what a demo was.

"After that summer in the Catskills, Barry and I started hanging out, playing stickball and cards," said Jack Keller. "Barry followed me like a puppy dog. First he followed me to George Paxton Music, then to Aldon. At Paxton's he went up to the receptionist and said, 'I gotta see George Paxton.' Well, George was in the back with the Ames Brothers and he wasn't going to see anybody. But the secretary only says, 'He's busy right now. He can't see you.'

"So Barry waits and waits, and finally he couldn't stand waiting any longer and he bursts into Paxton's office, proclaiming, 'Mr. Paxton, I've got a song you've got to hear.'" Laughing hysterically, Keller added, "George threw him out on his ear."

Although he never got to play for Paxton that day, he learned that he could take getting rejected. By the end of '58, he had sold his first hit, "She Say (Oom Dooby Doom)," recorded by the Diamonds on Mercury Records. He had achieved one of his goals by writing a hit song before his twentieth birthday.

By the end of the year, he had learned that Keller had landed a staff job at Aldon for $200 a week, and on the strength of his hit by the Diamonds, one of Kirshner's favorite groups, Mann landed his own deal at Aldon Music for $150 a week against future royalties. As 1960 began, Barry Mann had a steady income and a great place to write his songs and hone his dream of being a recording artist.

"My first memory of Barry was that I thought he should sing his own songs," Don Kirshner recalled. "To me he was like Darin and Carole and Sedaka—singer-songwriters who could become artists. I thought he had an incredibly different melodic structure with feeling, depth of emotion, and great counter melodies."

Barry's first success at Aldon was "Footsteps," a Top 10 song for Steve Lawrence, which debuted in March 1960. It had a catchy repeating chorus.

"He wanted to know how to note 'Footsteps, da-da-da, da-da' for the background singers," said Keller. "I helped him with that and we started hanging out together. We'd double-date and help each other in the office. He'd sing a lot of my demos and make them sound great."

Barry was a chain smoker and a scotch drinker. Not very tall, he still looked great in jeans and a jacket, which was his everyday uniform. His first trophy car was a Peugeot sedan.

"He was a talker, he could talk a blue streak," said old friend Artie Kaplan. "I was a good listener, so we got along well. He was very ambitious and totally driven. He had great ability to sit down with a lyric and knock out a melody like that. He formulated his music from within, that Plato thing. He was born with it."

• • •

A month after "Footsteps" debuted, a song Mann had written for singer-songwriter Teddy Randazzo called "The Way of a Clown" hit the charts. Don Costa, who Randazzo had become close with, produced it for ABC-Paramount. Ironically, the flip side of that record was written by a struggling newcomer named Cynthia Weil.

Cynthia Weil was born on October 18, 1937 (according to IMDb .com), and raised in Manhattan. A lanky five feet nine inches, she had dirty blond hair and a seductive look. Her parents sent her to the prestigious Sarah Lawrence College in Westchester, New York, where she studied acting. She even had a brief role on the early TV series *The Goldbergs*.

Shortly thereafter, deciding she could write for Broadway, she got a job with Broadway composer Frank Loesser's publishing company. Having little interest in writing for the pop market, she somehow was introduced to Randazzo and began writing with him. She happened to be working with Randazzo when Barry Mann came up to their office to discuss a song Mann had written for him. Cynthia immediately perked up.

"Who's the cute guy?" she asked Judy Tannen, a secretary who was working for Steve Lawrence and Eydie Gorme in the adjoining office. Tannen, whose previous job was switchboard operator at Mercury Records, knew the answer.

Thanks to author David Evanier, I was able to talk to some of Kirshner's old friends, like Joyce Becker and Harriet Wasser. Their background information was invaluable.

"That's Barry Mann," she informed Weil. "He writes for a friend of mine, Donnie Kirshner, over at Aldon Music."

Weil's next question left no doubt about her intentions.

"Is he married?" she asked.

"No. Why don't you go over there and try to see him again," said Tannen.

She made an appointment with Kirshner to show him her lyrics, and hoped to get a chance to meet Mann. Regardless of her real motive, Kirshner, impressed with her lyrics, hired her. Once at Aldon, she decided to check things out with the receptionist.

"She asked Faith the marital status of every male in the office," Keller said with delight. And after hanging around Aldon's reception area for several days, she *accidentally* ran into Barry again. "I guess you can say I stalked him," she told Keller. "Cynthia didn't have to break into the business," Keller pointed out. "All she had to do was pick the right guy."

Barry had been rooming with Artie Kaplan at a friend's midtown Manhattan apartment. At twenty-five, Kaplan was practically the elder statesman of the firm. That was the summer of '61. The Yankees were back atop the American League standings with their number three and four hitters, Mickey Mantle and Roger Maris, locked in a race to try and topple Babe Ruth's long-standing record of sixty homers in a season.

"Barry and I had a ball. We were both in our twenties and New York City was full of chicks," said Kaplan. "We had money in our pockets and we were in the music business and 'happening.' Then Barry met Cynthia and he was mesmerized immediately. And why wouldn't he be? She was five-nine or five-ten and very striking. She looked like she just stepped out of a *Dior* ad. Bright and delightful, she dressed very, very well.

"And that was it; they became a couple right away. She portended to really snag somebody, and he was a great catch. Or it was love at first sight? Whatever it was, Barry and Cynthia were destined to become a great team of writers."

Their love affair kindled as fast as their writing relationship took off.

"When she came in, it just became hot and heavy," said Kirshner. "They were really kind of opposites. She was sophisticated and he was more of a street kid, and I guess opposites attract. And one day it was there."

• • •

Right around that time, Kirshner had given assignments to King and Goffin, and now to Mann and Weil, to write the perfect song for his new discovery, Tony Orlando. Carole and Gerry landed Orlando's debut record, "Halfway to Paradise," but Barry and Cynthia earned the follow-up with their first hit as a songwriting team, "Bless You." Jack Keller produced the session at a new studio where the bugs hadn't yet been worked out.

Keller recalled an early problem at the session: "The song was supposed to begin with Tony coming in cold, singing the opening line, '*Every time I face the world*,' without any accompaniment. Then the string line was supposed come in, but for some reason, it just wasn't working."

Orlando picks up the story: "I'll never forget this. Jack runs out of the control room and he sits down at the piano and he starts playing the bass line to 'Hava Nagila.' He starts playing: bomp-bomp, bomp-bom-bomp, and he kiddingly starts singing 'Hava Nagila' and the orchestra and everybody laughs."

In effect, what Keller was doing, besides getting everyone to relax, was going from a cold opening to the bass line, and it worked.

"When you think that Jack didn't write the song, but yet he was making a huge contribution to Barry and Cynthia's first hit together," Orlando said. "And I remember that while I was singing the song, I looked behind the window of the control room and I saw Cynthia crying. That's how emotional she was about hearing her lyrics being recorded."

Orlando also felt like he had a special relationship with Mann and Weil. "Barry was very sure of himself," Orlando explained. "Cynthia was innocent, shy, and introverted lyrically. When she finally did put a lyric on the table, it was hard to believe that it came from this girl. There was a graciousness about her."

• • •

In the summer of '61, Kirshner tried another songwriting experiment and put Gerry Goffin and Barry Mann together to write a song.

"We were messing around and wanted to see how many songs we could write together in a half hour," said Goffin. "Within five minutes we wrote 'Who Put the Bomp,' a song that mocked rock and roll."

> *Who put the bomp in the bomp-a-bomp-a-bomp?*
> *Who put the ram in the rama-lama-ding-dong?*

It was a very clever knockoff of the Marcels' version of "Blue Moon," a huge hit earlier that year. Barry sang it on the demo, which was so good that Kirshner had no problem making a deal to produce it for ABC-Paramount. Mann's teenage dream of becoming a singing star was about to become a reality, but he was a little gun shy.

"I told him that this was his time," said Kirshner. "I said I could easily get the Marcels to do it, but Barry was right for it, and he sounded great on the demo."

Getting the song recorded, however, was no easy matter. Jack Keller was assigned to produce and knew he needed a street corner–type doo-wop group to back up Barry. To find them, he went over to the Brill Building and listened in the hallways for groups rehearsing.

"We found the perfect group," Keller recalled. "We tried them out in the stairwell to make sure. On the stairwell they sounded great, but it turned out that in the studio they were all a half a note flat. And none of them had the falsetto voice we needed to back up Barry's mock-talking segment."

Al Nevins asked Carole if she'd give it a try. After putting on her headphones, she sang less than two notes, when Gerry, who was sitting in the back of the control room, grabbed the mike and screamed, "Carole, what's wrong with you! You're fucking up the whole song!"

For the first time that anyone had ever witnessed, Nevins broke from his usually cool façade and flopped on the floor laughing. Goffin calmed down and Carole eventually nailed it.

"Who Put the Bomp" debuted on the *Billboard* charts August 21, 1961. Roger Maris had just hit home runs number forty-three and forty-four against the Washington Senators that week in his pursuit of Babe Ruth's single-season record. The song that started as a joke quickly rose to No. 7. It was a pretty amazing performance for a first-time artist, and everyone thought that like Sedaka, Barry Mann had a big recording career in front of him. It turned out to be the only hit he ever had. He even mocked his own failure to get a follow-up hit by recording "Teenage Has Been."

As good a lyricist as history has proved Cynthia Weil to be, she must be grateful every day of her life that she met Barry Mann. He has always had a tremendous capacity to write hit songs, no matter who the lyricist was. Between 1960 and 1963, twenty-seven of the thirty-one songs he had recorded were hits—an astounding batting average! Mickey Mantle wished he could hit like that. During that period it didn't seem to matter who brought him a lyric, because when Mann finished the song it was a hit.

He wrote "Footsteps" with Hank Hunter, "The Way of a Clown" with Howie Greenfield, "I Love How You Love Me" and "Patches" with Larry Kolber, "I'll Never Dance Again" with Mike Anthony, and "Who Put the Bomp" with Gerry Goffin.

Teaming up with Cynthia Weil made him even better. In their first two years writing together, they wrote "Bless You" for Tony Orlando, "Uptown" and "He's Sure the Boy I Love" for the Crystals, "My Dad" for Paul Peterson, "Blame It on the Bossa Nova" for Eydie Gorme, and the incomparable "On Broadway" (with Leiber and Stoller) for the Drifters. A year later, they would write the most played song of the twentieth century, "You've Lost That Lovin' Feelin'," for producer Phil Spector and the Righteous Brothers. They continued to write hits in four different decades. Spector's great arrangement of "Lovin' Feelin'" made the record the success it was, but he selfishly took a writing credit as well.

Artie Kaplan, who has gone on to become a successful musician, songwriter, and recording artist, and who is one of the most respected people in the business, reflects on the combined talent of Mann and Weil.

"That team was made in heaven," said Kaplan. "She was a great lyric writer and he was a great songwriter, and they always delivered for every date that came up. I'm totally convinced that both of them were the key to any threesome (with Spector) or foursome (with Leiber and Stoller) that were considered songwriters on a song. I always believed those two wrote it, or wrote most of it, or had the idea for it, and brought it home. They were just that talented. They were monster songwriters. They were born to be songwriters."

Fifty years later and still married in 2010, Mann and Weil were finally inducted into the Rock and Roll Hall of Fame. In their acceptance speech Weil told the story of the first time she laid eyes on Mann. The song he played for Teddy Randazzo that day, "was fine," she said. "But *he* was oh *so* fine. He was hot and he was cool. I guess you could say I built a career over lust that turned into love."

Take Good Care of My Baby

Take good care of my ba-a-a-by
Please don't ever make her blu-u-u-ue
Just tell her that you love her
Make sure you're thinking of her
In everything you say and do-o-o-o

Another Aldon song debuted on the charts the very same day as "Who Put the Bomp." It was by Goffin and King but almost was a collaboration of Carole and Cynthia's instead.

"When I first got there [to Aldon] hoping to meet Barry, Kirshner told me he had the perfect person for me to write with," Weil told interviewer John Brahney of Taxi, an independent A & R company. "I thought, here comes the cute guy! The door opens and in walks this little girl who looks about twelve."

Kirshner explained that the "twelve-year-old girl" was Carole King, whose husband, Gerry Goffin, worked days as a chemist. Weil agreed to meet at Carole's basement apartment in Brooklyn to try and write something together.

"I was this Manhattan girl who never went on the subway," Weil explained. "It was a nightmare. I had to change trains! I got out there, and Carole played me this great melody. By that time I was exhausted. Who could write? So I said, 'Why don't I take this home. I can play a little piano. Just make me a lead sheet. I'll fool around with it and I'll call you.'"

She took the two subways back home, and when she walked in, the phone was ringing and it was Carole calling to say that Gerry was mad she gave her the melody.

"I have to take it back," King said sheepishly. "Gerry really likes it and he says he has a really good idea for it."

"Oh, yeah. What's so good?"

"It's called, 'Take Good Care of My Baby.'"

• • •

Cynthia, Barry, and Gerry (far right) are huddled around Carole at the piano. Best friends, the two couples were enormously competitive.

After the enormous success of "Will You Love Me Tomorrow," the music industry started taking a close look at anything written by Goffin and King.

"Essentially, it put Scepter Records on the map and made any success they had after that possible," said Kirshner. "At that point I started to think we had the power to make or break a record label."

In the spring of '61, King and Goffin had hits with Tony Orlando's "Halfway to Paradise" and the Drifters' "Some Kind of Wonderful." The latter was the first Goffin and King song Leiber and Stoller produced. "Carole was the first girl that I could communicate with in a nonverbal way," Goffin recalled. "'Some Kind of Wonderful' was how I felt about her."

Leiber and Stoller were recognized as the best producing team in the business and it became a signal to the industry that Gerry and Carole were for real. A teenage singer named Bobby Vee recorded their next song, called "How Many Tears."

Vee, born Robert Velline, was only fifteen years old when he woke up the morning of February 3, 1959. He was excited about going to the rock-and-roll show that night in Moorehead, Minnesota, just across the Red River from his home in Fargo, North Dakota. But when he came home from school for lunch that day, he heard the news that Buddy Holly's plane crashed and that Holly had died along with the Big Bopper and Ritchie Valens.

The remaining acts, including Dion and the Belmonts and Holly's band, the Crickets with Waylon Jennings, arrived by bus around noon. They met with the radio station promoters, who decided to go on with the show.

"They made an announcement that if there were any local bands in the area that would help fill in to give them a call," Vee remembered when I reached him by phone. There were only a couple of bands in town, including Vee's, which was a garage band. "We didn't even have a name. We called the station and we just showed up and waited in the wings and that was it."

Then the host of the concert turned to Vee's group and asked for their name. Vee whispered something to him. Then the host blared into the mike, "Ladies and gentleman, here they are, the Shadows." Vee sang lead, and along with his brother, Bill, and two other band members, they did a few Elvis songs and a few Everly Brothers favorites.

"There were a thousand people there. It was sold out," said Vee. "I wasn't scared until I got onstage and heard, 'Here they are, the Shadows.' The lights come on and we're clawing away at the guitar and all of a sudden I felt myself relax. And I thought, *Wow, this sounds good.*' Afterward a guy came up and handed me his card and said if we were looking for work to call him."

The Shadows worked school dances on a regular basis after that, and on June 1, 1959, recorded what Vee calls the ultimate heartbreak song, "Suzie Baby," which he wrote. With only sparse promotion, the record became a big hit in Midwest markets, and before long it caught the eye of a young producer in Los Angeles named Tommy "Snuff" Garrett.

Although Garrett was only twenty-two himself, he had been around the block. He'd quit school at the age of fifteen and went to work for rock radio station KLIF in Dallas. Two years later, he was a disc jockey in oil-rich Wichita Falls, Texas, near Lubbock. While there, he became best friends with a young singer named Buddy Holly.

"Buddy used to give me his records to play before they were sent out by the distributors. When he gave me 'Peggy Sue' I played it for five straight hours," Garrett told me. "I went on the air and I said, 'Here's the new record from Perry Como.' And I played 'Peggy Sue.' Then I said, 'Here's the new record from Gale Storm.' And I played 'Peggy Sue.' The phones were ringing off the wall. It created havoc."

Garrett became so successful he added an afternoon TV show as well. He was making close to $500 a week—an enormous sum for someone so young—when Holly's plane went down. Garrett became so depressed he quit his job and drove to L.A. on a whim and soon after landed a job as a producer for Liberty Records.

"Our Minneapolis distributor told me about this really young kid named Robert Velline," said Garrett. "I listened to his song, 'Suzie Baby,' and it reminded me of Buddy right away. I picked up with Bobby where I thought Buddy left off."

When "Suzie Baby" first started to hit, Vee began getting calls from record companies wanting to sign him, but the call he got from Garrett topped them all.

"Everybody else was calling to talk about numbers and percentages and money and stuff that I didn't know anything about," Vee explained. "But Snuffy called and said, 'I'm sitting right here with Gerry Allison, the drummer for the Crickets, and I played him 'Suzie Baby' and it brought a tear to his eye.'"

Vee immediately felt connected to him. "Snuff Garrett was only twenty-two," said Vee, "but he lived big, thought big, and dreamed big."

By the time Velline had relocated to L.A. and Garrett changed his name to Vee, Garrett had produced two hits for singer Johnny Burnett, "Dreamin'" and "You're Sixteen." It didn't take him long to strike gold with Bobby Vee either. When 1960 came to a close, Vee had reached the No. 6 spot on *Billboard* twice, first with the remake of "Devil or Angel" and then with "Rubber Ball."

Garrett loved the melody and lyrics Goffin and King had written for "Will You Love Me Tomorrow," and got in touch with Kirshner looking for any other new songs they had. He chose Carole and Gerry's "How Many Tears" for Vee's next release.

"When we were about to record the song, Carole and Gerry called and said they were in L.A. and would love to come to the session," Vee recalled. "During the break, Carole sat down at the piano and played us a song they had just written, 'Take Good Care of My Baby.' We flipped out."

That Kirshner, a Jewish kid from New York, and Garrett, a good old boy from Texas, would become such bosom business buddies wasn't difficult to understand. They were both young and becoming very successful very fast. When Garrett invited Don out to L.A. to discuss "Take Good Care of My Baby," Kirshner accepted, and traveled all the way there by train.

"'We're going to make you a pallet,'" Snuff told Kirshner. "Well, he didn't know what a pallet was, and when I told him it was a bed on the floor, he laughed his head off."

Kirshner had an unresolved problem going into the deal with Garrett. He had already offered "Take Good Care of My Baby" to Dion to record. Dion Dimucci was approaching his twenty-first birthday in the summer of '61. He had already left his group, the Belmonts, to become a single act. His first record as a single, "Lonely Teenager," was a semi-hit and climbed to No. 12 on *Billboard* in late 1960, but his next three releases failed to reach the Top 40.

Dion's management and his record label, Laurie, knew his next release would be critical. They narrowed it down to "Take Good Care of My Baby" and one other. Dion went to Aldon's offices at 1650 Broadway to sit down in person with Carole and Gerry.

"I'll never forget sitting down and listening to Carole King," Dion later told me when I reached him by phone in Florida. "To hear her go through song after song—it was fucking unforgettable. It affects you right down to your soul."

Dion recorded "Take Good Care of My Baby" and even placed it on his next album. But for some reason it didn't work. His version of the song was slower than Carole's demo, and a little on the bluesy side. However, his next release turned out to be the biggest record of his career, "Runaround Sue."

Kirshner then gave the okay to Garrett for Vee to record "Take Good Care of My Baby." "Snuffy was concerned when he heard that Dion didn't release his version," said Vee, "so he asked them to write an intro. That was the kicker, the verse. It set up the song and made it an original piece of material."

Here's where opinions differ. Garrett remembers that *he* wrote the verse with Carole, even though he is not credited as one of the songwriters.

"It was in Donnie's office that I wrote the verse with Carole," Garrett recalled. "Gerry wasn't there at the time. She was pregnant and we sat down at the piano. I knew what I wanted and she gave it to me."

> *My tears are falling because you've taken her away,*
> *And though it really hurts me so,*
> *There's something that I've got to say . . .*

Goffin clearly remembers it another way.

"I wrote the verse at home at 2635 Brown St. when I wrote the song with Carole," he said. "His [Garrett's] memory fails him. In fact, when I wrote the verse I was a little embarrassed because I thought it was a little too cute. We wrote the song very fast, in one sitting. I wrote most of the melody and Carole wrote the chords."

The inspiration for the song came from the multitude of love songs out then involving three people, called triangle songs. Musically, Goffin said they were inspired by Vee's previous recording, "Stayin' In."

"When I wrote the punch line," Goffin recalled, "I said to Carole, 'I've got the line that's gonna make this a big hit'":

And if you should discover,
That you don't really love her,
Just send my baby back home to me.

"Take Good Care of My Baby" debuted for Bobby Vee on *Billboard* August 7, 1961, on the Liberty label. It stayed on the charts the rest of the year and was No. 1 for nearly a month. It was the first No. 1 record for both Vee and Garrett and the second for Goffin and King.

Only ten days after Kirshner gave Garrett the okay to record it, Goffin and King heard it on the radio while driving home from Connecticut.

"We knew it was a hit because it was out so fast," said Goffin. "I got goose bumps when I heard it on the car radio that weekend. We celebrated by going to this little restaurant in Sheepshead Bay for hot turkey sandwiches."

After the record was released, Aldon lyricist Larry Kolber, who wrote "I Love How You Love Me," stopped by the office to congratulate fellow lyricist Goffin.

"He paid me the greatest compliment," Goffin recalled. "He said, 'Thanks for putting *baby* back in the English language.'"

I Love How You Love Me

Larry Kolber was a levelheaded guy with an extremely quick wit. When he got out of the army in 1958 at the age of twenty-three, he was going to get a good job and finally make some money. He had studied journalism in college and had written for *Stars and Stripes* magazine in the army, so he thought he might try advertising or sales.

Soon after he was back in New York, he found himself in a long line of vets to collect a $20 unemployment check. He started chatting with the guy in front of him, Larry Martin, who was a songwriter. Martin said he had written a hit before he even went into the service, "Till We Two Are One," which was No. 7 for Georgie Shaw in 1954.

"The only songwriter I ever heard of was Irving Berlin," Kolber told him. "I can't believe I'm talking to a guy who actually made a living writing songs. I tell him in college I used to kid around and write dirty songs for a nightclub act in Greenwich Village. He said, 'Let's try to write something.' So we wrote a song called 'Forget Me Not.'"

Martin soon called Kolber and said he had met a guy named Don Kirshner, who was opening a publishing office with a guy who used to be with the Three Suns singing group. Maybe they should take "Forget Me Not" there.

"I was a whiskey salesman by then and had nothing to lose," Kolber recalled. "Kirshner heard 'Forget Me Not' and took 'Forget Me Not.' The next thing I know Martin calls and says we've got the next hit by the Kalin Twins. A quarter million records it sold. I figured this is it; my life is made."

It was one of Kirshner's first coups as a publisher. The Kalin Twins were coming off a Top 5 smash called "When." Everyone was trying to get the follow-up. Don had some contacts at Decca from when he brought Bobby Darin to them, and got the right man to listen to Kolber and Martin's song. "Forgot Me Not" rose to No. 12 and Kirshner thought he had found a hit songwriting team.

"That's when he asked me to sign," said Kolber. "I said, 'Why not? I'm too busy to be knocking on publishers' doors.' So he gave me a hundred bucks and I signed. I think Neil Sedaka and Howard Greenfield were the only ones there before me. Martin later left the business and became an insurance salesman. I had another job and money coming in, and didn't sweat it, so I kept going up there and Donnie kept getting bigger."

Kolber had a bird's-eye view of Aldon Music's rise to the top of the pop music world. And he credits Kirshner for most of that success.

"Donnie was a good guy, a talented guy," he said. "He had a lot of balls and a lot of heart. The kind of guy you wanted to be in business with. He had this great ability to captivate people he wanted to like him. [Phil] Spector became hot, and boom, he had Spector in his pocket. Deep down Donnie was a pussycat. The type that would cry at movies. But when he set his sights on getting a record—he got it."

About himself, Kolber liked to say, "I was a liquor salesman with a hobby." He was only a year younger than Kirshner, and the two became friends as well as colleagues. On weekends Don and Sheila and Larry and his wife would often go to the Concord Hotel in the Catskills. And Kolber would make a point of bringing Al Nevins rare brandy for his lavish parties. Kolber's sales career continued to flourish and he soon became a top gun for Four Roses whiskey.

In July 1961 all seemed right in Larry Kolber's world. There was a new hope in the country after JFK's "ask not what your country can do for you" inauguration speech. America was back in the space race after astronaut "Gus" Grissom became the second American to orbit the Earth that July.

And the Yankees were leading the American League again, with Roger Maris and Mickey Mantle locked in a ding-dong home-run battle that threatened Babe Ruth's record.

One day after completing a sales call on Broadway in July '61, Kolber decided to grab some lunch at Hector's Cafeteria across from Kirshner's office at 1650 Broadway. While there, he kept thinking about a song title and wrote it on a Four Roses cocktail napkin: "I Love How You Love Me," followed by these lines:

I love how your eyes close whenever you kiss me
And when I'm away from you, I love how you miss me
I love the way you always treat me tenderly
But, darling, most of all, I love how you love me.

Kolber looked at what he had written on the Four Roses napkin and knew it was special. He knew it was the best lyric he had ever written. But what should he do? Aldon was just across the street, but could he find a composer for his lyric?

"I wrote the lyric in seven minutes and I ran across the street and up the elevator wondering who was there," he said. "I needed a melody writer, any melody writer, and sitting there was Barry Mann."

Mann loved the lyric and wrote an upbeat melody nearly as fast. With Tony Orlando about to record, they raced the song into Kirshner's office, hoping to get a spot on Orlando's album. To their surprise, they weren't alone. A young, unknown producer was sitting in the corner of Kirshner's office. The young producer listened quietly to the song as Barry performed it.

"Then he asked Donnie if he could have it for a girl group he was producing in L.A.," Kolber explained. "I was pissed off because I was losing a shot at a Tony Orlando record."

The producer was Phil Spector, who at twenty-one had just moved to New York to work with Leiber and Stoller. Kirshner would have never said no.

Spector took the song to Los Angeles and had a backup singer, who was the girlfriend of a buddy, do the demo. Her name was Cherilyn Sarkisian, but in a few years would simply be known as Cher.

Phil Spector wrote his first song, "To Know Him Is to Love Him," while still in high school, after seeing that inscription on his father's tombstone. He had taught himself a few instruments and, with $40 he borrowed, he went into a demo studio with a few friends and cut the record. He called the group the Teddy Bears, and they soon had the No. 1 song in the country in December 1958.

After performing for a while, Spector longed for the thrill of producing the records rather than singing them. He gravitated to Lester Sill, probably the most connected rock-and-roll music man on the West Coast. Sill had helped groom Leiber and Stoller in a similar way a few years earlier and decided it was time to send Spector to New York. On Independence Day 1960, Spector flew to New York and went directly to Leiber and Stoller's offices in the Brill Building.

"Lester Sill called me and asked if I'd let Phil hang out and steal some of our ideas," recalled Jerry Leiber. "When he arrived, he had no place to stay and he wound up sleeping in our office that first night."

By the end of that first summer Spector had co-written "Spanish Harlem" with Leiber and was well on his way. A year later, sitting in Kirshner's office, Spector's first reaction to Mann and Kolber's "I Love How You Love Me" was that it would be perfect for the Paris Sisters, a girl group he was producing in L.A.

"I wrote the song for Tony Orlando," Kolber said. "But Kirshner wasn't about to turn down Spector because of his relationship with Leiber and Stoller."

After many e-mails and phone calls, I was able to reach Albeth Paris, whose memory of her time with Phil Spector and Don Kirshner was crystal clear.

Albeth, Sherrell, and Priscilla Paris grew up in San Francisco in the '50s, under the watchful eye of their mom, Faye, who sang opera before she retired to raise the girls. From the first, they were performers, dressing alike and singing and dancing at USO shows before they were even in their teens. Faye would have them learn all the hits of the day, and when the Andrews Sisters came to perform at the Warfield Theater in San Francisco in 1954, the girls, dressed identically, were sitting in the front row.

In those days, theaters like Radio City Music Hall in New York and the Warfield in San Francisco showed films with stage acts in between. It wasn't unusual for a headliner to come on five or six times in a day.

"We took a day off from school, we were so excited," said Albeth Paris, the oldest of the sisters. "We rehearsed Andrews Sisters' hits for days, hoping to meet them. They noticed us by the second show, called us backstage, and asked if we'd like to watch the next show from the wings."

The Andrews Sisters had their orchestra stop midway through their next show and one of them said, "We have three little girls back here that are about the ages we were when we started. Would you like them to sing a song?" The audience applauded dutifully.

"They had never heard us sing, but they knew we had learned their songs," said Paris. "We came out onstage—and my mother came from the audience to sit at the piano so we'd feel comfortable."

The orchestra played and they sang two of the Andrews Sisters' greatest hits, "Pennsylvania Polka" and "Rum and Coca-Cola." This time the audience really went wild. And in the crowd, to make the story complete, were two agents from MCA, who signed the Paris Sisters the next day.

For the next seven years, the girls honed their nightclub act, belting in three-part harmony. Their father got them false birth certificates so they could play all through the night at the clubs in Las Vegas, and they had recorded several times for Decca, but without a hit. Then their mom took them to meet Lester Sill late in 1960, and they signed on his new label, Gregmark. That's when Sill asked Spector to return to L.A. after his year of seasoning in New York.

This was years before Spector created his famous "Wall of Sound," and even before he became known for producing the Crystals. But he had a great idea for the Paris Sisters. He wanted their harmony to sound like his original group, the Teddy Bears, and he was looking for the Paris sister who could match the whispery tones of the lead singer from the Teddy Bears, Annette Kleinbard.

"He came out to our house and auditioned us individually to see who he wanted to sing lead," Albeth Paris recalled. "We sat out on our front step, he played a little guitar and we all sat around. He searched for the right keys and we took turns singing. Priscilla was the youngest and she had that sound—that wonderful plaintive sound. And she was the lead voice."

(Left to right) The Paris Sisters: Priscilla, Albeth, and Sherrell surround Phil Spector at the piano as he shows them how to record "I Love How You Love Me."

They rehearsed "I Love How You Love Me" at home several times, in the slow, haunting style that Spector created, which was far different from Mann's upbeat tempo. They went into Goldstar Studios at Santa Monica and Vine to record it, but they found Spector difficult to work with.

"He was always so outrageous," Paris explained. "His behavior was very erratic. He was always late and we always had to wait. We did numerous retakes."

But Spector knew the exact sound he wanted and he didn't care how much studio time it would take until he achieved it. Albeth Paris explained how he got that sound for "I Love How You Love Me."

"Sherrell and I overdubbed our voices, which wasn't common at all in those days. We didn't sing live with the band as we had in our earlier days with Decca. Instead we sang on top of the band's track. Then he took Priscilla in last, into a little sound-proof booth to sing the last track. He had her sing as breathy as she could."

In Richard Williams' 1972 book *Out of His Head: The Sound of Phil Spector*, Williams writes, "This might also be one of Spector's most important records. Listen to the distant quality of the strings—in that line of overtones without the basic note, it's possible to hear everything that Spector ever did with strings in later years."

When the record was released, it hit the ground running. The song debuted on *Billboard* Labor Day weekend of '61 and peaked at No. 5. The girls remained close with Spector and even stayed at his apartment in New York when they came in to promote their hit. When they stopped by Kirshner's office, he ushered everyone else out so he could hold court with the girls. "We were hot potatoes," Albeth recalled.

"We were all very close to Phil during those years," she said. "Priscilla in particular. He had a crush on her. We'd often visit him at his mansion in L.A. off the Sunset Strip. She was closest to Phil because she was the youngest, had the most passion, and made the biggest emotional connection. She used her artistic energies the same way he did."

When Larry Kolber heard how Phil Spector had slowed down his song to the same crawl that "To Know Him Is to Love Him" had, he wasn't happy.

"It was almost a funeral dirge," said Kolber. "At that moment I hated Phil Spector. Then wop, it's a huge hit! Who knew? Seven years later, Bobby Vinton does it all over again the same way and it's Top 10 all over again. I'm still getting paid for that song. I love Phil Spector!"

Kirshner didn't need to hear Spector's record to know it was a hit. He knew it as soon as he heard the title.

"You've got to understand," he explained. "'Will You Love Me

Tomorrow,' 'You've Lost That Lovin' Feeling,' 'Up on the Roof,' 'On Broadway,' 'Take Good Care of My Baby,' all say it in the title. And when Larry brought it to me I knew it was a hit because you can't say more to a girl, or a girl to a boy than 'I Love How You Love Me.' It says it all in the title. It's a caring, sharing, warm, sentimental feeling of love expressed in those six words. It was one of the warmest lyrics ever written by a liquor salesman, that I had ever heard."

Later that year, Kolber and Mann combined again with a country song called "Patches," about a guy who falls for a girl from the wrong side of the tracks. Because the lyric had both song characters committing suicide, no record company would touch it. Then an unknown label called Smash put the record out nine months later, in the summer of '62, with Dickie Lee singing. It quickly rode its way to No. 6 and Mann and Kolber had another hit.

The only thing that prevented Kolber and Mann from being a great songwriting team was Cynthia Weil. Once Barry moved in with Cynthia in July '61, it was pretty much the end of Barry writing with any other lyricist.

"I wrote two songs with Barry," Kolber lamented, "and both were monsters. He was a tremendous talent. Then Cynthia pops into the picture and she marries him. If I knew he wanted to get married, I would have married him. But he never even made a move on me."

Cynthia's mother, however, was never sure that Barry was the right one for her daughter. Walking down the aisle she whispered to Cynthia that it wasn't too late to change her mind.

As for the Paris Sisters, they never made a dime from "I Love How You Love Me." Spector's recording expenses for all the retakes were deducted from their royalties, leaving them with next to nothing. The record did, however, make them famous, and gave them a sound they became identified with.

"That was the start of people embracing that sound," Albeth Paris said. "Phil created that sound completely. That was his vision. We were belters, in a time warp. We were still singing the three-part harmony in our stage act. Our fans were disappointed because we couldn't re-create that sound in our show."

By the 1980s the Paris Sisters had stopped performing and were raising families. Priscilla moved to Paris, France, where she lived for twenty-five years before suddenly dying from a stroke in 2003. Albeth and Sherrell paid tribute to her in the liner notes on their *Everything Under the Sun* album, which was re-released in 2005 by Eric Records.

As for Spector, he and Sill became partners on their own label by joining their first names together as Nevins and Kirshner had with Aldon. Phil and Les started the Philles label, which became famous for Spector's productions with a girl group he put together called the Crystals. Subsequent arguments over Spector's excessive studio time and cost overruns broke up the partnership, but not before the Crystals recorded six hits in a row.

Mann and Kolber's song was just another big hit in a long line of hits that year for Aldon Music. Before 1961 would close, Aldon would also publish "Goodbye Cruel World," No. 3 for actor James Darren; "Run to Him," No. 2 for Bobby Vee; and Neil Sedaka's "Happy Birthday Sweet Sixteen," which peaked at No. 6. With songwriters like Carole King, Barry Mann, and Jack Keller now being recognized as the great talents they were, the industry began to take Kirshner's role in the process for granted.

That same year, after winning ten pennants in twelve years, Casey Stengel was no longer the manager of the New York Yankees. With Maris and Mantle in the lineup, nothing less than winning the World Series became acceptable.

"Donnie had a lot of talent," Kolber remembered. "They called him a great publisher with a great ear. He was, and he did. But he had a lineup like Casey Stengel. He had his own Maris and Mantle. He was a great manager, a great guy, a great talent, a great publisher, and had a great ear. But he also had the people who knew how to write."

Some Kind of Wonderful

By the summer of '61, Kirshner had his "Magnificent 7" staff of songwriters in place: Neil Sedaka, Howie Greenfield, Gerry Goffin, Carole King, Barry Mann, Cynthia Weil, and Jack Keller. Keller was the only composer of the group who didn't have a steady writing partner, but that soon was solved.

Part of Kirshner's brilliance was mixing and matching team members. Keller, for example, would write with Goffin every Tuesday and Thursday, with Greenfield Mondays and Wednesdays, and with Larry Kolber on Fridays.

The match-making merry-go-round produced amazing results. Mann and Goffin wrote "Who Put the Bomp" in one of their sessions, while King and Greenfield created the Everly Brothers hit "Crying in the Rain." The latter was the elusive Everly Brothers hit Kirshner longed for.

Kirshner was an equal-opportunity publisher. Once he signed you, he made sure you learned from everyone in the office. In 1961, nineteen-year-old Artie Wayne was a perfect example. Bobby Darin sent young Wayne to Aldon after hearing him perform backstage at an Alan Freed stage show.

"After hearing my songs," Wayne said, "Don gave my mother such a pep talk about my future, even I was convinced I couldn't fail. Donnie put me together with Howie Greenfield, who showed me how to tighten my lyrics; he asked Jack Keller to show me more interesting chords to play against my melodies, and he had Barry Mann show me how to sing harmony."

Things were so loose, love and happiness engulfed the place. Barry

Mann would crack everyone up impersonating Al Nevins' smooth style, and Kirshner's distinct walk and unbridled enthusiasm. They felt so comfortable, they could even tease the boss. Once a secretary asked Kirshner if he was aware that he was wearing one black and one brown shoe. As he looked down at his feet, someone said, "I bet you have another pair just like that at home." Everyone laughed, except for Don.

Each Friday Kirshner would summon everyone into his office to play the songs they had been working on all week. If someone was stuck trying to finish a lyric or a lyrical phrase, confused on how to finish a bridge in a song, or simply trying to write a better tune, someone else would make a suggestion. It was like being at songwriters camp. And it was brilliant. Many used a title from a Goffin/King song to describe how it felt. They said it was "some kind of wonderful."

"Don Kirshner was our father figure and we all wanted to please him," Sedaka recalled. "He knew how to provoke us, how to bait us, and how to inspire us. He had a certain bigger-than-life *joie de vivre.* He represented success."

Cynthia Weil put it another way: "We didn't know we were writing standards," she told *Bomp Magazine* writer Greg Shaw. "We were only trying to please Donnie."

During the summer Kirshner would round everybody up on Wednesdays to play softball in the "Music Man's League" at Randall's Island, which is right outside Manhattan.

"On the way to the field Donnie would have the car stop at a sporting goods store," Keller said. "He'd go in and buy a whole supply of bats and gloves and balls. Then the next week he'd do it all again because he couldn't remember where the equipment was from the week before. Bobby Darin would play second base and Donnie would play shortstop. That summer he must have bought enough stuff to outfit a major league team."

Often on Saturday nights the "Magnificent 7" and a few other Aldon regulars would get together at Keller's apartment in the ritzy Riverdale section of the Bronx. During the summer they'd have pool parties at Keller's place, or up in the Catskills at Esther Manor, the hotel owned by Sedaka's in-laws. After dinner everyone would gather at the piano and they'd all play their latest songs for each other.

"It was like the Garden of Eden," said Keller. "We were on top of the world. I use the phrase Garden of Eden because ego never came between any of us. We were competitive but we got along fabulously. That's why it was so successful!"

It worked because Nevins and Kirshner took care of all their problems, one way or the other. When Carole and Gerry couldn't pay the rent or needed furniture or a car, Don and Al were there for them.

"Al and Don were the parents and we all were the kids, competing for their love and their attention," Keller remembered. "We all would try to write the best song we could, and if they loved it, we felt loved. We [the kids] didn't have to think about anything except writing the next song. That was the beauty of that office. When you walked down the hall, Donnie was on the left side and you went that way if you wanted him to listen to your songs. Al was on the right side. He was the office psychiatrist, and he not only listened to your problems, he usually solved them too."

While Kirshner's office was bright and featured his red piano, Nevins' office was subdued, similar to a study or a lawyer's office, with bookcases and dark paneling. The only clue that he was in the music business was a sixty-six-key cocktail piano in the corner.

"If you went in Al's office with a problem," said Keller, "you'd always walk out feeling better. But if you went on too long, Al had this tiny little chiming bell on his desk, and when he felt you had spent enough time he would give it a little flick, and it would ding. That was your cue that your time was about up."

The generosity of the two partners did not stop with the "Magnificent 7." When song plugger Don Rubin wanted to get engaged, Nevins gave him the money for an engagement ring. When Tony Orlando's mother needed an operation, Kirshner paid the hospital bill. When songwriter Brooks Arthur's wife was having their first child, Kirshner paid that bill too, although Arthur had yet to write a hit song. When seventeen-year-old demo singer Ron Dante had his guitar stolen from his car, Kirshner bought him a new one. A month later, when the new one was also stolen, Kirshner bought him another.

Then there was the case of Darin and Kirshner's friend Dick Lord, who eventually became a very successful stand-up comedian. Lord worked for Aldon for about a year performing various tasks. One morning he was so upset about something he was crying at his desk. Nevins passed by and asked what was wrong.

"Look at my face," Lord said. "It's all red and broken out. I don't know how it happened. It's horrible."

"Wait here," said Nevins, who disappeared for a few minutes. When he returned, he handed Lord a piece of paper with the name and number of a dermatologist.

"Within a week my skin cleared up," said Lord, "but I must have gone back to that dermatologist three or four times. Finally I told Al that I was embarrassed that the guy never gave me a bill."

"Don't worry about it,' said Nevins. "It's been taken care of."

Time after time Nevins and Kirshner were there for their Aldon Music family. When it was discovered that Tony Orlando's ten-year-old sister Rhonda was crippled with cerebral palsy, Kirshner brought a car full of Tony's new friends to his house in Union City, New Jersey, to cheer her up.

"All these people became my sisters and brothers and took a personal interest in Rhonda," said Orlando. "They all had huge hearts and are all special people to me.

"Have you ever taken your wife or your friends or your kids back to your old neighborhood?" Orlando asked. "Well, for me, it's the sixth floor at 1650 Broadway."

Orlando went to explain what he thinks was Aldon's magic formula. "There was an unselfishness between these people, and Donnie nurtured all of our talent. He wasn't just a guy who had a great ear. Donnie 'father-hooded' that office, and gave birth to those songs. And trust me when I tell you he was the father and mother of invention."

Kirshner set the tone in that office, and part of that tone was a healthy competition between the writers. As an athlete Kirshner thrived on competition. He captained his basketball team in college and took those leadership skills with him to Aldon. He also made life fun. He was known to walk around the office barefoot, eating either pickles or peanuts.

Carole King defined Kirshner for the A&E biography *The Teens Who Stole Pop Music*: "Al was the classy guy and Don was the driving guy," she said. "In his own way Don had class, but he wasn't about class. He was about drive. And the combination was incredible."

While his team was writing songs, Kirshner was busy networking with the record companies, trying to find out who was scheduled to cut an upcoming album, and how many empty slots there might be to fill. Then every Wednesday night Kirshner would call the "Magnificent 7" at home and tell them who was on deck.

"The Everly Brothers are up," he'd tell them, meaning they were about to record an album. "See if you can get the follow up to 'Cathy's Clown.'" Or "Snuff Garrett's coming to town looking for songs for Bobby Vee," or "The Drifters are recording a new album in a few weeks." Then they would all scramble to see who could get the next record.

They didn't realize that they were always learning from each other, fighting off each other, competing with each other. The cubicles that they wrote in were actually half a dozen closet-size music rooms lined up in a row against one wall. They looked like telephone booths, only slightly bigger. Each room was barely big enough for an upright piano, a chair and an ashtray.

Some people thought that if you wrote a hit, you graduated to a room with a window. But the cubicles had no windows. The walls in between the cubicles were paper-thin and the writers could hear a good part of what was being created in the next room.

Paul Kaufman, Keller's boyhood friend who later would write "Poetry in Motion," worked briefly at Aldon as a songwriter. He remembered one day being in the cubicle next to Carole King.

"She was writing 'Will You Love Me Tomorrow,'" Kaufman said. "I heard the song through the walls and I got so depressed that she did it so easily that I stopped writing for that day. It was demoralizing. I thought to myself, 'How am I ever going to compete with that?'"

Another young writer, Artie Wayne, had a similar reaction the first time he heard Carole play that song. "I couldn't write another song for a month," he said. "I thought that I was wasting my time. That I had already heard the ultimate song."

Wayne also heard King and Goffin constantly arguing and yelling at each other. "They were always at each other's throats," he recalled. "Everybody knew about it because the walls were so thin. Then all of a sudden the yelling would stop and this beautiful music would come out. And you said to yourself, 'Shit, is that what it takes to get a hit?' Their relationship was so volatile, but it was understandable because their musical sensitivities were so far advanced that when something was ignited it took the music and the song to a place that nobody had gone before."

There were many days that Goffin and King were in the room right next to Mann and Weil. Hearing the team in the next cubicle propelled them to write something better.

At the beginning of their careers Mann and Weil were intensely competitive. They lived, ate, and breathed pop songs. Soon they felt like they were in a fierce competition with Goffin and King.

Once Kirshner told them who was about to record an album, they wrote as fast as they could to complete a song. Then they rushed to make a demo of the song the way they felt it should be recorded. Then they'd wait for Kirshner to call with the news of which team got the record.

For the team that won, life was good and they felt like they were both worth something. If they didn't get the record, they felt like they didn't exist. They became the songs they wrote. As the stressful competition intensified, the two couples would even vacation together, to avoid being beat out of a record by the other team.

"We were sort of friendly competitive," Goffin recalled. "When we first came to the office, we looked up to Barry because he had a hit before us. Then, after 'Will You Love Me Tomorrow,' we became closer." Translation: they had earned Mann and Weil's respect.

The friendship and the competition meant that while one team would win, the other—their best friends—were the losers.

"There was a camaraderie but the underlying competition was still fierce," remembered Artie Kaplan, who was very close with both couples. "When each of them had a success, it sometimes took a few months for them to talk to one another, but they always came back with warm ferocity."

As close as the two couples were, they were worlds apart when it came to their lifestyles. Here's how legendary rock writer Greg Shaw of *Bomp Magazine* described them:

"Mann and Weil were the hipsters of the Brill Building set," he wrote in 1982. "While Carole King and her friends were basically square middle-class types who wrote things like 'Take Good Care of My Baby" by day, and watched TV at night, Barry and Cynthia liked to hang around the Greenwich Village scene with poets, beatniks and jazz cats."

To this day, the two teams are still very close. In fact, through the years most of the Aldon graduates have stayed close. In 1990, when Orlando was inducted into the Hollywood Walk of Fame, among the many in Hollywood to cheer him on were Kirshner, Mann, and Weil. Also there was Brooks Arthur, who, along with Kaplan, was responsible for first bringing Tony to audition for Kirshner.

"Aldon was like an instant neighborhood, an instant crowd, an instant friendship that occurred there, an instant bond," said Arthur. "Every once in a while, God plants a miracle right in front of your face and says, *'This one's for you.'* These are the life-changing events. Aldon Music was such an event for all of us."

Run to Him

If someone else's arms can hold you
Better than my arms can hold you
Go to him, and show to him
All your emo-oh-tion

"Take Good Care of My Baby" made Bobby Vee a huge star, and everyone at Aldon was hoping to write the follow-up song for him. That's what Jack Keller had in mind as he drove to Gerry Goffin's Brown Street apartment in Brooklyn for one of their regular Thursday writing sessions.

Keller had the radio on in his car while driving there. A Peggy Lee song came on that caught his attention, so he turned up the volume.

"There was a drum riff at the start of the song that I just couldn't get out of my head," Keller recalled. "So when I sat down at the piano at Carole and Gerry's, that riff was still pounding in my brain."

He played a variation of the riff over and over until he had the making of a melody. Goffin picked right up on it.

"In innocence you do things that are really good or really bad," said Goffin. "And this was a really good one. I was trying to write something that was like 'Take Good Care of My Baby,' but Jack was smarter than me. He wrote a melody that was entirely different."

After an exhausting four hours, Keller finished the melody. He leaned back on the couch and stretched out his legs. Goffin lit up another cigarette and started pacing, as usual, working on the lyrics. In the background, Carole was in the kitchen working and watching the baby. And listening.

"Go ahead and take a nap," she told Keller. "I've heard you play it enough times to play it for Gerry while you sleep."

Four hours later, Goffin had nearly finished his pack of cigarettes when Carole gave Jack a gentle nudge. Then she walked over to the piano.

"The first thing I remember after waking up," said Keller, "was Carole at the piano saying, 'Jack, listen to your song.' Then she played and sang it for me. It was one helluva way to wake up."

Goffin might have had Bobby Vee in mind when he began writing "Run to Him" with Keller, but Kirshner had another idea. He wanted it for the Everly Brothers, a young rock-country-pop duo who had four No. 1 songs from 1957 through 1960. Kirshner had wanted to land a song with the Everlys since he opened Aldon's doors. He felt their broad appeal would assure that a hit on the pop charts would also cross over onto the country charts.

Vee's producer, Snuff Garrett, enjoyed staying at the Hampshire House on Central Park South when he came to New York. It was only a short walk from there to 1650 Broadway and his other stops in town.

"Snuff would gather demos and bring them back to L.A. to listen to," Vee remembered. "He told Kirshner he was going to come by his office. Don said he wouldn't be there at that time, but that he would leave a package of demos on his desk marked for Snuff.

"When he walked into Kirshner's office, there it was, a stack of demos marked 'Snuff Garrett and Bobby Vee.' And right next to it was one marked for the Everly Brothers. Garrett looked around, saw no one, so he grabbed them both."

When Garrett got back to Los Angeles, he couldn't wait to pry open his packages. "I was like a kid in a candy store," he recalled. "It was a game I played called 'Find the Hit.'"

As soon as he heard "Run to Him," he loved it and had Vee record it right away. He particularly loved Keller's chord progression. "It was way ahead of its time," Garrett said. He produced the record with a single guitar repeating a chord to capture the riff Keller wanted, and strings in the background to help build the song to a crescendo. He knew it would be a hit, but there were technical problems recording it that Garrett had to address first.

"There was some electric signal coming through the tape on the vocal track," Garrett recalls. "The engineer was going to fix it by going through the master, using another take. I went to New York and it took days and days and days. Then the engineer called me and played it over the phone. After thirty seconds I said, 'Holy shit. That's the wrong take! You cut the wrong take!'"

They eventually got the right take and fixed the problem. Garrett went back to L.A. and finished dubbing the record and finally had what he wanted.

"I was never so proud," said Garrett. "It was one of the three best records I ever produced."

"Run to Him" first appeared on the *Billboard* charts on November 13, 1961, and stayed there for fifteen weeks. For four straight weeks, from the middle of December through the middle of January, "Run to Him" was No. 2 but couldn't crack the top spot. Standing in its way was "The Lion Sleeps Tonight," the blockbuster performed by Jay Siegel, Hank Meddress, and the Tokens. Siegel, who sang in high school with Neil, said the genesis of his big hit was an old South African folk song the Weavers had recorded that had no lyric other than the word *wimoweh.*

"I had a wide range and could sing falsetto," Siegel said. "We [the Tokens] would sing 'Wimoweh' for our own pleasure on the street corners and everyone seemed to love it."

I was able to contact Jay Siegel through an acquaintance who grew up with Jay. One summer afternoon in 2006, my golf partner asked what I was working on. When I mentioned this story, he told me he was a friend of Siegel's, who lived nearby in Rockland County, New York, and he could arrange a conversation.

At the end of that '61 summer, the Tokens signed with RCA producers Hugo Perreti and Luigi Creatore, known to everybody in the business as Hugo and Luigi. The Tokens had previously been signed to Morty Craft's Warwick Records, for whom they wrote and sang the

Top 10 song "Tonight I Fell in Love." When they told Craft they were leaving, he wasn't pleased.

"I got you a hit record," he told the Tokens. "What can RCA Victor do for you that I can't?"

"Pay us," the four of them said in unison.

While auditioning for RCA, Siegel sang their lyric-less version of "Wimoweh," and Hugo and Luigi said they thought it could be commercial.

"I did some research and found out that the 'Wimoweh' African chant was describing a lion hunt," said Siegel. "The theory was that if everybody was quiet, the lion will sleep, and if the lion is sleeping they can make their kill."

Working with that background to shape the lyrics, Siegel reconstructed the melody and the group cut a demo. Before the song was released, Siegel brought the demo up to Aldon to play it for his old friends.

"We brought it up to Donnie's office, and Carole was there with Gerry," Siegel recalled. "We played the forty-five and Carole was looking at us and looking at us. We were old friends, so I asked, 'What do you think?'"

"'That's a fucking smash,' she finally said. 'It's a fucking smash.'"

She was right. "The Lion Sleeps Tonight" was the only thing that kept "Run to Him" out of the top spot. Nevertheless, Goffin and King were on a roll.

● ● ●

Kirshner continued to experiment with his songwriting teams. Near the end of '61, he somehow got Gerry to allow Carole to write a song with Howie Greenfield. True, Gerry had been writing with Jack Keller all along, but he was very protective of what Carole did. The result was something Don had been dreaming of since he got into the business—an Everly Brothers hit.

"Crying in the Rain" entered the charts in January '62 and didn't slow down until it reached No. 6. For Don and Phil, it was their first

Top 10 song in a year. They were so grateful that they shipped over a fifty-pound bag of Kirshner's favorite snack—peanuts. If you look closely at the photo below, you can see that Carole has a bump.

Celebrating their success with "Crying in the Rain" are (from left to right) Carole King, Gerry Goffin, Don and Phil Everly, Kirshner, and producer Jack Keller (below).

• • •

With Bobby Vee riding a wave after having successive No. 1 and No. 2 songs, Snuff Garrett was feeling like he was the hottest producer in the business. His regular New York visits continued and he called Kirshner one day with a request.

"Donnie, I'm looking for Bobby's follow-up to 'Run to Him,'" he said, "and I want to give your writers first crack. Can you have 'em all come into your office tomorrow night?"

"No problem, Snuff. When do you want everyone to come in?" Kirshner asked.

"Midnight," Garrett said.

"Midnight?" Kirshner gulped.

"Yep, midnight," Garrett said. "See you then."

At midnight the following night, all of Kirshner's "Magnificent Seven" writers were there except for Sedaka, who was on the road performing. Everyone sat out in the secretaries' bullpen area waiting to be summoned into Don's office to make their pitch. Goffin and King entered first. Carole sat at the piano and played five or six songs they were working on. Garrett was not blown away the way he had been when Carole first played "Take Good Care of My Baby." He asked for the next team.

In came Mann and Weil. Barry sat at the piano and pitched another half dozen songs without striking a chord with Snuff. Next Howie Greenfield walked in and represented several songs he had worked on with Neil. Again Garrett hadn't heard what he wanted.

Now it was after 1 a.m., when Jack Keller walked in alone.

"I've only got one song to play for you," said Keller, "that I think is right for Bobby." He then proceeded to play a ballad called "Please Don't Ask About Barbara."

"Man that's good," Garrett said when Keller completed the song. "I think that's the one."

Keller's lyricist on "Please Don't Ask About Barbara" was not Howie Greenfield or Gerry Goffin or even Hank Hunter, who Keller had written a few other hits with. His partner on this one was a lyricist named Bill Buchanan.

"Buchanan was a friend of Greenfield's and he asked Howie if he knew anyone to write the music for a lyric he had," Keller recalled. "Greenfield looked at the lyric and liked it, but suggested he change the title.

"What's wrong with 'Please Don't Ask About Susan'?" Buchanan asked.

"Nothing," said Greenfield, "except Jack Keller just split with his wife, Barbara, and I think he might go for it with Barbara in the title."

Keller did go for it and so did Garrett and Vee. "Please Don't Ask About Barbara" came on the charts the last week of February in '62.

Despite the haunting melody and Vee's pleasing sound, it never made it higher than No. 15. Vee thinks he knows the reason why.

"It came out at a time that Dick Clark just got divorced from *his* wife Barbara," Vee recalls. "I was doing a show in Ft. Wayne, Indiana, with Dick, and he leaned over and whispered to me, 'Why'd you ever put that song out?'"

"'Please Don't Ask About Barbara' never got played on *American Bandstand*," said Vee. "And that was the kiss of death."

The Loco-Motion

As 1961 came to a close, only "The Lion Sleeps Tonight" kept Aldon from totally dominating the charts. The company had three songs in the Top 10: "Run to Him" was No. 2; "Goodbye Cruel World," recorded by actor James Darren was No. 3; and Neil Sedaka's "Happy Birthday Sweet Sixteen," still on the rise, had climbed to No. 10.

Aldon was running on all cylinders when Nevins and Kirshner decided to expand and take the entire sixth floor at 1650 Broadway.

On Wednesday, January 24, 1962, the music industry's performance society, Broadcast Music Inc., known as BMI, held its tenth Annual Awards Dinner in the grand ballroom of one of New York's ritziest hotels, the Hotel Pierre, located across from Central Park. For songwriters, a BMI Award was the near equivalent of an Oscar.

BMI is the organization that keeps track of airplay, both radio and television, for music publishers and songwriters. Every time a song is played on the radio, the publisher and writers roughly divide two cents. It adds up quickly, especially for songs that become hits. For hits like "Up on the Roof," it can be an annuity.

On this particular evening, BMI was honoring ninety songs from 1961 for their "great national popularity as measured by broadcast performances." Aldon Music was taking home an astounding twelve of the ninety awards, four times more than any other publisher that year.

"Al and Donnie rented a couple of suites at the Pierre for everybody to change into their tuxedos and evening gowns," Artie Kaplan recalled. "Carole was still in her teens, and I remember Al's secretary,

Tenth Annual
AWARD DINNER

Given by

THE OFFICERS & DIRECTORS

of

BROADCAST MUSIC, INC.

* *

GRAND BALLROOM
HOTEL PIERRE
NEW YORK

* *

WEDNESDAY, JANUARY 24, 1962

Looking like a deer in the headlights, Carole King dons her silver fox wrap, as she gets ready to receive her first BMI Award.

Faith Whitehill, taking her to buy a dress that afternoon. Then Faith completed Carole's makeover by taking her to the beauty parlor for help with her hair and makeup. But even with her hair done, the formal dress, and a silver fox fur wrap, she still looked *so* young."

Jerry Wexler has a firm memory of Goffin and King getting their first award.

"They were just kids; Gerry Goffin in a tuxedo with Carole in

On January 24, 1962, almost exactly a year after "Will You Love Me Tomorrow" hit No. 1, Carole and Gerry got to receive their BMI Award for the song.

a formal dress," said Wexler. "They looked like they were going to a prom. Then he used a Yiddish phrase to describe the pride her parents must have had.

"*Shepping nachas* means to glory in the accomplishments of your children," he explained. "Her parents were overwhelmingly *Shepping nachas* that night. They were there at that BMI dinner, standing up cheering for them both, when only two years earlier they were trying to break them up."

As the Pierre's staff served *petite marmite* and Breast of Chicken Isabelle, Eddie Lane's orchestra played sixteen bars of each song as it was announced while the writers and publishers walked up to receive their awards.

The Aldon songs being honored that night were:

"Breakin' in a Brand New Broken Heart"	Jack Keller/Howard Greenfield
"Calendar Girl"	Neil Sedaka/Howard Greenfield
"Goodbye Cruel World"	Gloria Shayne
"Happy Birthday Sweet Sixteen"	Neil Sedaka/Howard Greenfield
"I Love How You Love Me"	Barry Mann/Larry Kolber
"Just for Old Times Sake"	Jack Keller/Hank Hunter
"Little Devil"	Neil Sedaka/Howard Greenfield
"Run to Him"	Jack Keller/Gerald Goffin
"Take Good Care of My Baby"	Carole King/Gerald Goffin
"Where the Boys Are"	Neil Sedaka/Howard Greenfield
"Who Put the Bomp"	Barry Mann/Gerald Goffin
"Will You Love Me Tomorrow"	Carole King/Gerald Goffin

Each time an Aldon song was announced, the songwriters and publisher marched to the podium to accept their award while the orchestra played the song. Kirshner could have logged several miles before the night was through.

As people started to mingle after the program was over, Kirshner went out of his way to congratulate Gene Pitney, the twenty-year-old songwriter of "He's a Rebel." Kirshner knew that Pitney was writing for George Goldner's label on another floor at 1650 Broadway, but he didn't know that Pitney was about to breakout as a star himself.

Thanks to Charlie Feldman at BMI, I was able to reach Pitney by phone. He remembered that night vividly. Sadly, Pitney passed away shortly after our conversation.

"By the end of the evening everyone knew who Don Kirshner was," said Pitney. "He was a big guy, and in a tuxedo he made quite a dashing figure. So when he came across the room and headed directly for me, I didn't know what to make of it. Then he said the nicest thing to

The Aldon boys put on their best smiles and hold up their BMI Awards. From left to right, they are: Barry Mann, Jack Keller, Al Nevins, Don Kirshner, and Howie Greenfield.

me. He said, 'I just won twelve awards, but yours was the best song of them all.' I'll never forget how magnanimous he was."

As Kirshner was about to leave the Grand Ballroom, a fellow he remembered seeing once before in his office—a songwriter he had met who had promise—confronted him.

"Congratulations," Berry Gordy said to him. "I want you to know that I'm going to Detroit and I'm going to try and build a company [Motown] the same way you've done it here. I just hope I can have half your success."

Also there that night was Philadelphia's Jerry Blavat, maybe the hottest DJ in the country at age twenty-two. When he was only sixteen, Blavat was managing Danny & the Juniors who had the smash hit "At the Hop." Blavat reminded Kirshner about the first time they met at the Turf restaurant in 1958.

"That's where I first met Bobby [Darin] and Donnie—before any of us were anybody," Blavat recalled, when I reached him at WPEN in Philadelphia. "We were all trying to make it one way or another, and despite rejection after rejection, Bobby and Donnie never got down. You could feed off their determination. They knew they were going to make it."

Kirshner gave Blavat his famous bear hug that night, and told him he'd call him when he had a special record to give him in advance.

After the awards dinner, everyone went to Al Nevins' luxurious apartment at 57th Street and Sutton Place to celebrate. Also attending the party was Dick Asher, a young attorney Nevins and Kirshner had hired away from the law firm that was representing them, who later on would become head of CBS Records and Polygram Records. Asher recalled a conversation he had with Kirshner earlier that day.

"Donnie was complaining to me about his finances," said Asher. "He asked, 'How come I have all of these hits and only $500 in the bank?' Well, I had totally forgotten about that conversation until we were leaving the party that night. We came out of the building and they had one of those long canopies that extended from the building to the street. And at the end of that canopy was a big black limousine. So my wife, the joker, says to me, 'Oh, honey, there's our car.' Of course it wasn't our car. It belonged to Donnie, the man who was complaining about how poor he was. All I could do was chuckle."

● ● ●

In March '62, Mann and Weil served notice they had begun to write more than just pop music. The result was "Uptown," recorded by the Crystals and produced by Phil Spector. It was Spector's first attempt at his famous Wall of Sound.

The song touched on social issues, dealing with a young man who had a very hard time of it during the day at his job downtown. But when he returned uptown at night, the world was his. The castanets and the Spanish tone of Spector's music intimated that "home" was probably Spanish Harlem.

Kirshner didn't really *get* "Uptown." It wasn't his kind of a song. When Barry and Cynthia first brought it to him, he couldn't imagine the spectacular production Spector would build behind it.

"So I told Barry and Cynthia, 'Why don't you just write another 'Little Darlin','" Kirshner recalled. "But after it was a hit, I told them, 'Write some more of those songs that I don't understand.'"

Cynthia's inspiration for the lyrics was the sight of a young garment worker pushing a cart down Seventh Avenue. For Spector, "Uptown" could have easily been the Spanish Harlem section of New York. And like the record "Spanish Harlem" that Spector co-wrote with Jerry Leiber, he borrowed from Leiber and Stoller's arrangement, using a single-string Spanish guitar and castanets, with violins in the background. "Uptown" never rose higher than No. 13 on *Billboard*, but has maintained a cult following ever since.

● ● ●

On March 3, 1962, just a few months after Aldon swept the BMI Awards, Cameo-Parkway Records, a fast-growing label in Philadelphia, released two songs by a rocking sixteen-year-old female singer named Dione LaRue. Cameo-Parkway's owner, Bernie Lowe, changed LaRue's name for recording purposes to Dee Dee Sharp.

Sharp introduced her two new hits at an industry dinner, which is discussed at length in the preface of this book. At seventeen, she was less than a year older than I was when I attended that event with my father. The two songs she introduced were "Slow Twistin'," which she sung as a duet with the great Chubby Checker, and her own raucous dance song, "Mashed Potato Time."

There was no doubt about Sharp or the two songs. Both stayed on the charts for four months, with the former reaching No. 3 and the latter No. 2. Kirshner was well aware of Cameo-Parkway, and was in fact present at Sharp's unveiling that night in Philadelphia. He had been there to try and convince Bernie Lowe to use some of the songs by Aldon's writers.

When "Slow Twistin'" and "Mashed Potato Time" took off, Kirshner called his top writers into his office. "There isn't a hotter singer in the country right now than Dee Dee Sharp," he told them. "Cameo-Parkway is going to come out with a follow-up to the 'Mashed Potatoes' this summer. Let's give them a song they can't turn down."

At that time Kirshner was still seeking a signature sound for

Aldon to start its own label. He found it, by chance, in Eva Boyd, an eighteen-year-old-nanny/housekeeper.

Eva Boyd was born June 29, 1943, in Belhaven, North Carolina. Her family was close to the church and she grew up listening to and singing gospel, rhythm and blues, and the rock and roll she heard on the radio. She always enjoyed singing and was part of the family gospel group, the Boyd Five.

When she was sixteen, during summer vacation in 1959, she visited her eldest brother, Jimmy, in Coney Island. The following year, she quit school and took the bus back to New York, where she found work as a maid. Jimmy's wife was friendly with Earl-Jean McCrea of the Cookies, who were singing demos for Carole King and Gerry Goffin at the time.

With baby Louise already at Carole and Gerry's feet and a second child on the way, the Goffins hired Boyd to be their live-in nanny for $35 a week. She shared a room with Louise.

By the spring of '62, the Goffins had written one successful song after another. All Kirshner had to do was give them an idea and they'd create another hit. In this case, it was to write a follow-up to "Mashed Potato Time."

It didn't take Goffin and King long before they had the makings of their own new dance, and their nanny was humming along while they wrote.

"I had the song inside me for a while," Goffin remembered. "I was going to write it with Jack [Keller], but then I realized it wouldn't have the same rock-and-roll feel as it would if I wrote it with Carole."

He kept it in his head for nearly two years and remembered it when Kirshner asked them to write another dance song for Sharp.

"When I sat down to write it," recalled Goffin, "I said, 'This is going to sound stupid, but what the hell.' Then we asked Eva, our babysitter, to try it. She wasn't a demo singer or anything, but we knew she had sung gospel. Carole played her the song and she started singing along and doing a little dance that reminded me of a train. She chanted: 'Everybody's doin' a brand new dance now. Come on baby, do 'The Lo-co-motion.'

"No one could sing like Eva," said Goffin. "At first she was the gruffest, but then she became a big star."

When the song was completed, King and Goffin decided they wanted to record Eva doing the demo. She sang it as if she owned it—as if it were written for her. So they brought Eva to their favorite demo studio, Dick Charles, at 47th and Broadway, for a 10 a.m. session. Artie Kaplan was there to play an important sax solo on the session.

"I remember Carole coming in and she'd put Louise in the playpen in the middle of the studio and then do her thing: play the piano, direct traffic, tell the girls what to sing," Kaplan recalled.

The "girls" were the Cookies: Earl-Jean McCrea, Margaret Ross, and Dorothy Jones, who would back up Eva. They also achieved fame on their own and for backing up Ray Charles. Besides Kaplan, the only other musicians playing on the session were Charlie Macey (who was Al Nevins' former guitar teacher) on bass guitar, and Buddy Saltzman on drums. And of course, Carole on piano. Kaplan, though, stood out with his saxophone solo in the middle of the record.

They started the session at 10 a.m. and by 1 o'clock Kirshner had sent Kaplan on a bus to Market Street in Philly to play the demo for Bernie Lowe at Cameo-Parkway. Among other jobs, Nevins and Kirshner were training Kaplan in the art of song-plugging.

Bernie Lowe was no stranger to a hit song. Before he founded Cameo-Parkway, he had been a very successful songwriter in his own right. Along with writing partner Kal Mann, he wrote Elvis Presley's No. 1 hit "Teddy Bear" for publishers Hill and Range. Between then and the day Kaplan arrived with the demo of "The Loco-Motion," Lowe had built Cameo-Parkway into the top independent record company in the country, with artists like Chubby Checker, Bobby Rydell, Dee Dee Sharp, and the Orlons. Since Cameo published most of its own songs, it would take something special for Lowe to give up the follow-up to "Mashed Potato Time" to another publisher.

"I wanted to meet Bernie Lowe, but the secretary wouldn't allow me into the inner office," said Kaplan. "I sat in a waiting room while they took the demo in to him. I heard him place the needle on the record. He listened to about a minute of the song. I heard the needle come up off the record and the secretary put the demo back into its sleeve. Then I distinctly heard him say, 'I didn't hear the hook.'"

The hook is a repetitious chorus or a repeating phrase that can pull listeners in and keep them there. "The Loco-Motion" is that kind of a song, yet Lowe claimed he didn't hear the hook.

"The secretary brought it back to me and just said, 'No, thank you.' So I got on the bus and went back to New York," said Kaplan, who remains skeptical about Lowe's rejection. "I doubt that Bernie Lowe didn't recognize that "The Loco-Motion" would be a hit. He certainly was aware of who Goffin and King were."

Dave Appell (pronounced Apple), who was a staff writer for Lowe and did much of Cameo-Parkway's A & R work, isn't so sure that Lowe was being a shrewd businessman when he claimed he didn't hear the hook in "The Loco-Motion."

"I can't tell you how many hits he turned down," says Appell. "He wouldn't put a song out unless his teenage daughter, Lynn, liked the record."

Lynn Lowe confirmed that she did help select records to be recorded for Cameo-Parkway. Ironically, in 1964 one of my best friends, Ronn Owens, now a popular talk-show host in San Francisco, was dating Lynn, so Lynn and I also became friends. Years later, I was able to track her down and confirm the story.

When Kaplan returned with news that Lowe had turned down the demo, Kirshner's first thought was to shelve the record until he could figure out whom to send it to next. But Carole and Gerry loved the sound they achieved with Eva, and encouraged Kirshner to sign her as he did with Tony Orlando, and to have it produced by Aldon Music.

"Larry Utall, the president of Bell Records, was trying to convince Donnie to start Aldon's own label as an adjunct to the publishing company," Kaplan remembered. "That's the way Dimension Records was born. "The Loco-Motion" became the first release on Dimension, and it was distributed by Bell Records."

When "The Loco-Motion" reached No. 1, Kirshner (far left) and Nevins, along with Carole and Gerry, and of course Little Eva, posed on a locomotive. This promotional shot, taken by William "PoPsie" Randolph, graced the cover of Cashbox Magazine.

When the Goffins took Eva to Mirasound to make a master recording for the new violet Dimension label, they couldn't reproduce the same sound they had captured on the demo. Instead, they decided to use the demo as a master. Carole and Eva overdubbed backup vocals, and even though the record was essentially the demo, it was ready for release.

If there were mistakes and tape hiss on the record, it didn't matter, Carole felt, because it was "happening." Carole loved the energy from the demo, so tape hiss and all, they went with it. That's how Aldon's first record label, Dimension Records, began.

"From a two hundred-dollar demo," said Kaplan, "to a multi-million-dollar enterprise. God bless America."

Dee Dee Sharp did have a hit with her follow-up. It was a song called "Gravy (for My Mashed Potatoes)," and it debuted on *Billboard* on June 16, two weeks before "The Loco-Motion." While it was a near sound-alike of its predecessor, "Gravy" did get as high as No. 9, but it was left in the dust by "The Loco-Motion," which was No. 1 by August, and graced the cover of *Cashbox*.

Kirshner, Goffin, and King were trying to decide if they should identify the singer of Dimension record No. 101 as Eva or Eva Boyd when Gerry had an idea.

"She was less than five feet tall," said Goffin, "so we just decided to call her Little Eva."

The song broke in Philadelphia first—not by Dick Clark on *American Bandstand* but by Jerry Blavat on WHAT 1340 radio. Blavat, who talked faster than a speeding bullet, called himself "The Geator with the Heater, the Bog Boss with the Hot Sauce," and he referred to his audience as "yon teens." Here's how he first introduced "The Loco-Motion" in his machine-gun style:

"Greetings and salutations to the entire population of this here fantastic nation," he began. "Don't be shamed . . . mention the Geater's name . . . goin' on a 'Loco-Motion' just the same . . . Here she comes, Little Eva . . . From out of nowhere she's a star thanks to Carole King and Gerry Goffin . . . and my main man, Donnie Kirshner."

When they all got together to take promotional pictures for the release of Aldon's first record on the Dimension label, they had a great idea and all stood on the front of a locomotive. Kirshner, always a good sport, wore an engineer's hat. Or maybe he just wanted everyone to know that he was driving this train.

When Little Eva's song reached No. 1 that August, it replaced another Aldon song in the top spot that nearly didn't see the light of day—Neil Sedaka's "Breaking Up Is Hard to Do."

Next Door to an Angel

Do do do, doobie bop bop bop,
Oh do bop she don don . . .
I'm living right next door to an angel
And I'm gonna make that angel mine

By the spring of '61 Neil Sedaka was unstoppable. A month earlier, he had released "Calendar Girl," his fifth straight hit, and now with the song peaking at No. 4, *The Ed Sullivan Show* was beckoning.

Ed Sullivan was perhaps the most powerful man in show business. His Toast of the Town gossip column was syndicated in more than 500 newspapers across the country, and his prime-time Sunday night variety show by the same name was often the highest-rated program each week. Sullivan might have been a stiff host on TV, but behind the scenes he was a power broker. If you were an actor or a singer, Sullivan could make you or break you, like Walter Winchell before him. When Sullivan called, you never said no.

Sullivan not only wanted Sedaka for his program, he wanted to make him the feature performer of the night, giving him the opportunity to show off his versatility. Neil would perform three different numbers. The first was to be a piano selection from Chopin, which would display his Juilliard training. The second would be the hit of the day, "Calendar Girl," and the third was to be a tribute to his Brighton Beach, Brooklyn, roots, "My Yiddishe Momma."

Sedaka had performed "My Yiddishe Momma" regularly on tour and it was "a real showstopper," he said. But Sullivan decided he didn't want Neil to do it. He thought the song was "too Jewish."

"There was a bit of a squabble during rehearsals," Sedaka told

Wayne Hoffman of *The Forward* in February 2004. Sedaka told him, "Sullivan, whose wife was Jewish, said he didn't want to put it on the show, and his son-in-law, who was the producer, was also against it."

Sedaka's manager and the producers exchanged heated words. They threatened to walk out. Finally, two hours before airtime, Sullivan bowed to the pressure and approved all three numbers.

"I think they didn't want to be seen as anti-Semitic," Sedaka said. After performing the song, the audience response was overwhelming. "I knew it would go over great because the sentiment of the song is absolutely beautiful."

Sedaka's string of consecutive hits would continue for another two years. He would close out 1961 with two more, "Little Devil" and "Happy Birthday Sweet Sixteen." But one thing still eluded him—he was still searching for his first No. 1 song.

Between his traveling, appearances, and picking up awards, Neil Sedaka found he had less and less time to write in 1962. His partner, Howard Greenfield, was having tremendous success writing with other Aldon composers while Sedaka was on the road. When Sedaka did write something he liked, it wasn't always easy to get Greenfield's attention. Such was the case with "Breaking Up Is Hard to Do."

"I wrote the title, 'Breaking Up Is Hard to Do,' and the melody to go with it, and I was playing it for Howie week after week, but he wasn't interested," said Sedaka.

It had been more than six months since Sedaka introduced a Top 10 song and he might have been getting a little anxious. He thought his title was perfect for the teenage market and he continued to press Greenfield to write a lyric.

"When he finished it," Sedaka related, "Howie chose to continue with the sad theme of the title I gave him, even though it was an up-tempo melody.

Don't take your love away from me
Don't you leave my heart in misery
If you go then I'll be blue
'Cause breaking up is hard to do

"I took it in to play for Barry Mann to get his opinion. I played it along with several other new ones. Of them all, "Breaking Up Is Hard to Do" was his least favorite."

In Mann's defense, Sedaka hadn't yet included his famous opening lines. "The night before the session, I called up my arranger, Alan Lorber," Sedaka recalled, "and I told him that I wrote an obbligato line—the Neil Sedaka trademark dooby-doos, and he wrote them in."

Doo doo doo, down dooby-doo, down, down
Come-a, come-a . . .

On the way to the studio the next morning, Sedaka made an important stop. "I picked up the Cookies, who were the background vocalists on most of my early hits and I taught them their parts in the car on the way to the studio."

"We were used to learning on the fly," said Margaret Ross Williams, who was with the Cookies at that time. "It wasn't all that unusual for Neil to try to teach us our parts on the way to the studio. It was always exciting to work with him."

In 1962, music was still being recorded in four-track. Sedaka was a huge fan of Les Paul, who was the first to use the over-dubbing technique in recording his records with Mary Ford. Their version of "How High the Moon," with Mary Ford's voice over-dubbed several times, changed the way records were being produced.

Sedaka borrowed from Les Paul's innovation and became one of the first singers to multi-track his own harmonies. The background tracks had both Sedaka and the Cookies, which left room for Sedaka's lead vocal on the other two tracks.

"The 'bread' to begin with was the 'down, dooby-doos,' Sedaka explained. "Then the meat of the song followed, then another piece of bread. I used a similar technique on most of my early songs."

"Breaking Up Is Hard to Do" debuted on both *Cashbox* and *Billboard* on June 30, 1962, just in time to be played over and over on the beaches across the country Fourth of July weekend. A month later, it was No. 1 and stayed there until the end of August, when it was unseated by Goffin and King's "The Loco-Motion."

Twelve years later, Sedaka released it again, as a ballad, almost as an afterthought in his *Hungry Years* album. It reached the Top 10 all over again and will be one of the standards for which he will always be known.

Less than a month after "Breaking Up" hit No. 1, Sedaka married his girlfriend of four years, Leba Strasberg. He first met her in 1958 at her parents' hotel in the Catskills, Esther Manor. Still in his teens, Neil had a job singing in the lobby of the hotel.

"I was sixteen when I first met Neil and he told me he had just written 'Stupid Cupid' for Connie Francis," Leba recalled. "I thought, 'It's ridiculous that I would know someone that writes songs.' It was just foreign to me. Nice Jewish girls were supposed to date doctors, lawyers, and maybe engineers—but not songwriters."

I also reached Leba through Neil's production office, and she graciously agreed to talk about the early days and what it was like to date a star on the rise.

Before long, Leba was answering Neil's fan mail. Her parents didn't approve at first, but they grew to adore Neil. When Sedaka finally got around to asking for Leba's hand, it was Howie Greenfield who convinced her.

"The two of them called me from Brooklyn when I was in Monticello [the Catskills]," she remembered fondly. "It was really Howie that asked me to marry Neil. By the time Neil asked me, I didn't believe him. I said, 'Put Howie on the phone.' And Howie said, 'He's serious. He really wants to marry you.' So Howie sealed the deal."

They were married on September 11, 1962. Sedaka's parents danced at the wedding, but there was no denying that they had an unusual relationship. His father, Mac, was a hardworking cab driver. His mother, Eleanor, watched over Neil's career closely. She quickly adapted her lifestyle and dressed in the latest New York fashions.

"His mother would sometimes walk into Aldon's offices with both her husband and her quote-unquote 'business advisor,'" said Aldon songwriter Toni Wine. "They were very chummy and arm in arm. It seemed very unusual."

Ben Sutter, a former washing-machine salesman, was the business advisor in question. Neil's mother was determined to have Sutter become Neil's new manager. When Sedaka first signed to be a recording artist for RCA, he also signed a management contract with Nevins under the newly formed Aldon subsidiary, Nevins-Kirshner, Inc. But as Sedaka grew more popular and his songs more successful, his mother grew more dissatisfied with the type of appearances Neil was getting. While Bobby Darin and Connie Francis were playing the Copa and similar nightclubs, Sedaka was sent out of the United States.

"They sent him to Australia and South America and England, but not here," said Leba Sedaka. "They were his publishers, his producers, and his managers and had never seen him perform. We thought there was a conflict of interest."

At that time, Sedaka was second only to Elvis Presley in record sales. Kirshner, though, has no recollection of managing Neil.

"Total nonsense," he said in defense when I asked him about it. "I wasn't in the managing business," he said. "My main business was music publishing and record production. If it was anyone booking his dates, it was Al."

If that was the case, it's difficult to believe that the right hand didn't know what the left hand was doing at Aldon. Artie Kaplan, has no doubt, however, that the company was holding Sedaka back.

"I think they were afraid that a career as an artist might take away from Neil's writing and record sales," Kaplan reasoned. "They were in the publishing business, not in show business. Regardless, Neil deserved better management. I don't know that Ben Sutter was the answer, but Neil deserved better than what Nevins-Kirshner, Inc. was doing for him. It's interesting that after he left Nevins-Kirshner, Inc., he started appearing at the Copa and other clubs."

Jack Keller, who had produced most of Sedaka's recording sessions, was scheduled to produce Neil's next recording, "Next Door to an Angel," but an eighteen-day bout with mononucleosis prevented him from being at the session.

"His mother made Neil tell Al and Don that he wanted a new manager," recalled Keller. "Don was not happy. He felt they were ungrateful."

With Keller out sick, Nevins and Kirshner co-produced the session. Also there were Kaplan and Lou Adler, who was Aldon's West Coast man. Nevins and Kirshner, along with Kaplan and Adler, were all upstairs behind the control board. Sometime during the session, Eleanor Sedaka and Sutter walked in and sat on the visitor's couch, just below the control board. Kirshner peered over the board, saw them, and began to seethe. *How did they have the nerve to come to the session?*

"Ben Sutter was a low-life second-rater," said Kirshner. "This so-called friend of Neil's started berating and abusing Howie [Greenfield] and I told him three times that if he does it again, I'm going to punch him out. Then he said something rude to Howie, who was a gentle type of kid, and I jumped over the console and decked the guy. I remember Al looking at me, holding me back, and I said, 'Okay, Al. Okay, Al.' 'Cause I would always listen to him. But not this time, because the guy was so obnoxious that I just lost it."

Artie Kaplan jumped on Kirshner's back to keep him from getting out of control.

"He could have killed him," said Kaplan. "Sutter was an old guy, but on the other hand, he might have been carrying a gun. Meanwhile, Lou Adler threw a real good punch at Ben."

Once things were under control, Nevins found amusement in the situation.

"When they carried the guy out, I remember Al just wagging a finger at me like a mother saying, 'I told you not to do it,' " said Kirshner.

The disturbance didn't harm Neil's performance any. "Next Door to an Angel" entered the charts October 6 and stayed on them the rest of the year, peaking at No. 5. For Sedaka, though, it would be his last Top 10 number for a dozen years, until "Laughter in the Rain" started the "Sedaka is back" campaign in 1974.

For Aldon, it was only one of two dozen big hits they had in '62. And the Goffins were about to deliver their fourth No. 1 song in two years, "Go Away Little Girl."

19

Go Away Little Girl

In the fall of '62, having written three triangle love songs that Bobby Vee successfully recorded, Gerry Goffin was looking to strike gold again.

"After 'Take Good Care of My Baby,' I got the idea of writing a song using the expression 'little girl,'" Goffin recalled. "When I wrote 'Go Away Little Girl,' I had Bobby Vee in mind. Carole and I wrote it in about ten minutes. I thought for sure Snuffy Garrett, his producer, would love it too. But he didn't."

Goffin might have thought that Garrett turned it down, but Kirshner never gave him the chance. As soon as Kirshner heard the demo, he immediately thought of his pal Steve Lawrence. And again his instincts were right, although it's hard to believe that it wouldn't have been a smash with Vee also.

"Over the course of our relationship Don would send me a lot of songs," recalled Lawrence. "If I liked one, I'd send it to [arranger/producer Don] Costa. One day Donnie called me very excited about a song that Carole King and Gerry Goffin had written. When he played 'Go Away Little Girl' for me, I just loved it. Who could resist a line like, 'Go away little girl before I beg you to stay'?"

My first memory of Steve Lawrence and Eydie Gorme was on Steve Allen's late-night TV show, Broadway Open House, *in 1956. They were so young and gorgeous—both of them—and funny. And could they ever sing! In 1964, when I was eighteen, they were appearing at the Latin Casino in Cherry Hill, New Jersey, just across the bridge from Philly. I took a date and every penny I had saved and saw a show I'll never forget.*

The same day Kirshner delivered the demo of "Go Away Little Girl" to Lawrence, Costa and Lawrence went right to the studio and recorded it. It debuted on the charts on November 10, 1962, reached No. 1 the second week of January, and remained in the Top 10 clear into March.

Unfortunately, the ride to the top was not as happy for Goffin, who was dogged by a negative article that appeared in *Time* magazine about his lyrics.

"They thought 'Go Away Little Girl' was a sick song. 'Go Away Little Girl' was an expression, and not about somebody with some underage kid," said Goffin. "They [*Time*] actually came to me and said, 'So you like to make love to little girls?' They did the article and kind of laughed at all my songs. It really depressed me."

Fortunately, no one else had that perspective. In fact, in 1971 "Go Away Little Girl" was No. 1 all over again for Donny Osmond. Ironically, it also was recorded by Johnny Mathis, who Kirshner originally had in mind for "Will You Love Me Tomorrow."

For insiders in the record business, Steve Lawrence and Don Costa's names were connected for years, but for the general public, Lawrence's name would forever be linked to someone else.

Born and raised in the Bronx, Eydie Gorme was born Edith Gormezano, the daughter of immigrant parents. Her mother was from Turkey and her father was a tailor from Sicily. She grew up in a home where several languages were spoken and she became fluent in both Spanish and English. She also happened to be a distant cousin of Neil Sedaka's.

Her musical talents were recognized early. She was only three when she first sang on the radio, and by 1950, at age nineteen, she began a professional career singing with bandleader Tommy Tucker.

In 1953, Gorme became a regular guest on Steve Allen's late-night TV talk show, *Broadway Open House,* the forerunner to *The Tonight Show.* She joined another singer who was already appearing on the show named Steve Lawrence. In '54, Allen's show went national on NBC, and Lawrence and Gorme started seeing success on the pop charts. They also started seeing each other. Neither of them, though, had a

Top 10 hit before Kirshner started looking out for them. For Gorme, her biggest song came thanks to a phone call she got from Brazil in '62.

"We were in L.A. doing a couple of TV shows, staying at the Beverly Hills Hotel, and we got a call from Tony Bennett, who was in Brazil," said Gorme. "All he said was, 'There's a great new thing here. It's called the Bossa Nova. Get on it.' And that's all he said and he hung up. Swear to god. He always talked in these cryptic messages. So I 'got on it' and started listening to Astrud Gilberto."

It was Gilberto who made famous the classic Brazilian jazz number "The Girl from Ipanema." Having done her homework, Gorme arranged a date to record some jazz-oriented bossa nova songs. Shortly before going into the studio, Steve and Eydie had dinner with their close friends, the Kirshners.

"We were always together with Sheila and Donnie. We vacationed together, we lived together, all our kids were raised together," Gorme remembered. "At dinner that night, Donnie asked me what I'm doing and I told him. Next thing I know, Stevie's handing me this song, 'Blame It on the Bossa Nova,' he got from Donnie, who had Barry Mann write it."

It was amazing how fast Kirshner could turn a dinner conversation around and have a hit on the charts. Any piece of information you gave him was a potential hit song in the making.

Said Gorme: "Nobody had been presenting me with pop songs. I said to Donnie, 'I don't really do this type of thing.' Then Steve said, 'I think you'd do it great.' I did it and it was a hit, and then the record company put it out as the title of my jazz album. It turned out to be the only pop song in the album."

"Blame It on the Bossa Nova" entered the charts the third week in January '63, the same week Lawrence's song stood at No. 1. It made it all the way up to No. 7 and helped bring the bossa nova rage to America.

A few years later, Kirshner's writers gave Steve Lawrence another song he loved. This one was written by Jack Keller and Howie Greenfield and was the theme song to a new TV series, *Bewitched*.

"Bewitched" is one of the songs that Lawrence is most proud of recording, yet for more than forty years his version of the song was never heard.

"The studio [Columbia Screen Gems] was in a big hurry to get the song out with the first episode of the show," said Keller. "By the time Steve recorded Howie's lyrics, they were pretty set on using the instrumental version."

The song, like the series, has lasted more than 40 years, and thanks to director Nora Ephron's film by the same name, the world is now aware of Greenfield's lyrics – and Lawrence's sensational version of the song.

"First of all, I thought it was a terrific song," said Lawrence. "Don Costa wrote a great orchestration so that it really surrounded me and propelled me in the studio. As a vocalist, you are inspired initially by the song that's on the page. If the composer and the orchestrator meet each other properly, they can make the song an experience. In the case of 'Bewitched,' it just walked out of the studio."

Of all the hits Keller has written, "Bewitched" is the song that made him more money and brought him more smiles than any other.

Up on the Roof

When Gerry Goffin was six years old and his brother, Al, was two, his parents separated, eventually divorcing. Like their parents, the brothers were also separated. Gerry went with his father, Jack, a traveling salesman, and Al stayed with their mother, Anita.

When Gerry wasn't in school or traveling with his dad, he worked in his grandfather's cellar. His grandfather was a furrier, and he had Gerry down in the basement making skulls of fox heads for fur wraps. The boys remained separated for five years, but somehow Gerry managed to always watch out for his little brother.

"I hated it when they got divorced," Goffin recalled. "My mother was a little *schizo* and my father said he couldn't take it anymore. But she was a hardworking lady and worked as a bookkeeper the rest of her life."

By the time Gerry started writing full-time, he was the only one at Aldon with family responsibilities. Nevins was single and Kirshner had just gotten married. Sedaka was going with Leba, and Greenfield was unattached. Barry Mann hadn't yet met Cynthia Weil, and Jack Keller was a divorced bachelor. While everyone else was enjoying a freewheeling lifestyle in the music business, Goffin went home to his tiny three-room apartment to change diapers and write songs.

"Gerry was a deep thinker," said Tony Orlando, who worked closely with Carole and Gerry in '60 and '61. "He was complicated and he was a genius. And he was harder on himself than he ever was on anyone else."

He was also a worrier who paid attention to, and was affected by, world events. By September 1962, the Cold War between the United

States and the Soviet Union was about to explode. Both countries raced to control outer space. Evidence came in that the Russians had begun to build a missile base just ninety miles south of the U.S. in Cuba.

"Life is meant to be enjoyed," Goffin said, "but there are so many downers."

While the rest of the Aldon songwriting commune continued to distract teenagers with light and airy songs, Goffin's preoccupation with his own problems and the Cuban Missile Crisis led to his creation of "Up on the Roof."

When this old world starts getting me down
And people are just too much for me to face
I climb way up to the top of the stairs
And all my cares just drift right into space . . .

Carole had written the melody first and suggested he write something about getting away from it all. The idea for the lyrics came to him while sitting on a friend's rooftop on West End Avenue in Manhattan, overlooking the Hudson River. They reflected how peaceful it was up high, away from it all. But he was stuck for one final rhyme.

"I went to Jerry Leiber," Goffin recalled. "He was like the big daddy. I needed a rhyme for *roof,* and he said, 'How about *proof?'* Then I had it: 'I found a paradise that's trouble-proof.' And he laughed and I laughed too. Then I wrote 'There's room enough for two up on the roof.' I was very proud of myself. Looking back, I think it's my best song."

Jerry Leiber has some fond memories of working with Goffin and King on the song before he produced it for the Drifters.

"Most writers would hit you with three or four songs. Not these guys. They always came with their best shot," said Leiber. "They always hit the mark with me. I don't think they ever brought me anything I didn't like. And if I liked it, I recorded it."

He liked "Up on the Roof" immediately, even though the bridge of the song needed some work. Together he and Gerry came up with the solution. Said Leiber, "I suggested: 'On the roof's the only place I know / where you just have to wish to make it so.' I was always afraid that people would think that I lifted that line from Snow White."

He and Mike Stoller produced the song with the Drifters' Rudy Lewis singing lead. As good as the record turned out, Goffin had hoped for someone else.

"I loved Ben E. King's voice and I kept waiting for him to sing one of my songs, but he never did. I thought he was a great singer, a very soulful singer," Goffin lamented. "We kept praying Jerry and Mike would get Ben E. to sing it, but he had left the Drifters by then."

The Drifters were started in 1954 when Atlantic gave Clyde McPhatter permission to also have his own group. He organized the group in partnership with his manager, George Treadwell, under the business entity Drifters Inc. so he could share in the profits. When McPhatter decided to leave the group, he sold his half to Treadwell, who only paid the other group members $100 a week. When the rest of the group also quit, Treadwell bought the contract of the Five Crowns and called them the Drifters so he could fulfill contract obligations at the Apollo Theater.

The baritone of the new group was Benjamin Earl Nelson, who would later be known as Ben E. King. On March 6, 1959, the group went into the studio to cut four songs for Atlantic, with Leiber and Stoller producing. Nelson was tapped to be lead singer when Charlie Thomas developed stage fright. Of the songs they recorded that day, "There Goes My Baby," which Nelson co-wrote, became a classic. It marked the first time strings were prominently featured on an R & B song.

Nelson was unhappy about the pay and all the travel, but stayed with the group long enough to record the Doc Pomus and Mort Shuman hits "This Magic Moment" and "Save the Last Dance for Me" before he went out on his own as Ben E. King. Rudy Lewis became the Drifters' new lead singer, and held that position when Goffin and King's "Some Kind of Wonderful" and "Up on the Roof" were recorded. He also sang lead a few months later when the group recorded "On Broadway," written by Mann and Weil with help from Leiber and Stoller.

"Up on the Roof" climbed to No. 5 in '62, and has lived a long and lasting life on the play lists of DJs around the world ever since. It is one of the standards for which Goffin and King will always be remembered.

About three months later, in March '63, Leiber and Stoller produced another classic Aldon hit, which nearly didn't happen. "On Broadway" was Barry Mann's attempt to write a song in a Gershwin-esque style. From the start, Mann and Weil thought they had something special, but making it into a hit record was another story.

Phil Spector, who had so much success producing Mann and Weil's "Uptown," took a crack at "On Broadway" with the Crystals again singing. But as good a musician as Spector was, and as good an ear as he had, he just couldn't make the record work.

Gerry Goffin was the next one to try it. He produced it with both Freddie Scott trying one version and the Cookies singing another.

"I was a little jealous that Cynthia copied my lyric style just like I had copied Jerry Leiber's lyric style and Doc Pomus'," said Goffin. "I fought my jealousy and I cut two different versions. I thought they both were good."

So did Scott. "I couldn't see anything different in the Drifters' version than what I recorded," he said. "I thought Gerry and I had put out a hit." (A few months later, Scott got his hit with King and Goffin's "Hey Girl.")

But Kirshner didn't agree that the Freddie Scott version of "On Broadway" was a hit. His golden ear told him that something wasn't quite right, so he went to the one guy he knew might be able to fix it. He called Jerry Leiber and asked him for a favor.

"A couple of very talented writers of mine wrote a song for Phil Spector," Kirshner told Leiber. "Phil fell in love with the song and he put it out, but he recalled it because it wasn't a hit. We all thought it would be a hit and we were all wrong. I still think it's a hit, but there's something wrong with it and I can't figure out what it is."

Leiber came over to 1650 Broadway and listened to the song in Kirshner's office.

"It was not a hit the way the way I heard it," said Leiber. "It didn't build properly. There was no denouement that really worked. It just sort of went through on an even keel and it just didn't kick anywhere hard enough to make it happen."

Leiber told Kirshner what he thought was wrong and how it might be fixed, and Don asked if he and Stoller would rewrite it. Leiber said they'd be glad to, but only if the original writers were involved in the process. So they made a date with Mann and Weil to work on the song together. The young couple was thrilled to be rewriting their song with masters.

"Jerry [Leiber] would write lyrics in a much more abstract way, kind of throwing out lines," Weil told UPI's Steve Sailer many years later. "I was always very linear. I had to be a good girl and finish verse one before I would allow myself to have the pleasure of verse two. But Jerry said, 'Just loosen up, woman, and let's just write the song. We'll throw out lines that we think are good, and then we'll see where they go and if we can use any of them.'"

Leiber got Weil to loosen up enough to allow a successful rewrite to take form.

"Mike [Stoller] changed a couple of chords and a couple of notes, and I rewrote the lyric and they were thrilled," Leiber recalled. "When we finished, I said that we liked it so much that we were going to make a record of it with the Drifters, and it was a smash."

Leiber, who is very proud of his roots in the black neighborhoods of Baltimore, first became famous writing "Hound Dog" for Big Mama Thornton, which was later covered by Elvis. When I asked him which lines he wrote and which lines Weil wrote from "On Broadway," he responded by reciting a few lines from the song:

"'How you gonna make some time? When all you got is one thin dime. And one thin dime won't even shine your shoes.'" He then explained that "anything in there that sounds really black is mine, and if you don't know the difference between white and black, then you won't know what mine is."

Mann's Gershwin-esque style stayed in the record. The record also became noted for the guitar solo in the middle played by Phil Spector, of all people.

"Phil was coming to our sessions," Leiber recalled. "He came to this one and brought his guitar. We had four guitar players on the floor already, but no one was able to nail the solo correctly. At one point he said, 'Can I play?' I looked at Mike and we both said, 'Well, I don't know.' He said, 'Come on, I can do it.' I studied with [jazz guitar great] Barney Kessel.' I said, 'Why didn't you say so?'"

Spector went out and plugged in, and he kept pointing to his guitar and motioning with his mouth, "Can I play?" when the solo came up.

"We did maybe twenty, thirty takes," said Leiber. "I think I had George Barnes and Bucky Pizzarelli out there, two of the greats. I pushed the intercom, and said, 'On this next take, this kid is going to take a crack at the solo. Okay?' Nobody objected. We let him take the solo, and we both liked it. And that's the guitar solo on 'On Broadway.'"

The record debuted the first week of spring in 1963 and peaked at No. 9. Fifteen years later, it was Top 10 all over again for George Benson's wonderful jazz version, produced by Quincy Jones.

"I've had a lot of songs that peaked at No. 5, 8, or 9," said Leiber, "but not many that last for 40 years."

21

The Part of a Fool

In the latter part of 1961, Jack Keller thought he had written another smash with a song called "The Part of a Fool." He had reunited with Hank Hunter, with whom he had written "One Way Ticket (to the Blues)" and the Maguire Sisters hit "Just for Old Times Sake." Keller got Barry Mann, fresh off of his "Who Put the Bomp" success, to sing the demo. "It was the best demo I had ever heard," Keller said without reservation.

Kirshner flipped when he heard it. With the demo in his hand and Keller at his side, Kirshner decided to offer the opportunity to record "The Part of a Fool" to Jerry Wexler and Ahmet Ertegun at Atlantic Records. Ertegun and Wexler thought of Kirshner as a competitor, not a friend, and their relationship was definitely tepid. But the four of them settled in to listen, and apparently Wexler and Ertegun agreed that the song had hit potential. The problem began when Kirshner told them what he wanted them to pay him for the song, which was more than the going rate.

Neither Wexler nor Ertegun nor Keller nor Kirshner recall exactly what Kirshner asked for, but whatever it was, they refused. At that point, things got stupid.

"Don stood up, grabbed the demo, and said, 'Then I'm not going to give it to you,'" Keller recalled. "The next thing I know, the three of them were on the floor wrestling for the demo."

Kirshner won the wrestling match but lost that particular war. He was able to retrieve the demo and leave in one piece. The song eventually was recorded by Robin Luke for Dot Records, but never charted. This incident was in some way typical of Kirshner's competitive relationship with the duo from Atlantic, especially Wexler.

"I was never pissed off at Donnie, but we never were too affectionate," said Wexler, who took great pleasure in trying to outwit Kirshner. "Carole King would come to my office and demo a song on my piano and I would secretly tape it. Then I'd say under my breath, 'Fuck you, Donnie, I'm cutting this.'

"In order to get a Carole King song as an exclusive from Donnie," Wexler explained, "you had to promise him the earth. You had to give him the B side *and* promise him the follow-up. If I recorded Carole's demo and put it out by the Drifters or Aretha Franklin [without Aldon's permission], he wouldn't do a thing. I never gave a shit because I knew he wouldn't stop me if I gave him a hit record."

Because of Aldon's rapid success, Kirshner had the kind of leverage Wexler described. In addition to asking for the earth, the sun, the moon, and the stars, he could also ask for more than the traditional two cents per 45 rpm sold that a music publisher got. And, as publisher, he also had the leverage that came with being the owner of the copyright of the song—the right to control the terms around the first recording of the song, including which label recorded it first and how much they paid for that privilege.

Once a song was released, anyone could record it and pay the publisher two cents per copy without asking permission. But for that first release, the copyright owner could ask for more, though rarely did, unless, like Kirshner, he believed the song was the most important element of any hit.

"I remember I got pissed off one day about a Gene Pitney record," said Kirshner. "His producer, Aaron Schroeder, really got me hot. I started asking for three or four cents because I thought the key to that business was the song, and we were getting so little. I always had the balls to try to change things, like copyright licenses."

As music publishers, Nevins and Kirshner would own the copyright to the work of a songwriter they had under contract for twenty-eight years. In return they would split two cents per record sold with the songwriters. If a record sold a million copies, the publisher received $10,000 and the songwriter(s) $10,000. In the 1920s and '30s, a music publisher's primary concern was selling sheet music. But by 1958, that was far from the case.

At one point in the '30s, for every dollar earned, the publisher took two-thirds and the writer got one third. (For sheet music, then and now, the writer earns a flat 10 percent of the sales). In the '40s, '50s, and '60s, the publisher would split with the writers 50 percent each. The fee formula changed dramatically in the '70s and the '80s. The writer was now taking 75 percent and the publisher getting 25 percent.

"But I'll tell you one thing, however they divided it, Donnie gave those writers their start," said Herb Moelis, who, along with Dick Asher, were Aldon's attorneys. "He found those writers. This is not a case where any writer will say to you, 'Donnie and Al got all the money and I went broke.'"

When Nevins and Kirshner opened Aldon Music, it associated itself with BMI (Broadcast Music Inc.), the up-and-coming organization that kept track of the writers' and publishers' performance fees. BMI was in direct competition with ASCAP (the American Society of Composers, Authors and Publishers). In the '50s and '60s, in order to enroll as many new songwriters as possible, BMI gave publishing firms like Aldon incentives to invest in new writing talent. It handed out subsidies that were to be used as cash advances for the writers. Kirshner and Nevins later hedged their bets with ASCAP by starting a subsidiary, Nevins-Kirshner, Inc., set up to hire songwriters who were already ASCAP members.

When new writers joined Aldon, they usually were offered $50 a week against future royalties in a standard five-year contract. When a royalty check came in, say for $10,000, the writer would have his or her cost to the company deducted from his check. If the writer had been with the company for one year, the deduction on a $10,000 payment amounted to $2,600.

"The $50 contract—in those days it was a lot of money," said Kirshner. "I always believed in the longevity of copyrights. I figured if it took a year or two to build someone, then what do I have them for—three years? But that $50 contract I signed Goffin and King to—that was the best investment in the modern world."

As publishers, Nevins' and Kirshner's expenses went beyond the $50 weekly draw they paid the writers and their expenses for rent and supplies at 1650 Broadway. They had union payments, and the costs associated with recording the demonstration records. Those costs included studio time, musicians' costs, paying the demo singer and the backup singers, and hiring a sound engineer of choice. They also paid for retaining legal council.

Any contract a songwriter signed with a publisher was good for only twenty-eight years. The twenty-eight-year expiration gave the writers a second chance to recapture ownership of their material. After twenty-eight years, the songwriters had a choice of either regaining ownership of their copyrights or reselling them. If their songs were being played and earning money, the writers could usually expect to get ten times the annual profit for those copyrights, just like any other asset was valued.

When Jack Keller first signed with Aldon, he knew enough to have Larry Green, one of the best lawyers in town, look at the contract. Green said it was ridiculous. He sent back to Aldon a forty-four-page contract, which Nevins basically agreed to. The standard Aldon contract asked the writers to forego their renewals after the twenty-eight-year period expired. Thanks to Green's contract, Keller was the only Aldon writer who got to keep his renewals.

"Now it's 1961 and they call me in and introduce me to Tony Orlando and tell me I'm going to produce his first record," said Keller. "They tell me that I'll get a royalty and my name on the record. They make up the production contract for me to produce Tony Orlando and the lawyers slipped in, in paragraph two, that everything is retroactive to the original contract and this goes in its place. I thought it was going to be just for the songs I produced. That cost me at least a million in 1988, when the renewal period came up."

According to former Aldon attorney Dick Asher, Nevins and Kirshner weren't trying to take advantage of anyone.

"In truth, the contracts they signed were no different than the contracts that everybody was signing at that time except the really big writers," said Asher. "Al and Donnie probably had as much greed as anybody else, but I don't think they intentionally gouged anybody."

But it wasn't the terms of the contract that drew the teenage writers to Aldon, it was the atmosphere of a songwriting commune they found so alluring. Kirshner had copied what the great publisher Max Dreyfus did in the 1920s when he hired Jerome Kern, George and Ira Gershwin, and Cole Porter.

"Donnie sprang out of nowhere," said Atlantic Records partner Wexler. "When rock and roll came in and the big-band era died, and the era of the song plugger ended, nobody thought that you could sequester songwriters in rooms like they did in the old days and have them turn out music. Somehow Donnie and Al did it. You could say, sure they had great songwriters, but they had the format. Look, these kids were running around with songs and anybody could have picked them up. Anybody that had the vision. It was Al and Donnie that had that vision to put them under contract and give them a weekly stipend."

Wexler's partner, Ahmet Ertegun, wasn't as impressed. "They had these kids [the songwriters] all lined up. You couldn't miss," Ertegun recalled when I reached him by phone. "Don Kirshner was a—how should I say it—a person who recognized an opportunity to make money. He wasn't just lucky, but he wasn't a genius. In a sense, he was like a scavenger. When he saw these young kids getting their songs recorded, he saw an opportunity to talk them into letting him publish their music."

As respected as Ertegun was in the business, his comments sound like sour grapes. Of the more than one hundred people in the industry I interviewed for this book, no one else came anywhere close to sharing those feelings—not even his partner, Jerry Wexler. In fact, most people agreed that Kirshner did have a "golden ear," a unique talent to know when a song was a hit and an even greater talent of finding and guiding talented songwriters to their ultimate success.

Kirshner's hard-line negotiating with Wexler and Ertegun could have cost him more than he thought. Years later, that pair was instrumental in creating the Rock and Roll Hall of Fame. And while they graciously invited Goffin and King into the Hall (and later Mann and Weil), they also worked to keep Kirshner out. When I questioned each of them on this, Ertegun was steadfast that Kirshner did not belong in the Hall. Wexler was wavering, but sounded like he didn't want to rock the boat.

• • •

Just about the time that Nevins and Kirshner were getting Aldon Music off the ground, the payola scandals hit in 1960. ASCAP, which was tied to the old Tin Pan Alley days, was jealous of BMI's rise to prominence on the coattails of rock and roll and asked the House Oversight Committee to look into a possible pay-for-play scheme.

The record companies freely admitted they were paying disc jockeys and program directors to get their songs on the air. Congress decided that pursuing the DJs was its easiest path. Rock pioneer Alan Freed became its biggest-name victim. When he refused to sign a statement denying payola involvement, he was fired by WINS in New York. Other big-name DJs who were caught in the scandal included Murray "The K" Kaufman (also of WINS) and Joe Niagara, known as the "Rockin' Bird" at WIBG in Philadelphia.

Dick Clark, host of *American Bandstand,* was also targeted, but he surprised the investigating committee by sharing the details of his financial involvement in the music business and then announcing he had given up all outside interests in it. Because Clark came clean, he got off with a modest reprimand from House Oversight Chairman Orrin Hatch, who told Clark, "You're not the inventor of the system or even its architect. You're a product of it. Obviously, you're a fine young man." Freed wasn't as fortunate. His career was over and he died five years later a broken man.

As publishers, Aldon had an interest in getting its songs played, but Aldon didn't have nearly as big an interest as the record companies. For every 45 rpm sold, Aldon was receiving two cents (which it split with the songwriters) while the record companies were keeping about 40 cents per copy, and approximately $2 for every album sold.

The major labels got around payola by leaving the business of payola in the hands of artists' managers and business agents. By doing that, monies spent for promotion and chart positions of records couldn't be traced back to the record company. Nobody was clean. Promotion was promotion, and in the music business, everybody had their hand out.

It Might as Well Rain Until September

In 1960, Lou Adler and Herb Alpert were partners when they produced the hit song "Alley-Oop" by the Hollywood Argyles. It didn't take long for Kirshner to have an idea for a follow-up and he contacted Adler.

"I went into New York to listen to material, said Adler, "and met with Kirshner while I was there. "Donnie said, 'If you're ever looking to get into the publishing business, let me know.' Not long after that, Herbie and I went our separate ways and I called Don up."

Kirshner couldn't have hired a more perfect music man for the West Coast. Adler, who was already producing Jan and Dean, wanted Kirshner to meet a young kid who was writing songs about the California beach life. In August of '62, Adler brought the kid, Brian Wilson, and his group to New York to meet with Kirshner.

At the time of the meeting, Wilson's new group, the Beach Boys, already had a moderate hit in L.A. with Wilson's first song, "Surfin'." They also had a national hit with their next song, "Surfin' Safari," also written by Wilson. Even though Wilson was there to discuss becoming a writer for Aldon Music, the possibility also existed for the Beach Boys to record for the company's new Dimension label.

Artie Kaplan was assigned to take Wilson to breakfast the morning of the meeting with Kirshner and soften him up by telling him how great it was to work at Aldon Music. When they came back to the office, Wilson waited in an unoccupied room and was soon joined by the rest of his group. A short while later, a gorgeous fifteen-year-old girl, with dark eyes and dark brown hair down to her waist, accidentally walked in. It was Toni Wine, who Kirshner had signed as a songwriter and demo singer.

"There was a sign outside the door that said, 'Game in session. Do not disturb.'" Wine recalled. "Of course, I had to disturb. A tall, cute, blond kid opened the door. And there were three other blond kids in the office. On the back of the door was a hoop, and they were throwing rolled-up pieces of paper at it. One of them said to me, 'Do you want to play or root?' I said, 'Root.' It was Brian Wilson and the Beach Boys and they were all wearing these cute pinstripe button-down shirts."

Despite the fun, Wilson was not at all amused when he finally met with Kirshner.

"Brian was pretty turned off at that meeting," Adler recalled. "There was a discussion of money, and whatever it was that Donnie had offered, Brian thought it was very low. What I remember from the meeting was that Donnie said to Brian, 'Don't come on like Tarzan.' And that's the last he ever saw of Brian Wilson."

After the meeting, Kaplan remembered seeing Wilson as he was leaving the office. Wilson told him Kirshner offered him $50 a week. "Can you imagine," asked Kaplan, "how big Aldon would have been if we signed the Beach Boys?"

Paul Simon was another young talent who tried to impress Kirshner, but somehow missed the mark. Simon, who was Carole's first writing partner at Queens College, found it difficult competing against King and Goffin, Mann and Weil, and others who already had Don's ear.

"He was on the bench," said Kirshner about Simon. "He couldn't crack the lineup." Simon eventually went in another direction. Although his "Hey Schoolgirl," recorded with Art Garfunkel, reached No. 49 in 1957 (they were billed as Tom and Jerry then), Simon didn't write another Top 40 hit until "Sounds of Silence," in the fall of '65.

In Simon's defense, he was probably just about as raw as Carole was as a songwriter when Kirshner first met her. But by '62 Kirshner didn't have the time or the patience to train another "project" like Paul Simon. Had it been two years earlier, Kirshner would have probably welcomed him with open arms.

"I remember some great artists and songwriters walking into and out of our office without us signing them," said Kaplan. "One day Berry Gordy and Jackie Wilson went back to see Don. Another time, Gary U.S. Bonds came in and shortly thereafter walked out. For all I know, his No. 1 song "Quarter to Three" might have walked out the door with him. A few years later, I asked Don about the ones that got away, and he told me, 'If you didn't pass on some of the great ones, you weren't seeing the right people.'"

In the summer of '62, Goffin and King wrote an upbeat tune with a downbeat message, called "It Might as Well Rain Until September." They wrote it for Bobby Vee, but for some reason his producer, Snuffy Garrett, wasn't that interested. Instead Vee released Jack Keller's "Please Don't Ask About Barbara," followed by one entitled "Punish Her."

King had recorded the demo of "It Might as Well Rain Until September" and Kirshner thought it was a hit exactly as it sounded on the acetate. He decided to make the demo into a master and put it out on the new Dimension label. But King, who was not fond of singing in front of an audience, had no desire to promote the record. Besides, she had just had her second child. So with no promotion whatsoever, "It Might as Well Rain Until September" hit the *Billboard* charts and stayed there for nine weeks, peaking at No. 22. *Cashbox* had the song going a little higher.

With that kind of success despite no promotion of the song, one has to wonder why Carole King did not have another hit record until she scored with "It's Too Late" nine years later, in '71, as part of the *Tapestry* album she recorded for Lou Adler's label. Was she more valuable to Kirshner as a songwriter than a singer?

"Donnie released the demo and it caught Gerry by surprise," theorized Jack Keller. "The song went to No. 22 with nobody knowing who she was. I don't think Gerry wanted Carole to perform, to be a star. I think he was afraid to lose her."

Goffin, respectfully, disagrees. "Carole had kids at the time and she couldn't go out on the road to promote it. It's as simple as that," said Goffin. "I was very proud of her. She never had great chops [for a singer], but they were soulful chops, especially for a white Jewish girl. Besides, our writing was more important to us. In retrospect, nobody talks about that song anymore."

Right around that time, Carole and Gerry started working on a soulful ballad that took nearly a year to get released. Just as George Gershwin had been the inspiration for Barry Mann's "On Broadway," Gershwin was also the inspiration behind Goffin's pleading lyrics in "Hey, Girl."

"I just thought of a *Porgy and Bess* type of guy, where she says, 'Porgy I love you, Porgy I want you to stay.' That type of thing," Goffin recalled.

Freddie Scott, a young R & B singer who originally came to the office as a songwriter, recorded "Hey, Girl." Born in Providence, Rhode Island, Scott grew up in Augusta, Georgia, listening to his grandmother's gospel group, the Gospel Keys. He came to New York in 1951 when he was seventeen and soon became one of the headliners at the Apollo Theater, on 125th Street in Harlem. One thing led to another and by 1962 he had signed with Aldon.

"'Hey, Girl' was written as a follow-up to Chuck Jackson's big hit, 'Any Day Now,'" said Scott. "I went to Carole and Gerry's house and we worked on it and we worked on it and we worked on it. Carole was meticulous working on a song. She'd just bear down until it got done. But for some reason, 'Hey, Girl' stayed on the shelf for over a year."

For some reason, Chuck Jackson's people turned the song down, and Scott's brilliant demo wasn't pushed anywhere else. Goffin felt he knew why.

"It wasn't the type of song that Donnie liked," he said. "It was too slow. He liked something with rhythm. It took us months to put that song out."

Artie Kaplan had the great tenor sax solo on the record, and it was he who encouraged Kirshner to release the song. Phil Spector was also intrigued.

"Phil told us he got the rhythm and the beat of his whole Wall of

Sound from 'Hey, Girl,'" said Goffin. It was the famed Wall of Sound he used while producing 'You've Lost That Lovin' Feelin',' which turned out to be the most played record of the twentieth century.

I asked Goffin if "Hey, Girl" was an early indication that his marriage with Carole was coming apart, as some reports have asserted. The song has been paired with a song from Carole's *Tapestry* album, "It's Too Late," which may have been a response to Goffin's pleading lyrics in "Hey, Girl."

"'Hey, Girl' was written five years before we split up," said Goffin. "I just wrote songs from situations that I made up in my head. That's when I was writing good. When I wrote songs from experience, that's when I started writing not so good."

When "Hey, Girl" was released, it made an immediate splash. The song became No. 1 on the R & B charts and reached No. 10 on *Billboard*. Once more King and Goffin had made a star of an unknown. For Scott, it was a memorable time.

"We had a little celebration at the office and also had one at Carole and Gerry's house," he recalled. "But the night I remember best was celebrating at Broadway Joe's with Marvin Gaye and Richard Pryor. Joe Namath was a co-owner and everyone who was anyone was there."

A few years later, Goffin and King would eventually write a song for Spector that he produced for the Righteous Brothers called "Just Once in My Life." It was the follow-up to "You've Lost That Lovin' Feelin'." Mann and Weil might have landed the first one with Spector, but King and Goffin got the follow-up, which evened the score between the competitive couples. Spector took a writing credit on the song, which he also did on 'Lovin' Feelin'.' It was a practice that hasn't gone without some controversy.

"I know he didn't write a goddamn thing on 'Just Once in My Life,'" said Goffin. "He took a third [of the writing credit]. Sometimes that pisses me off and sometimes it doesn't. And then I realized that it's worth it to get a Spector sound."

The main reason "Hey, Girl" sat on the shelf so long was that Kirshner had other things on his mind. It was the spring of '63. In five years, he had gone from being a total unknown to the prince of pop music. And now he was about to sell his company.

Breaking Up Is Hard to Do

As 1963 rolled in, Don Kirshner was starting to realize the magic he had created at Aldon and the power he was attaining. Eydie Gorme's "Blame It on the Bossa Nova" had just reached No. 7. She was another non-rock-and-roll performer who Kirshner had put on the charts. Previously his songwriters had made hit singers out of movie star James Darren ("Goodbye Cruel World"), TV star Paul Peterson ("My Dad") from *The Donna Reed Show*, and unknowns like Little Eva ("The Loco-Motion") and Dickie Lee ("Patches").

"It was a heady experience to know I had the kind of power to take people that had never had hits before and to make them stars," Kirshner said. But after nearly five years building Aldon, the challenges were fewer and fewer.

"It wasn't fun going to the BMI Awards dinners anymore," he recalled. "There was no fun, no joy in Mudville for me anymore. No more horizons. It was not the same driving up to my house hearing 'The Loco-Motion' [on the radio] or 'Up on the Roof.' It wasn't exciting to me anymore. It wasn't as thrilling as it was in the old days. I felt I had gone as far as I could go there. Sixteen Fifty [Broadway] was becoming too limiting."

He also was concerned about his partner's heart condition. Al Nevins was spending less and less time in the office due to his rheumatic heart. Attorney Dick Asher recalled a business trip he made with Nevins to Europe, early in '63, which enlightened him about Nevins' condition.

"When we were overseas, we used to walk a little and he'd have to stop and catch his breath. Then we'd walk a little more," said Asher.

"Another thing that bothered me was that he had this special pillow made with arms because he needed to sleep sitting up. At the time, I was naïve to all this, but apparently his heart problem must have been serious."

Kirshner felt like he was running Aldon almost single-handedly. Despite that, he took his first vacation in years, staying in L.A. at the Beverly Hills Hotel. As soon as he and Sheila arrived, Kirshner went to visit a business associate, Bobby Darin's new manager, Steve Blauner, at Blauner's home in Bel Air. Relaxing and sitting by the pool were not part of Don's makeup.

Again, thanks to author David Evanier, I was able to reach Steve Blauner by phone. He filled me in on the night Darin opened at the Copa and the role he played in the sale of Aldon Music.

"Donnie was always complaining that Nevins was always on vacation and that Donnie was left doing all the work," Blauner remembered. "I kept telling him, 'You can sell out and start all over again.'"

Blauner's home was originally built for a film called *Strangers When We Meet* with Kim Novak and Kirk Douglas. It had four different levels separated by a series of small landings. When Kirshner arrived, he went immediately up to the top landing, for privacy, to call the office.

"I'll never forget this," said Blauner. "After his call, he came to the top of the landing and looked down, and said, 'Nevins went to Puerto Rico. There's nobody minding the store. Okay, I'm ready to sell. What do I do?'"

Just before Kirshner had left on his "vacation," he had sent Artie Kaplan on a forty-day trip through England with Little Eva to promote her new record on Dimension, "Let's Turkey Trot." While there, Kaplan became aware of a new group from Liverpool that was attracting attention.

"The Beatles were in Hamburg that month and they were starting to make some noise," recalled Kaplan. "Noel Rogers, our music man in England, gave me a number of their records, recommending that we make a deal. He said Brian Epstein, the Beatles' manager, was looking for a music publisher in America."

Nearly a year earlier, on January 14, 1962, Epstein had signed to manage the Beatles. No one knew it at the time, but it was an event that changed music history. In August '62, Epstein replaced Pete Best on drums with Ringo Starr and offered Kaplan's friends at Decca Records the opportunity to release the Beatles' music in the U.S. They turned down the offer, signing the Tremeloes instead. In October, "Love Me Do" was released in Europe and the Beatles were off and running there.

Impressed with what he had heard, Kaplan brought the Beatles records back with him to New York for his meeting with Kirshner and Nevins. They, along with Aldon attorney Herb Moelis, sat down in March '63 to hear the details of his trip.

"I played a Beatles record for them—I think it was 'Please, Please Me'—and I said, 'Noel Rogers recommends we get involved and sign these guys.' They all started to smirk among each other because they knew something that I didn't," said Kaplan.

What they knew was that Aldon Music was about to be sold. The Beatles were put on the back burner.

"And to think," said Kaplan, "we could have and should have signed the Beatles."

More than one major media concern was interested in buying Aldon. The big companies were becoming aware of the value of copyrights in music publishing. And by this time, in 1963, Aldon had amassed more than 200 hits.

"They were looking for publishing companies to buy, and we were the hottest thing since sliced bread," said Kirshner. "There was nobody near us. I was coming home every day, pinching myself that the major papers were doing two-page articles on us."

The first bidder, according to Kirshner, was Leonard Goldenson, chairman of ABC.

"All of a sudden, ABC started offering to buy the company," Kirshner recalled. "Goldenson offered me a lot. We're talking a million, two million, three million. You multiply that fifty times today."

By this time Kirshner was living like a mogul, even if he wasn't as wealthy as one yet. But the royalties were starting to flow in, and he and Sheila were very comfortable. There was no financial urgency to sell.

"Then Steve Blauner introduced me to a young guy by the name of Bert Schneider," said Kirshner. "He was Abe Schneider's son, who was the chairman of Columbia Pictures."

Bert Schneider and Columbia Screen Gems had decided Aldon would be a perfect fit, and knew if they could woo Kirshner, they'd be able to buy Aldon. Schneider appealed to Kirshner's ego and invited him to have dinner with a few special friends. The dinner was set at Lutece, the premier French restaurant in Manhattan, located on tree-lined East 50th Street near Second Ave. *Time* magazine called it "America's best French restaurant."

If Kirshner felt uncomfortable five years earlier meeting Nevins for the first time at the House of Chan, he definitely felt out of place at Lutece (pronounced *Lou-tess*). Just the name itself evoked elegance and luxury. When he walked in, he passed the small zinc bar with a Paris mural overlooking the area. Soon famed owner Andre Surmain greeted him and in his delightful French accent tried to make Don feel at home.

"Yes, Mr. Schneider is expecting you," Surmain said with a smile. He led Kirshner passed the main dining room, called Le Jardin, whose topiary trees yielded a cathedral-like feel, up the carpeted steps of the townhouse to one of the two small private dining rooms. He was joining Schneider in Le Petit Salon, which had hand-finished suede walls and crystal chandeliers that gave the room both warmth and privacy.

As Don walked passed all the fancy French décor, he began to sweat. He would have preferred meeting at a good steakhouse. And when Kirshner arrived at the table, he was overwhelmed by who was joining them for dinner.

"Don," said Schneider, "I'd like you to meet two of Hollywood's greatest stars, Joan Crawford and Anthony Quinn." Kirshner, nearly speechless, froze in his tracks. Finally he managed a faint hello and a nod of his head. He wasn't sure what to do. Finally he nodded toward Crawford, not knowing whether to shake her hand or not, and eventually did stick his hand out for Quinn to shake.

Once Kirshner realized he was running out of challenges at Aldon, he'd given some thought to being a motion picture director, a successful one. By bringing these stars to the meeting, Schneider was feeding into that mindset.

"You've got to understand," said Kirshner, "when I was an usher, I'd be seeing these people on the screen, and now Bert takes me to dinner with Joan Crawford and Anthony Quinn. That's a very heady experience for a kid in his twenties. They wanted to romance me, and I was reeling."

They settled in after a few glasses of French wine, specifically selected by Surmain. Kirshner ordered caviar soup with Madeleine Island scallops and sautéed sea bass for his main course. Quite a change for a guy used to ordering in pastrami on rye from Carnegie Deli.

It was at that dinner that Kirshner decided to sell. He also saw this as a way to retire his father, Gilbert, from his Harlem tailor shop. But most of all, Kirshner saw this as an opportunity to expand his horizons. He was coming along as part of the deal. He'd get $75,000 a year (about $1 million today), a big corner office, and he'd become director of music for Screen Gems.

He told them he needed to oversee the music on all film and all television projects. Getting screen credit was a must, and his name would have to be on every song sheet. He was to have complete creative control or he wouldn't sign.

"I knew how to ask pretty well in those days," Kirshner said. "I said to myself, I was a great music publisher, and why couldn't I become a great director like an Otto Preminger or Richard Brooks or a Carl Foreman."

When the deal was announced, it was reported that Kirshner and Nevins split somewhere between two and three million dollars.

"That's about the right amount, but the deal was part cash and part stock in Columbia Pictures," said one of the major participants in the deal, who requested anonymity.

Steve Blauner, the man who brokered the deal, wound up getting a finder's fee.

"My best friend was Bert Schneider, vice president and treasurer of Screen Gems. I put the two of them together and Screen Gems bought the company," said Blauner. "Donnie said, 'You have to take a fee.' I said, 'I don't want anything. You're a friend of mine and he's a friend of mine.' But Donnie kept insisting and insisting, and I ended up getting half of what he insisted."

If Kirshner negotiated the deal before consulting with Nevins, it's likely Nevins had his own list of demands when he found out.

"I'm sure he didn't want to sell," said Artie Kaplan. "He had financed the whole Aldon operation. He enjoyed coming to the office and being the business half of such a successful company. If they sold, he would have nowhere to go. And because he financed Aldon from the start, he probably told Kirshner that he was taking out the first million in cash for himself. He was nobody's fool."

The deal was announced April 12, 1963. It would include the entire Aldon catalog of copyrights and all the songwriters under contract. The only problem was many of those writers' five-year contracts were nearly up. Kirshner had to move fast to re-sign them.

Sedaka and Greenfield's renewals would come up in '64, and Goffin and King's and Jack Keller's would come up in '65. So Kirshner sent them all what became known as the "eighteen-month telegram." In the telegram he told them he had sold the company to Columbia Screen Gems and that he wanted them all to sign eighteen-month extensions of their contracts. He told them the deal would be great for them because now they'd also be able to write for movies and television. Jack Keller, however, knew that the Garden of Eden was no longer pure. Kirshner was offering them an apple.

"I was a terrible businessman," said Keller. "We loved them [Don and Al] like you loved your mother and father. But once in a while there's a time in your life when you realized your parents were assholes and you didn't have that love anymore. In this case, we realized we were all under their spell."

Keller was the first to accept Kirshner's extension. It wasn't until a month later that he realized he had lost the leverage he had—that they all had—in the situation.

"He had to get me before Barry and Cynthia walked in the door because they were the tough ball-breakers," Keller explained. "The truth is the truth. My motivation was—which wasn't far from the other kids—that we just loved to be able to write and do what we were doing. We were on top of the world."

By this time, Gerry and Carole had moved to a tract house at 15 Waddington Ave. in West Orange, New Jersey, not far from the Kirshners' home. Kirshner knew it was imperative to get King and Goffin, who had written four No. 1 hits, to sign a renewal. He went to their house and decided to make them an offer he thought they couldn't refuse.

"I think he offered us a million dollars," said Goffin. "I was taking flying lessons at the time and got my pilot's license. I told Don if he wanted us to sign, that he had to go up with me."

Kirshner, who was terrified of flying and often took the train cross-country just to avoid going up in a plane, vividly recalls what happened next.

"So I said to Gerry, 'If I go up in this plane with you, if and when we land, will you sign with me?' He said, 'Absolutely!' So I said, 'Okay, I gotta call Sheila before I turn purple.' It was one of the worst experiences of my entire life."

Although Goffin and King were rewarded handsomely for re-signing, they soon became much less enchanted with Kirshner and their new employers.

"He screwed us both. All of us," said Goffin. "We were stuck writing for Screen Gems. They gave us assignments. We couldn't write what we wanted."

Kirshner eventually got everyone to sign the renewals. Within a few months, nearly everyone had moved over to Columbia's offices at 711 Fifth Ave. The May 18th edition of *Cashbox Magazine* had a picture of the major participants of the deal on the cover, including Greenfield, Mann and Weil, King and Goffin, and Keller. The writers, after all, were a major part of the assets of the deal.

Shortly after the deal closed, Charles Koppelman, a failed song-writer Kirshner had turned into a song plugger, was on the phone to London. He was telling Brian Epstein about the merger. Epstein, who still didn't have a publisher for the Beatles in America, invited Koppelman to fly over and discuss publishing the Beatles songs in the U.S.

"I called him because they had recorded a couple of Gerry and Carole's songs," Koppelman said. "They had done 'Chains' and I had this good vibe about the Beatles."

Lou Adler flew in from L.A. and was set to fly to London with Koppelman when longtime Screen Gems executive Marvin Kane squashed the trip.

"He was a music guy and a good guy, but he was from the old school," Koppelman said, referring to Kane. "He had no concept of the revolution that was happening. Donnie asked me to tell him why we were making the trip. Kane listened, and then said, 'You mean you're going to waste maybe $2,000 to fly over and sign some group from England?' The trip was cancelled and the deal was killed."

Koppelman was shocked Kirshner didn't reverse Kane's call. "To me it was symbolic of one thing," Koppelman said. "Donnie no longer had control of his own destiny."

Selling Aldon to Screen Gems probably seemed like a sweet deal to Kirshner at the time. Little did he know that it would wind up costing him hundreds of millions in royalties. Of course there was no way for Kirshner to know that oldies stations would spring up all over the country and play Aldon's songs over and over for the next fifty years.

Aldon's Last Hurrah: This could be the last time Aldon was one big happy family—when Cashbox *put them on the cover, May 18, 1963, announcing their sale to Columbia Screen Gems. Noticeably missing are Neil Sedaka (who was on tour) and Al Nevins, who didn't want to sell. Just about everyone in the photo became unusually successful by music business standards. This photo is a portrait of winners the likes of which no people in the music world could ever have imagined so early in their lives.*

Among the group pictured above are (1) Don Kirshner, (2) Charles Koppelman, (3) Don Rubin, (4) Cynthia Weil, (5) Barry Mann, (6) Artie Kaplan, (7) Lou Adler, (8) Gerry Goffin, (9) Larry Kolber, (10) Jack Keller, (11) Howie Greenfield, (12) Eva (Little Eva) Boyd, (13) Carole King, and (14) Tony Orlando.

24

One Fine Day

As Kirshner moved over to the new offices, he seemed to be going in all directions at once. Al Nevins took his share of the deal and went his own way, only striking a consulting pact with Screen Gems. Less and less could Don call on Al for advice. And then the unthinkable happened. On January 25, 1965, Al Nevins had another heart attack. This time it was fatal. He was only forty-eight.

"I mean, I never dreamed, I thought he'd live to be sixty or seventy without ever a thought of him dying," Kirshner told me. "I got the call and he was gone."

It was a huge loss to all, especially the songwriters, who loved Al Nevins for his kindness and generosity through the years. Nothing would be the same again.

At Screen Gems, Kirshner went from being master of his own domain to answering to the Columbia/Screen Gems executives in Hollywood. Yes, he had the big corner office in the new building, and yes, he was still in charge of the music, but at what cost?

When the deal was announced, Kirshner got all the publicity in the trades. *Cashbox* had them on the cover. *Billboard* and *Variety* did big, splashy features on Kirshner, declaring him the new genius of the publishing world. And of course, *Time* magazine ran the story calling him "the Man with the Golden Ear."

The amount of publicity he received was a double-edged sword. Sure, it looked good for Screen Gems, but privately many of the executives in California started complaining that Kirshner's ego was out of control. More and more he was called out to the West Coast to discuss strategy, leaving him less and less at home running the store.

Being distracted, he was forced to depend on the song pluggers he had trained. Kirshner was one who did not overlook how important this job was.

There are so many ingredients that go into the making of a hit record, from the artist's ability to put the song over, to the writers' ability to write the song, to the arranger's, producer's, and the sound engineer's ability to capture the quality of the song. And most of all—and always overlooked—is that the promotion department of that company has to go out and really bring that record home.

"In the old days, the publishers used to control the business and they would tell the record companies what to record," said Jerry Wexler. "Every major publisher would have the plugged song: the song where they focused all their energies. The main effort of their song pluggers was to bring it to the bands to be played on the radio. Records were almost a secondary concern."

Kirshner always plugged the hot songs for Aldon and assigned others to people like Artie Kaplan. One of his assignments was to plug Aldon songs with Dick Jacobs and Henry Jerome at Decca Records.

"To me, those guys were the biggest thing in the music business—mainly my idols from the '40s and '50s," Artie Kaplan recalled. "Dick Jacobs was an arranger for Tommy Dorsey, and Henry Jerome was a famous bandleader at the Edison Hotel on 47th Street. Alan Greenspan, the former Fed chairman, was a saxophone and clarinet player in that band. I used to listen to them on the radio when I was on the road with lesser bands in the early '50s. We'd hear: *From the Edison Hotel, here's the music of the Henry Jerome Orchestra with Jolly Joe Grimm singing 'Got a Date with an Angel.'*"

Kaplan felt like the hotshot kid on the street when he'd go up to see Jacobs and Jerome at Decca's offices representing Aldon as a song plugger. He had a crew cut and wore a nice tweed jacket and his shoes were always shined. When Kirshner heard what *he* thought was a great song, he'd keep it in his own private stash to plug himself, making it unavailable to other song pluggers at Aldon. Only when Kirshner released a song were others allowed to plug it. So off Kaplan would go to sit in Jacobs and Jerome's office and play them the demos made at Aldon that week, the ones that Kirshner didn't keep for himself.

"The Decca guys thought we were peculiar because they were from a different era," said Kaplan. "I would play something like 'Up on the Roof,' and Dick Jacobs would throw it back across the desk and say, 'I'm sorry, I can't use that.' They never took a song from me. They just got a kick out of me because I was the new breed. They didn't understand it, but they wanted to see what kind of terrible songs I had to offer. Eventually many of those songs they deemed to be 'terrible' became monsters."

• • •

With Kirshner so busy, he needed a lieutenant he could trust to run the office—one who wasn't tied down writing songs. He settled on a former songwriter who had more chutzpah than even Kirshner had. The job went to Charles Koppelman.

Before Charles Koppelman became a music publishing magnate and sold his empire to EMI for $320 million, before he became a sought-after advisor by Michael Jackson (regarding his publishing catalog), before he was asked to join the board and become the CEO of Martha Stewart Living, before he discovered and signed the Lovin' Spoonful, Charles Koppelman was a nineteen-year-old kid with a jump shot who talked Don Kirshner into a job.

Koppelman was the type of kid who other kids gravitated to. He could talk just about anybody into anything. And no one called him "Charlie" more than once. In the spring of 1960, even though he wasn't much of a singer, Koppelman formed a singing group with Artie Berkowitz and Don Rubin, two friends from Adelphi College.

"They were both extremely musical. Artie would sing on high holy days with the cantor and Don was a guitar-playing singer-songwriter," Koppelman recalled. "I was mainly interested in playing baseball, basketball, and stickball, but I got involved because they were my two best friends."

They started writing a few songs together and called their trio the

Ivy Three. Because Koppelman's next-door neighbor in Laurelton (Queens) was an editor at *Cashbox Magazine,* Charles became familiar with the various record labels based in New York.

"I started reading *Cashbox* for fun, and learned by osmosis that there was a business of music," Koppelman said. Then one day during spring break, Koppelman called Rubin and Berkowitz with some news.

"Fellas, we have an audition today and we're going into the city," Koppelman told them. "When we got to 1650 Broadway," recalled Rubin, "Charles says, 'You guys wait down here in the lobby.' We're waiting downstairs ten minutes, twenty minutes, a half hour. Forty minutes later, Charles comes down and says, 'Okay, we're all set.' I found out years later that we had no audition that day—that Charles arranged the audition while we were standing downstairs, by going from one office to the other."

Koppelman had luck with a small label called Shell Records, which was owned by a dentist. They auditioned for the writing-producing team of Lou Stallman and Sid Jacobson, who had a few hits under their belt.

"Charles had the idea for the song 'Yogi,' based on Yogi Bear from *The Huckleberry Hound Show,*" said Rubin. "Charles gave them the idea for the song and helped them write it. Lo and behold, we record the song and it becomes a big hit. It goes Top 10, we go on *The Dick Clark Show,* we get booked on a tour with Jan and Dean, and Johnny and the Hurricanes. We did a follow-up that bombed and a follow-up to that that bombed. And that was it. We were done."

But while promoting the record, they were booked as the main entertainment one weekend at Grossinger's Hotel in the Catskills. That's where they met Kirshner.

"We were playing basketball there that weekend and we met a guy who was a pretty damn good basketball player," Rubin remembered. "He introduced himself as Don Kirshner, and we sheepishly tell him that we're the group singing there that night."

Fast-forward six months to the BMI Awards dinner in January '61 at the Pierre Hotel. Koppelman is there to pick up his award as a co-writer for "Yogi."

"They called my name and I got my award," Koppelman said. "During the evening, I kept seeing Kirshner stand up to get awards. On the way home that night, I said to Donald, 'That guy Kirshner and his writers, they looked pretty normal to me. They didn't look like weird music people. Why shouldn't we be able to do that?'"

By then, Berkowitz, the third member of the Ivy Three, had gone into the insurance business with his father. Koppelman and Rubin decided to go home and write a new bunch of songs and see if Kirshner would hire them.

"We accumulated about twenty songs," Koppelman recalled, smiling. "We went to 1650 Broadway, and up to Aldon Music to try to see Don. We got to the receptionist's window, and she asks if we have an appointment. I said we didn't, and she said, 'Well, he doesn't see anyone without an appointment.' Just then another woman walks by, and I say, 'Can you please tell Mr. Kirshner that Charles Koppelman is here—the guy with the jump shot.'"

They waited about four minutes before Kirshner opened the door and came bounding out. He gave Koppelman a hug and invited them in.

"I told him we were writing songs and that we had met with another publisher in that building who was interested in us," said Koppelman. "It was half true. He said, 'Why would you do that? Why don't you just sign with us?'"

They signed for $25 a week each and wrote songs in cubicles next to Carole King and Gerry Goffin, Howie Greenfield and Jack Keller. Kirshner even listened to their songs occasionally. Mostly Kirshner would play demos of other records for Koppelman and ask his opinion.

"We were also-rans at Aldon," said Rubin. "We got a few songs recorded, though—the B sides of a Jan and Dean and a Tony Orlando. After about a year of splitting $50 a week with Charles, I decided to get married, but I couldn't afford an engagement ring. Al Nevins, may he rest in peace, gave me the money—$1,500 bucks. I didn't have the nerve to ask Kirshner. If they believed in you, they stuck with you and took care of your personal needs."

Jack Keller had become friendly with Koppelman and Rubin and would often join them for stickball games. One day the three of them were sitting on the curb, dreaming of where they'd like to be in ten years. Both Rubin and Keller said they wanted to be writing and producing hits. Then Koppelman stunned Keller with his answer, giving some insight into what he was thinking.

"I want to be bigger than Kirshner," Koppelman said.

After writing at Aldon for two years without a hit, in February '63 Kirshner called Koppelman into his office and told him he was selling his company to Columbia Screen Gems and that he, Kirshner, would be running a new division there.

"I can use a good, young executive at Screen Gems," Kirshner told him. "How much do you need to take home?"

"He's been paying me $25 a week," thought Koppelman, "so he can't be thinking less than that."

Koppelman told Kirshner he needed $115 a week take home. Three months went by with no word from Kirshner. Finally, Kirshner's office tracked down Koppelman. They asked him to meet Kirshner the next day at Columbia's offices at 711 Fifth Ave. at 3 p.m., and to wear a suit. The next day, he went straight to Paul Sergeant's men's store in Brooklyn and bought one for $25.

"Don met me at the elevator on the floor they sent me to," recalled Koppelman. "He put his arm around me and walked me into a big office and introduced me to Stan and Bert Schneider, who ran Screen Gems. Then he escorted me out and said, 'Listen, I just sold my company. You go over to 1650 Broadway, sit in my office, and you run the publishing company,' adding with a grin, 'the guy I had running it just quit.'"

A few months later, when everyone had moved over to the new offices at 711 Fifth Ave., Koppelman talked Kirshner into hiring Rubin, and the pair became song pluggers.

"That was basically our big break," said Rubin. "We gave up songwriting and Donnie taught us the business. Now we were making $150 a week each, and we're taking Goffin and King songs around and pitching them. We got to know everybody. Now we had offices and we dressed up every day. We were *mensches*."

One of their early scores as song pluggers was with a Goffin and King song called "One Fine Day." But Kirshner had kept the demo in his private stack, which meant he and he alone was going to pitch it to the major labels. On the demo, Carole was on piano with Little Eva singing the vocal. It was a sure-fire hit, but Kirshner had just sold his company and he was distracted running the new division for Screen Gems. So Koppelman "borrowed" the demo from Kirshner's desk.

"Koppelman was the only one who had the balls to take a demo off Donnie's stack," said Artie Kaplan. "He pulled 'One Fine Day' out of the pile and knew exactly where to take it."

He headed straight to Hank Medress and Jay Siegel of the Tokens, who now had a multi-record deal producing for Capitol Records. The Tokens' production company was called Bright Tunes Music, and was located down the street from Aldon at 1697 Broadway, next to the Ed Sullivan Theater.

After several failures, the Tokens' production budget was running out and Capitol was losing its patience. Then the Chiffons and their manager walked into Bright Tunes with "He's So Fine." Capitol turned it down, and so did eleven other labels before tiny Laurie Records agreed to release the record. "He's So Fine" was No. 1 for the entire month of April in '63 and stayed on the charts for fifteen weeks. When Koppelman grabbed "One Fine Day" from Kirshner's stack, he instinctively knew it was the perfect follow up for the Chiffons.

"We not only convinced them to record the song," said Koppelman, "but we convinced them to use Carole's demo track for the record. They replaced Little Eva's track with the Chiffons' voices, then added Artie Kaplan's baritone sax and Charlie Macey on bass guitar and released it."

"One Fine Day" became another Top 5 record for Carole and Gerry, and Koppelman and Rubin were on their way to becoming two of the hottest song pluggers in the business.

"Years later," Koppelman recalled, "I asked Kirshner why he hired me as an executive, because we were terrible songwriters. He said that he realized that every time he asked my opinion about a song, I was usually right. He knew I had the instinct to recognize a hit."

Among those impressed by Koppelman and Rubin was one of the most famous producing teams around, Hugo and Luigi. Hugo Peritti and Luigi Creatore were cousins who began working together by chance. After some early success at Mercury, they started their own label, Roulette Records, along with Morris Levy, who was rumored to have ties to the Mafia. They had auditioned a young singer named Jimmie Rodgers while working at Mercury and wanted to sign him, but the home office said they already had too many "boy singers." When they started Roulette, they remembered Rodgers.

"But we needed to hire a detective agency to find him," Creatore recalled. "He was working in a lumber camp in Oregon. When we got him to New York, he was haggard and hadn't eaten in days."

Rodgers recovered and recorded "Honeycomb" at that session, which was No. 1 for a month. A few months later, "Kisses Sweeter Than Wine," another Top 5 song, followed. A few years later, RCA came to Hugo and Luigi with a five-year deal for a million dollars. Creatore wasn't sure about how Levy would take the news.

"Morris said, 'If yous [sic] want to better yourselves, I can't stand in your way.' We gave him back our stock and parted as friends."

Levy was notorious for his ties to the Mafia. His story was captured in the chapter "Lullaby of Gangland" in Fredric Danner's book about the music business, *Hit Men*. Originally from the East Bronx, Levy co-promoted shows at the Brooklyn Paramount with DJ Alan Freed, owned the famous jazz club Birdland, and made a tidy fortune from publishing copyrights he had "acquired" over the years.

"Morris was more like a groupie for hoods. He was a lovable rogue," Creatore told me in a phone interview. "He admired all these people, but he didn't know half of them. If he was as connected as they say he was, every one of our songs would have been hits and we would have had all the money in the world. When we went to RCA, Roulette floundered pretty badly. If he had mob money behind him, it would have made it. But Morris did enjoy that characterization of himself."

Levy could be very persuasive when he wanted to. When I spoke to Gene Pitney, he told me about the time Levy was trying to sign him to Roulette. While Pitney was appearing in South Florida, Levy invited Pitney to relax in the hot tub of his Florida home.

"He turned up the temperature in that tub to near boiling," Pitney recalled. "And then he said, with a straight face, 'I'll turn it down when you sign.' Until he actually turned it down, I wasn't sure if he was kidding or not."

After meeting Koppelman and Rubin while promoting King and Goffin's song "The Old Crowd," Hugo and Luigi were duly impressed and suggested that Levy hire them away from Kirshner.

"They reminded us of ourselves when Hugo and I were just starting out," Creatore said. "Young and full of fire." Levy called them in and offered them each $225 a week. Don Rubin picks up the story from there.

"We go to Donnie and say, 'Don't take this the wrong way. We love you. We owe everything to you. You gave us our start, but we're still making $150 a week, and we're married now. Morris Levy just offered us $225 a week. Just match it and we're staying.'"

Kirshner couldn't believe what he was hearing. He got so insulted that his anger bubbled over. His face turned red and he finally responded.

"If you guys are telling me you're even thinking of leaving," he said while getting more and more upset, "I'm, I'm, I'm calling both your mothers!"

Kirshner didn't match the offer, and Koppelman and Rubin moved over to work for Levy. Kirshner retaliated by hiring Wally Schuster away from Levy. Schuster was a talented song plugger and music man. It was Schuster who first brought Carole Bayer Sager to Kirshner.

Six months later, using losses from the Brooklyn Paramount as an excuse, Levy fired Koppelman and Rubin, telling them he had to cut back. Jack Keller, though, thought there was another reason for their exit.

"I had heard," said Keller, "that when Morris fired them, Koppelman had the chutzpah to say, 'You can't fire us. We have a contract.'"

"It turned out to be the best thing that could have happened to us," said Rubin. "We wound up starting our own business."

It's a business that has made them more successful than either of them had ever dreamed and wealthier than they had ever hoped. Charles Koppelman has since become one of the most successful publishers in the world, and no longer has to identify himself as "the guy with the jump shot."

25

Groovy Kind of Love

With Kirshner now going in all directions, the songwriters abandoned the new offices and pretty much wrote from home. The new Screen Gems offices were beautiful, but felt antiseptic compared to the cubicles that 1650 Broadway had. Going into the office was no longer fun. With everyone going their own way, so to speak, Kirshner depended more and more on demos to sell his songs. Which is one reason he had under contract two of the best demo singers in the business: Toni Wine and Ron Dante.

Kirshner first became aware of the demo when he tried to sell the first song he ever wrote to pop star Frankie Laine, in 1954. Kirshner was a wide-eyed twenty-year-old, and Laine was a star who had had forty-four records on the charts in the previous seven years—three reaching No. 1. He told Don to make a "demonstration record" and he'd listen to Kirshner's song. Don "borrowed" $50 from his father and somehow got the demo made. Even though Laine turned down his song, Don was exhilarated by the process and realized just how important a demo could be.

"I was the first one to shorten the word to *demo,*" said Kirshner. "When Aldon began to click, they called me the 'King of the Demos.' I had killers doing our demos, like Bobby Darin, Carole King, and Neil Sedaka on piano and Toni Wine, Barry Mann, and Ronnie Dante singing them. In the old days, the great songwriters like Hoagy Carmichael ["Stardust"] would demonstrate their songs. My writers did too, but I shortcut it with spectacular demos. This innovation of demonstrating your wares became the showcase that turned the industry inside out."

• • •

Toni Wine showed early signs of being a gifted child. She was also blessed with physical beauty. She began studying piano at the Juilliard School of Music at the age of five, and when she was ten she played Carnegie Hall. She was on the fast track to becoming a concert pianist when in August 1958 her mother took 11-year-old Toni and her brother for a one-week vacation to the Catskill mountains. Their hotel: the Esther Manor.

This shot of Neil Sedaka and Toni Wine was taken in 1963. Imagine how much younger they looked five years earlier, when they first met at Esther Manor.

"Sitting in the main room playing piano and entertaining the *alter-cockers* was a young singer named Neil Sedaka," Toni recalled. "This was before anybody knew who Neil Sedaka was. He's playing a song and I start singing along from my chair. He encouraged me to come over, and he made room for me to sit with him. And there I was sitting alongside and singing harmonies with Neil. Little did either of us know that three years later we'd both be writing for Aldon Music."

That leap to Aldon happened quite innocently. One day after school a few years later, Toni was visiting her mom, who worked as a secretary at MGM's recording offices.

"Someone needed a background voice on a record, so I went with my mom to Associated Studios at 723 Seventh Ave," she said. One thing led to another, and young Toni found herself singing demos for others. She was just fourteen, but she had grown into a beautiful young woman, with long, straight brown hair and deep brown eyes.

One day in 1961, songwriter Paul Kaufman (Jack Keller's boyhood friend) was working on a song in the adjoining studio at Associated when he heard Toni sing and asked her if she'd like to work with him. Kaufman was overwhelmed with her talent and called his old buddy Jack Keller, who was also working at Associated that day, to come over to the session to hear her.

"Jack was really excited, and he asked my mom if I could meet Don Kirshner," she recalled. "I remember Kirshner's office vividly. The piano was on the right and Donnie was straight ahead. He had already heard some of my demos. My mom and I walked in, and he said to me, 'I love your voice. Do you by any chance, write?'"

Toni played and sang her version of several current hits. "I love your feel," Kirshner told her. "I want you to write for me too."

At Kirshner's urging, she changed her last name from Wein to Wine, which was how it was pronounced. And even though she was only fourteen, just like Carole King, Kirshner paid her $50 a week against future royalties. Between her amazing voice and her very striking looks, Kirshner thought she had star potential.

"You're in this family," he told her. And just like all the other teenagers Kirshner discovered, Toni Wine became part of the Aldon family. It was an experience she'll never forget.

"I grew up—I was raised in that office," she remembered. "That was my education. They all watched over me. Aldon was Room 610 at 1650 Broadway. You got off the elevators and you made a quick right and you were in the magic land."

She also marveled at how Kirshner managed all of his writers and how he inspired and encouraged them.

"He'd call the writers into his office to play for a particular producer or artist," she said. "Watching his vision come to life was special. He was remarkable in putting people together. "His vision was his greatest gift. He started with a handful of seeds that he believed would grow. He knew what would work and how to get it done. He was a magic man, that's what he was!"

About the same time Toni Wine was welcomed into Aldon in the early '60s, a sixteen-year-old, male demo singer named Carmine Granito also joined the "family." Soon he changed his name to the more commercial-sounding Ron Dante.

"Charles Koppelman and Don Rubin actually were the first in the office to hear me, and I was signed the next day," Dante recalled. "When I met Kirshner he wanted to know about my family. He was truly interested. He was going to pay me a certain amount per week, but when I told him I had to help support my family, he paid me more."

In Dante's first six months at Aldon, somebody stole his beautiful guitar out of the trunk of his car. Kirshner immediately replaced the $300 model. "About three months later, somebody stole it again and he replaced it again," Dante said. "Don and Al's kindness and generosity went beyond what I had ever imagined."

As a writer, Dante was able to get songs on the flip side of hits by Gene Pitney, Bobby Vee, and Jay and the Americans. When the British Invasion hit, Dante stretched his singing abilities and became one of Madison Avenue's top jingle voices.

Throughout the '60s, he continued to be sought after as a demo performer and was chosen by producers to be the anonymous lead singer of a group called the Cuff Links in '69. Dante was actually the only voice on the album, but he wrote the vocal arrangements by overdubbing his own voice ten or twelve times. The result was the Top 10 song "Tracy."

● ● ●

Toni Wine was hired primarily because she was a great demo singer, even at the age of fourteen. Sometimes she'd spend the weekend at Carole and Gerry's to learn the songs she'd record the following week as demos. Carole King ran her demo sessions a little differently than everyone else.

"She would come in and give everyone a lead sheet, then sit down and play the song on the piano with the feeling she wanted to convey," said Buddy Saltzman, who was the drummer on many King and Goffin sessions. "Then we'd experiment and try to play it with the feel she was looking for. We'd make notations on our lead sheets, and after a few takes we'd be close. Carole was very bright and very laid back—until her husband walked in. Then all they'd do is fight."

Flanked on either side of Don Kirshner are (left) Toni Wine and twenty-two-year-old Carole Bayer (Sager). Above them is Jack McGraw, Screen Gems' London rep who convinced the Mindbenders to record Toni and Carole's song "Groovy Kind of Love."

Besides being a wonderful demo singer, Wine also became a heck of a songwriter. A few years after joining Aldon, she teamed with a new songwriter, Artie Kornfeld, to write a mid-level hit for the Shirelles called "Tonight You're Gonna Fall in Love with Me."

"It wasn't a huge hit," said Wine, "but it was half a hit. And wow! What could be better than hearing your song on the radio when you're sixteen?"

Kornfeld went on to co-write "Dead Man's Curve" (with Brian Wilson and Jan Berry). He also co-wrote the classic song by the Cowsills, "The Rain, the Park, and Other Things."

Wine's songwriting took a step up in '65, when Kirshner paired her with a twenty-two-year-old high school substitute teacher named Carole Bayer (Sager). They produced a song that went all the way to No. 1, "Groovy Kind of Love."

I was able to find Carole Bayer Sager thanks to the Songwriters Hall of Fame. We traded e-mails and she agreed to a phone interview in 2007, in which she couldn't have been nicer and was quite forthcoming.

"Don was bigger than life and he gave me my first big break," Sager recalled. "Toni and I were a good match. We wrote a lot of good songs, we felt, but we had some stiff competition to have them heard. We liked the word *groovy* and one day decided to write a song with 'groovy' in the title. Toni handed me a beautiful melody and I finished the song."

Sager lived with her parents across the street from Carnegie Hall at the Alwyn. That's where she and Wine wrote "Groovy Kind of Love" in just twenty minutes.

Jack McGraw, Screen Gems' music man in England, helped make "Groovy" a hit. He already had placed two songs ("Ashes to Ashes" and "Off and Running") by Toni and Carole in the hit film *To Sir with Love*, and he was trying to get the producers to use "Groovy Kind of Love" also. The Mindbenders, a rock group, were in the film, and McGraw sold them on recording the song. It broke first in England and then quickly rose to No. 1 here.

"It just happened that fast," said Wine. "And on my nineteenth birthday, June 4, 1966, the Mindbenders' version went to No. 1. I called my mother when it reached the Top 10 and told her she was quitting her job."

Wine would continue to write and earned a reputation as one of the best backup singers in the business. She was part of the famous Ooh and Ahh Girls, who were highly sought-after backup singers. And in 1969, she kick-started Tony Orlando's second singing career when she co-wrote "Candida." Before Tony Orlando had the group Dawn as his backup singers, Toni Wine was one of three who sang background on "Candida" as well.

By the time Toni had reached her nineteenth birthday, more than just her songwriting had blossomed.

"The background voices for 'Candida' were me, a girl named Robin Grean, and Jay Siegel [lead singer of the Tokens, turned producer]," Wine recalled. "When the song became a hit, we were all doing what we were doing in New York and couldn't tour with Tony, so they hired Telma [Hopkins] and Joyce [Vincent] to become Dawn. In reality, for the whole first album, which included 'Knock Three Times,' the background singers were me, Robin, Jay Siegel, and a girl named Linda November."

● ● ●

While Toni Wine was moving into songwriting's big leagues, Sedaka and Greenfield, Goffin and King, and Mann and Weil all saw their production slow appreciably.

For Sedaka, "Next Door to an Angel" reached No. 5 in 1962, but he didn't have another song in the Top 10 until 1974. Goffin and King hit a dry spell until Aretha Franklin's "Natural Woman" reached No. 8 in '67. Mann and Weil had a semi-hit with "We've Gotta Get Out of This Place," for the Animals (No. 13) in '65, but for the most part, both the record companies and public were looking first to England for their music.

And just when they might have needed him most, Kirshner's attention turned toward a new Screen Gems project: the Monkees.

26

Sugar, Sugar

With all the publicity he had received, Kirshner was getting quite a reputation, and his ego swelled a little more once he began guiding the musical career of the Monkees.

In 1965, producer Bob Rafelson approached Bert Schneider with an idea. Rafelson was inspired by the Beatles' first film, *A Hard Day's Night,* which not only featured the group's songs but showed their happy-go-lucky wackiness as well. He wanted to do a TV series with four actors who would play a wacky American foursome. Schneider agreed and the two formed their own company, Raybert Productions, and sold the show to Screen Gems.

Screen Gems put out a wide casting call and finally settled on Americans Micky Dolenz, Mike Nesmith, Peter Tork, and Englishman Davy Jones. The company planned a weekly TV show, which would feature the group's slapstick antics and a song or two.

For the music, the company relied heavily on Kirshner. And he delivered. He selected and executive-produced all of their songs, several of which were written by Jeff Barry and Neil Diamond, two of the decade's greatest songwriters. For their first single, Kirshner carefully picked "Last Train to Clarksville," which was written by Tommy Boyce and Bobby Hart, who were new in the Kirshner stable.

After "Clarksville" went to No. 1, Kirshner somehow talked Neil Diamond into giving the Monkees "I'm a Believer," even though he wanted to record it himself. At the time, Diamond was already a successful performer, having struck with "Solitary Man" and "Cherry, Cherry," the latter reaching No. 6. Talking him into giving up "I'm a Believer" may have been Kirshner's greatest accomplishment for Screen Gems.

The Monkees, individually and as a group, were not easy. They didn't like to be told what to do or how to do it. Yet Kirshner was determined to "manage" them.

Thanks to the songs and arrangements chosen by him, both the Monkees' music and TV show took off. Soon everyone was taking credit for the success. Among those, Kirshner was one of the first in line, and the Monkees didn't like it one bit.

The first producer Kirshner chose to work with them was the great Snuff Garrett, who by now had produced more than two dozen Top 10 songs. Garrett found the foursome so difficult that after just one session he quit and flew to his mother's home in Texas to hide out.

"Kirshner's people called all weekend, but I never picked up the phone," Garrett recalled. "Finally on Monday they sent a brand-new Cadillac convertible just to get me to finish the session. Let me tell you, those kids [the Monkees] were assholes."

Jeff Barry, who had produced dozens of hit records with Leiber and Stoller's Redbird label, was the next producer Kirshner tried. It didn't take Barry long before he realized the group was more trouble than the job was worth.

Barry had brought in some of the best musicians in New York to make them sound great on record—a practice done by all the record companies—but the boys, inexperienced as they were, only wanted to play their own instruments and called a press conference to let everyone know. Not only did they want to play their own instruments, they also wanted to pick their own songs and choose their own producer. In other words, they wanted to manage themselves.

Kirshner next employed the mild-mannered Jack Keller to produce their next album. Whatever problem the group had, they seemed to want to take it out on Kirshner.

"Once Don sat in on a session," Keller recalled. "During a break, Mickey Dolenz walked back to the control room and poured a Coke on top of Kirshner's head. The ice slowly dripped down his face, yet he never moved or said a word. It was the most controlled I ever saw him."

Kirshner was determined to patch up his relationship with the group. Despite his fear of flying, he got on a plane and flew to California to present the boys with a million-dollar royalty check at a meeting at the Beverly Hills Hotel. Instead of graciously accepting it, they practically threw him out of the room.

Mike Nesmith felt Kirshner was simply looking for another photo-op. He took the opportunity to complain once again about playing their own instruments and choosing their own songs. Colgems Records' attorney, Herb Moelis, who was at the meeting, set Nesmith off by saying, "You better read your contract." Nesmith got so angry he literally punched a hole in the wall. "That could have been your face," he told Moelis, and then walked out of the room.

At that point, the Monkees would have said black if Kirshner said white. They went to Bert Schneider at Screen Gems and demanded Kirshner be fired. Schneider said he'd think about it.

In January '67, the Monkees were in Hawaii on tour when Kirshner released their next album, *More of the Monkees*. It was a collection of songs the group had recorded with different producers in the last year. The Monkees were hot, and Kirshner was right to get another album out to a public hungry for their songs. The mistake Kirshner made, however, was not telling the Monkees that it was coming out. Nesmith called it "the worst album in history," even though it contained the hits "I'm a Believer" and "You're Not My Stepping Stone."

About the same time, Kirshner also released "A Little Bit Me, a Little Bit You" as their next single without their consent. At this point, Screen Gems had agreed to let the group have approval on what songs were released.

The Monkees went ballistic when they got back to Los Angeles and vehemently demanded Kirshner be fired. This time management agreed. Despite the fact that he had personally selected the group's first three singles—all million-sellers—and their first two albums, which combined sold over three million copies, Kirshner got the ax.

It didn't matter that both "A Little Bit Me, a Little Bit You" (No. 2) and their next single, which was also a Kirshner selection, Goffin and King's "Pleasant Valley Sunday" (No. 3) were successful. Kirshner was gone, and it probably was no coincidence that the Monkees never had another song rise above No. 3.

He subsequently sued Screen Gems and won a large breach-of-contract settlement. The year was 1968 and Don Kirshner, at the age of thirty-three, was out of work for the first time since he and Al Nevins first shook hands and created Aldon Music.

Over the years, it's possible that Kirshner embellished one part of the story of his volatile meeting with the Monkees. He has often noted that he brought a special record to that meeting for the Monkees to record: "Sugar, Sugar," written by Jeff Barry and Andy Kim. And according to Kirshner, the Monkees wanted no part of any song Kirshner selected for them and turned it down.

Back in New York, and on his own for the first time in a decade, it didn't take long for Kirshner's phone to ring. Norm Prescott and Lou Scheimer, a couple of animators, had started a company called Filmation.

"They called Don, and told him they were doing a cartoon show featuring the characters from the *Archie and Veronica* comic books," recalled Ron Dante. "Don immediately said, 'You should have them all sing and call them the Archies.'"

Being available, Kirshner signed on as the musical supervisor and consulting producer. In that moment he had created the Archies, and he hired Dante along with Toni Wine to be the lead voices of the group.

There's reason to question if Kirshner actually had "Sugar, Sugar" written for the Monkees. If the Monkees turned down the song in January '67, then why did it take him more than two and a half years to release it, in July '69? Could he have decided to archive a great song that long just to get back at them?

Said Jeff Barry: "All the so-called music critics complained about how silly the lyrics were [for 'Sugar, Sugar']. What did they want? We were writing it for a Saturday morning cartoon show."

Regardless of when it was written or for whom, "Sugar, Sugar" turned out to be the biggest hit of the year. It stayed on the charts for twenty-two weeks and was No. 1 for a month. Selling eight million copies, RCA proclaimed that it was the biggest-selling single in the company's history.

And once again it proved that Kirshner certainly knew a hit song when he heard one.

When I kissed you girl, I knew how sweet a kiss could be
(I knew how sweet a kiss could be).
Like the summer sunshine, pour your sweetness over me
(Pour your sweetness over me)

Sugar, ah honey honey
You are my candy girl
And you've got me wanting you.

As contracted studio performers hired to be two of the singing voices on a weekly TV show, Wine and Dante didn't receive any royalties. It's a fact that that has rubbed Toni Wine the wrong way for a long time.

"My reward was a dozen roses," Wine said. "That was all I received. Where did the artist's royalties go? They didn't go to Ronnie or me."

For Toni Wine, getting paid with roses instead of royalties, was the clinching sign of how drastically things had changed since her days at Aldon Music. To her, that was the signal that they weren't in Kansas anymore. "That's the day the music died—the day they sold the company," she said.

● ● ●

Kirshner might have been out of a job, but he wasn't out of ideas. He would wind up coming back bigger than ever. In 1971, he approached Barry Diller at ABC with an idea for a weekly late-night

TV show called *In Concert*. Diller, one of the hottest programmers in television at the time, liked Kirshner's plan of a rock-and-roll variety show, a la Ed Sullivan. Other than *American Bandstand*, there was nothing on TV like it—especially late night.

Diller's strategy was to try Kirshner's show out as a Friday night replacement for talk show host Dick Cavett at 11:30 p.m. Cavett was getting killed in the ratings by Johnny Carson, so Diller felt he had nothing to lose. The shows kicked off in November and December 1972 with an all-star rock cast. Featured in those two programs were Alice Cooper; Blood, Sweat, and Tears; Chuck Berry; the Steve Miller Band; Bo Diddley; Seals and Croft; and the Allman Brothers Band. Kirshner pulled out all the stops.

Diller looked like a genius when *In Concert* literally doubled Cavett's ratings, and eventually overtook Carson on Friday nights. After those first two shows, Diller made it a weekend staple on ABC late night.

After two seasons, it became syndicated as *Don Kirshner's Rock Concert*. Kirshner was to be the host, and in the inaugural show, September 27, 1973, Don wanted to make a big splash. He did it by getting the Rolling Stones to make their first American TV appearance in four years. But it wasn't easy.

In a 2009 interview, Kirshner told *Rolling Stone*: "I was a nervous wreck because the Stones were being offered a million dollars by the other networks. I got Mick Jagger on the phone and he says, 'So what are you giving me?' I said, 'Three hundred.' He says, 'Three hundred grand?' I said, 'No, three hundred dollars a man.' He laughed, and said, 'Chap, I love your work and I'm gonna do it for you.'"

On the day the show debuted, legendary *New York Times* columnist John J. O'Connor wrote:

"In the television syndication business, a lead time of at least six months is considered normal in finding buyers for a new series. In less than five weeks, one new syndicated series has, so far, signed up 113 stations with access to about 84 percent of the national audience. That record-breaking pace provides still another indication of both the new success of rock music on television and the continuing success of Don Kirshner in the music business."

Enjoying enormous success, the show ran for a decade. Anybody who was anybody in rock and roll appeared on the program. It helped launch the careers of Santana, Aerosmith, Jimmy Buffett, Al Green, Van Morrison, and the Bee Gees, among others. It also marked the first appearance on American television by the Who.

Kirshner also insisted on including comedians on the rise, with fresh, cutting-edge material. Billy Crystal and Jay Leno were two who received their first big break on *Don Kirshner's Rock Concert.*

For years it was a can't-miss event for American teens. As hip as the show was, that's how un-hip Kirshner appeared to be as its stiff, Ed-Sullivan–like host. In fact, he was so out of place that Paul Shaffer made a living imitating Don on *Saturday Night Live.* But according to Kirshner's attorney, Herb Moelis, after the show ran for a decade, ABC asked Kirshner to replace himself with a younger, hipper host. "His ego got the best of him," Moelis said. "He refused to be replaced and the show was cancelled."

For Don Kirshner, the glory days were over, but he wasn't about to throw in the towel.

Beats There a Heart So True

. . . And through all eternity
She'd be good for only me,
Beats there a heart so true?

Like everyone else, Jack Keller had a hard time writing hit songs once the British Invasion set in. Although he wrote a pair of No. 1 songs for Connie Francis, his biggest hit just may have been a TV theme song.

In 1964, Screen Gems came out with a new TV series starring Elizabeth Montgomery called *Bewitched*. The studio execs asked Kirshner to have his writers come up with a theme song for the show. Kirshner asked them all to watch the pilot episode of *Bewitched*. On the pilot, the producer used the Frank Sinatra song "Witchcraft" and played it under the opening credits. But the execs wanted their own signature song.

Like everything else, Kirshner made this a competition and had all the teams turn in their best shot. Keller and Greenfield's version was the overwhelming choice. In fact, for future TV shows like *Hazel* and *Gidget*, Kirshner went directly to Jack and Howie for a theme song, bypassing King and Goffin and Mann and Weil, who didn't like the idea of being assigned TV theme songs. Keller also later would write "Seattle," the theme song for *Here Come the Brides*. That song was also a hit for Perry Como in 1969.

When *Bewitched* was completed, singer Frankie Randall recorded it first for RCA. An instrumental version was also recorded. Screen Gems decided to go with Keller's melody alone and left Greenfield's lyrics on the table. By the time Don Costa produced Steve Lawrence's sensational version of the song (used in the recent *Bewitched* movie), Screen Gems was set on using the instrumental version.

For more than forty years, that instrumental version of "Bewitched" has delighted viewers. In 2005, Keller re-recorded "Bewitched" with a hip-hop beat, hoping to make it a hit all over again. He even put it on his phone machine.

Throughout the remainder of the '60s and '70s, Keller continued to write and produce, scoring another Top 10 tune in 1970 with "Easy Come, Easy Go," performed by Bobby Sherman. "I showed it to Davy Jones [of the Monkees] first, and he said he'd think about it," recalled Keller. "While he was thinking about it, Bobby Sherman cut it and released it."

Ever since Jack Benanti first took a liking to Keller in 1956, and invited him to hang around the office and help Benanti select songs for his client, Frank Sinatra, Keller dreamed of someday writing his own song for Ol' Blue Eyes. Then in 1968, it happened with a song called "When Somebody Loves You." Keller thought it was perfect for Frank, but for some reason, he couldn't coax Howie Greenfield to finish the song. So Keely Smith (who teamed with Louie Prima) helped out and finished the song. With Nelson Riddle putting his signature arrangement on the ballad, Sinatra loved it and chose it for the title song of his next album. Keller couldn't have been any prouder. Now he felt his resume was complete.

After moving to Los Angeles, Keller had great success producing several albums for the Monkees. One of which contained his own song "Your Auntie Grizelda." In 1984, Jack was ready for another change; he moved to Nashville, became a fixture in the community, and once again enjoyed writing success. When he first arrived, a writer for the newspaper *The Tennessean* asked him how it felt competing with Nashville's songwriters. "I don't mind going to the back of the line and waiting for my turn again," he said.

When Jack Keller was a boy, he realized he never knew his grandfather on his father's side. Jack's dad, Mal Keller, died when Jack was fourteen. It marked the fourth consecutive generation of Keller men who hadn't lived long enough to see their grandchildren born.

Fully aware of the heart problems that ran on his side of the family, Keller constantly monitored himself. Through a good diet and exercise and a doctor's watchful eye, Jack Keller was hoping that someday he'd live to play with his grandchildren. He and his wife, Robi, raised four children, the first two of which were adopted.

In 1998, Keller felt a tightness in his chest. He knew what was happening and didn't waste any time, driving himself to the hospital in less than five minutes. A triple bypass followed, which provided him with a new lease on life, literally. A few years later, the first of three grandchildren was born.

In March 2004, he had a wonderful reunion with Tony Orlando, Toni Wine, and Ron Dante, thanks to an oldies cruise that Keller joined as a performer.

The warm reunion on the cruise ship led the Kellers to go out of their way to be at any of Orlando's shows within driving distance of Nashville. On February 10, 2005, they packed up the car and drove four hours to Evansville, Indiana, to see Tony and Toni perform. This time Orlando not only introduced Jack in the audience but asked him to come up to the stage to play something. He chose to do just one song, "Bewitched," which received a huge ovation from the crowd.

After the show, Keller surprised Orlando with something he brought with him that stirred memories from many years ago.

"Forty-four years after I first met Jack, he pulls out of his suitcase a letter I wrote to him when I was sixteen years old," Orlando said. "This letter was pristine perfect. There wasn't a wrinkle on it. Where he kept this letter completely amazes me. It contained the program I sang from my very first nightclub show at the Safari. When he showed me this letter, the impact it had on me was how important I was to him, that he would have kept something so pristine perfect for forty-four years. Then he pulled out a picture and asked, 'Isn't this your uncle Johnny?' I hadn't seen my uncle Johnny in twenty-two years, yet this photo was as if it had just come out of the Polaroid."

Later that week in 2005, after arriving back in Nashville, Keller contracted a low-grade fever that he couldn't seem to shake. In order to produce a three-day session that week, he managed to control the fever by attacking it with Advil, but once he stopped taking the pills, the fever returned.

By February 18, after several blood tests yielded few clues, Keller said, "My [blood] platelets are low. That's all I know, other than they don't think it's cancer."

"I'm worried about him," said Artie Kaplan. "I don't like the sound of this."

On March 2, Keller went in for more tests. This time he was hospitalized. By Monday, March 7, he had the bad news and shared it. He had been diagnosed with NK T-cell leukemia. The "NK" stood for "natural killer." The average patient diagnosed with this strain of leukemia lived for only fifty-five days, but Jack was sure he could do better.

"The doctors are confident they can get the fever under control and that I can return home," he told me. "If I can do that, I can get everything [his affairs] in order. I was worried about my heart all those years and something like this gets me."

Keller made the news as easy on the listener as possible. He was strong enough to do that. When he ended his conversation that day with his boyhood friend Artie Kaplan, he closed with, "I love you, man." Kaplan made plans to fly to Nashville.

The next two weeks were good ones for Jack Keller. The fever subsided and he indeed was able to return home to get things in order. During that time he started getting phone calls from all of his old pals. Gerry Goffin called first, then Jerry Leiber. Don Kirshner called several times. Keller's childhood friend Brooks Arthur called and patched up an old squabble. Toni Wine flew to Nashville to be with him and stayed for a week.

Through the process of writing this book and the dozens of conversations we had, Jack Keller and I had become close. He encouraged me to come to Nashville to gather photos and other mementos he had for the book. I was worried about his health, so I booked my plane ticket as duly ordered.

Time was fleeting and friends knew it. "You'll never guess who called. It was unbelievable," Keller told me on March 19. "I answer the phone and I hear this voice say, 'Jack, it's Carole King.' We talked like it was 1963 again. It was wonderful. She gave me the closure I needed with her."

Before that phone call, Keller and King hadn't been in touch for nearly thirty years. In 2002, King came to Nashville for a seminar, and Jack stopped by to see her at its conclusion. He asked if they could have a cup of coffee, but her manager whisked her off and they never talked. Keller was concerned that he had lost an old friend. But her phone call changed all that. "Now I know everything's right with us," he said.

"And did I tell you, who else called? Barry and Cynthia called. Carole must have embarrassed them into it. And Jerry Leiber called. He told me I was a great songwriter. Can you imagine, the great Jerry Leiber, telling me that?"

On March 20, Kirshner, the person who had brought them all together, talked with Jack by phone. "I told him what Jerry Leiber said," recalled Jack. "You know what Donnie tells me? He says, 'I was the first one who ever told you that you were a great songwriter.' You gotta love him."

For someone who was dying, he certainly was enjoying saying good-bye to everyone. Then the fever returned and he went back to the hospital.

On Thursday night, March 31, 2005, 11:30 p.m., Keller called me from his hospital bed. He had never called that late before.

"Maybe you better get here a little sooner than we had planned," he said. "I don't think I have that much time."

At 8:30 a.m. the next morning, Friday, April 1, 2005, with his entire family at his bedside, Jack Keller said, "I'm going to rest a little now," and he closed his eyes for the last time. Only twenty-seven days after being diagnosed with leukemia, he was gone.

Ironically, Paul Kaufman, his childhood friend with whom he wrote his first song, passed away thirty-four days earlier from cancer. Both gone at age sixty-eight.

The funeral was at Congregation Micah in Brentwood, just outside of Nashville. Artie Kaplan and longtime friend Bob Feldman drove up from South Florida. Tony Orlando and Toni Wine flew in and dozens of other close friends and relatives arrived.

The service was set for Monday, April 4. Before it began, arriving guests could hear a tape of Jack Keller hits playing over the speaker system as they walked into the chapel. One of them was the beautiful ballad, "Beats There a Heart So True," which he wrote in 1958 with Noel Sherman. It was recorded by Perry Como with the aid of a forty-three-piece orchestra and the Ray Charles Singers. In what may have been Keller's most beautiful melody, the song appropriately spoke of devotion:

Someone who'd be miles away,
Still within her heart I'd stay
Beats there a heart so true?

The song began and ended with the sound of a beating heart. In his liner notes, as part of a four-CD box set he made up for his friends, next to "Beats There a Heart So True" Keller wrote, "This is one of my all-time favorite recordings." Jack liked it so much he featured it on the first CD of the box set. The title for the four-CD package was a phrase his father, the bandleader, always used in his advertising: "Music for All Occasions."

The busy red cover of the box set read: "Music for All Occasions Written by Jack Keller—TV Themes—Golden Oldies—Jazz—Swing—Disco—Bubblegum—Novelty and Motion Picture Title Songs—4 CDs—80 Songs—80 Recordings—With personal memories from the composer."

Rabbi Ken Kanter of Congregation Micah was the first to speak: "From Music Row in Nashville to Screen Gems studios in Hollywood to the Brill Building in New York, Jack wrote for everybody," he said. "From Reba McEntire to Connie Francis, from Bobby Vee to the Monkees, from Ernest Tubb to Frank Sinatra, his music crossed all generations and knew no bounds."

Tony Orlando spoke next.

"He was the first person to teach me the importance of class," said Orlando. "Jack sat me down and said, 'This is how you wear your jacket; this is how you tie your tie.'

"All I ever wanted to be was like Jack Keller. All I ever wanted to do was to walk into a room and to have the same impact," Orlando continued. "And by trying it Jack's way I walked the streets of Pompeii, worked for seven presidents of the United States, found my dream with a star on the Hollywood Walk of Fame, and sang for the Queen of England . . . Thank you, Jack, for igniting a spark in my life. Thank you, my professor, my friend. I can never thank you enough."

The final speaker, Alexis Berk, was a young woman who arrived in Nashville five years earlier, barely out of rabbinical school. She was to be the junior rabbi at Congregation Micah. The Kellers immediately welcomed her to their home with open arms.

"There is nowhere else on earth like that home. It is full of paradox," Rabbi Berk began. ". . . And there was no one else like Jack. Right up until the end, Jack told it like it was. Last Thursday, I made my last visit to Jack. He was tired and things were not looking optimistic. He recounted to me the reports from the doctors and I echoed that it sounded like they were saying he might die soon. He agreed, sort of. Wondering what was on his mind, I took a page from his own book and just decided to get right to it. I asked him if he wanted to talk about dying. And before I could settle in for what I thought might be a poignant conversation, he simply responded, 'What's there to talk about?' Then he flashed that wide, fleeting smile . . ."

When the family returned home after the service, they found that a spread big enough to feed an army had been delivered with a handwritten note from Don Kirshner, explaining why he could not be there. It read in part:

> Jack Keller was a friend I was privileged to work with, know and love. Above and beyond that, he was one of the finest and most underrated songwriters of our generation. Because of his musical brilliance, he is leaving a timeless legacy throughout the globe on record, film and television.

We are all a lot richer from knowing Jack, who touched our lives in so many ways. —*Don Kirshner*

● ● ●

In the months before Keller died, he had been back in touch with Gerry Goffin, trying to write one last song together. Keller sent Goffin an unfinished melody that Goffin started to work on, but also couldn't finish. After Jack passed, Goffin sent it on to Artie Kaplan, who gave it hands and feet and completed both the melody and the lyrics. Goffin decided to call it "Hits in Heaven."

> *And when I reach that very end*
> *I know we'll be together my old friend,*
> *So say a prayer for me and ask heaven to be kind,*
> *And we'll have hits in heaven, yes we'll have hits in heaven,*
>   *one more time.*

● ● ●

Jack Keller: November 11, 1936–April 1, 2005. Beats there a heart so true.

Love Will Keep Us Together

After the '60s everyone drifted in different directions, but the impact of working together had left an indelible mark. It seemed like everyone who was ever associated with Don Kirshner during the Aldon years met with tremendous success. Here's what happened to some of them.

Neil Sedaka and Howard Greenfield

After writing together for what seemed like an eternity, in 1972 Sedaka and Greenfield knew it was time to move on. Neil hadn't had a hit since the end of '62, and with the Beatles changing the face of pop music, no one knew how to write a hit song anymore. Greenfield's lyrics in "The Hungry Years" were a clue to their unhappiness:

> *We spun so fast we couldn't tell the gold ring from the carousel*
> *How could we know the ride would turn out bad,*
> *Everything we wanted, was everything we had . . .*
> *I miss the hungry years . . . those days of me and you,*
>   *we lost along the way . . .*

After RCA dropped Sedaka, he decided to move to England, where he was getting more respect. Howie's other writing partner, Jack Keller, had moved to L.A. to produce the Monkees for Kirshner, so Greenfield started his new career in Los Angeles too.

In 1973, Sedaka and Greenfield reunited to write "Our Last Song Together," in which Greenfield cleverly combined lines and titles from many of their hits over the years. Sedaka told Howie to write fast because he was leaving for London the next day. The lyrics reflected the breakup:

Yesterday is yesterday,
The past is dead and gone,
Nostalgia just gets in the way,
Let's stop hanging on . . .

When Greenfield returned with the lyric, Sedaka was tweaking a new tune on the piano. In a matter of minutes, they wrote what indeed turned out to be their last song together: "Love Will Keep Us Together." It was a song befitting a great team.

While "Our Last Song Together" didn't crack the Top 40, "Love Will Keep Us Together" was a smash for the Captain and Tenille. Near the end of the song, they cleverly inserted "Sedaka is back" as a tribute to Neil.

Indeed, by 1975, he was well on his way back. In October '74, Sedaka began his comeback with the release of "Laughter in the Rain," written with Phil Cody. It was his first No. 1 song in thirteen years.

In 1986, Greenfield tragically became one of the first Americans to die from AIDS. According to Brian Gari, a friend of Sedaka and Greenfield's, Neil was in India at the time, and was unable to return in time for the funeral.

The circumstances of Greenfield's death caught Artie Kaplan totally off guard.

"It was shocking," said Kaplan. "Absolutely shocking. He was with a guy [Tory], who was one of the best-looking guys I've seen in my whole entire life. They were together for years and years. They traveled around the world. They had an apartment in New York, a home in Beverly Hills, and an apartment in San Francisco.

"I knew Howie since high school. He was always gay. But I don't think he was a promiscuous guy. He was a *haimisheh* guy, a stand-up guy, a mensch. I just don't see him carousing in bathhouses. Howie was a wonderful man. And he was the most prolific lyric writer I had ever met. The guy could write standing on his ear. Seeing Howie's success with a number of different composers, I somehow feel that Howie was more instrumental in pushing them in the right direction musically as well as lyrically. My only regret is that when I was in the office I didn't play the piano well enough to ask Howie to write with me."

When Sedaka received the Sammy Cahn Lifetime Achievement Award from the Songwriters Hall of Fame in 2005, he opened his acceptance speech by thanking Greenfield for knocking on his door that October day in 1952. Therefore, it seemed out of place that Sedaka neglected to mention Greenfield in recent New York–area appearances.

"In 2007, I saw Neil perform at Westbury [New York]," Brian Gari related. "After the show I asked him why he never mentioned Howie during the performance. Neil told me that he felt he deserved much more recognition for the songs because he was the one who recorded them and he was the one who traveled the world to promote them."

Regardless, the songs will always live on. Sedaka is still loved and adored by millions. And Howie Greenfield will ultimately be remembered as one of the greatest lyricists of the twentieth century.

Bobby Darin

Darin never had another No. 1 song after "Mack the Knife," but he did reach the Top 10 five more times. "Beyond the Sea" (No. 6) was his follow-up to "Mack" in 1960, and in '61, he hit with "You Must've Been a Beautiful Baby" (No. 5)—the same song Bobby auditioned for Kirshner in Natalie Twersky's living room six years earlier. After that came "Things" (No. 3) in '62, "You're the Reason I'm Living" (No. 3) in '63, and his final hit in '66 was his country version of "If I Were a Carpenter" (No. 8).

By 1966, Darin had completely changed his style to a folk-country sound, which disappointed many fans that came to see him in Las Vegas. He also had a successful acting career in the early '60s. Besides the romantic comedy hit *Come September,* in which he met his future wife Sandra Dee, Darin won much acclaim for his supporting role in *Captain Newman,*

M.D., playing a shell-shocked soldier. For his performance, he took the Best Actor Award at the Cannes Film Festival and was nominated for a Best Supporting Actor Oscar in 1963.

Although his music and acting careers flourished, he continued to worry about his weakened heart. In January 1971, he underwent successful open-heart surgery, but a similar surgery intended to repair two heart valves was not successful, and on December 20, 1973, Bobby Darin was gone. Afraid he wouldn't live to thirty, he died much too young at thirty-seven.

Kirshner and Darin had stayed close through the years. They both had met tremendous success since their first meeting in 1955. An only child, Kirshner always felt Darin was like a brother to him. "There was no one like him," he said, pausing for a breath. "And there never will be."

Barry Mann and Cynthia Weil

Of all the writers who learned and grew under Kirshner at Aldon Music, this pair was possibly the most productive after the sale of the company to Screen Gems. They wrote hits in every decade of the twentieth century from the '60s on. Their biggest success, though, came thanks to Phil Spector.

In 1964, Spector was producing the Righteous Brothers (Bobby Hatfield and Bill Medley) in Los Angeles. He asked Barry and Cynthia to fly out to see if they could write a song for the guys who were nicknamed "blue-eyed soul." They decided to try and write something that sounded like the Four Tops hit "Baby I Need Your Lovin'."

They stayed in L.A. for more than a month and the song they finally submitted to Spector was "You've Lost That Lovin' Feelin'." Only it didn't sound like the smash hit we all know today until Spector put his magic to it. Spector, correctly, took a songwriter's credit as well.

"I remember Barry singing the song for me when they got back to New York," said Artie Kaplan, "and I liked it. But of course that wasn't the Phil Spector version that I heard."

While preparing to record the song, Hatfield realized that his singing role was reduced to only taking part in the choruses and the bridge, while partner Bill Medley sang the meat of the song. "What am I supposed to do [while Medley is singing all those solos]?" Hatfield asked Spector.

Without missing a beat Spector, replied, "You'll go to the fucking bank."

When Spector finished the song, he called Mann and Weil and played it for them over the phone. According to Kaplan, they weren't that impressed either. But the song was not only a hit for the Righteous Brothers but for half a dozen other performers, and took down the title as the number-one played song for the century. BMI estimated that it has had more than 14 million airplays through early 2010.

Ironically, two years later, Mann and Weil's follow-up, "(You're My) Soul and Inspiration" out-sold "You've Lost That Lovin' Feelin'," and went higher on the charts.

Other classics they've written include "I'm Gonna Be Strong" (Gene Pitney, '64), "Here You Come Again" (which was Dolly Parton's comeback song in '77), "Sometimes When We Touch" (Mann wrote with Dan Hill, '78), "Don't Know Much" (Linda Ronstadt and Aaron Neville, '80), "Just Once" (James Ingram, '81), "Somewhere Out There" (along with composer James Horner, performed by Ronstadt and Ingram, '86), and "Wrong Again" (Weil with Tommy Lee James, performed by Martina McBride, '98). "Somewhere" also won a Grammy Award for Song of the Year.

Since then they have written an unproduced Broadway musical. Mann, who had the style, voice, and looks to be a singing star, never did have another hit of his own after "Who Put the Bomp." In 2005, they brought an Off-Broadway revue of their songs to New York, called *They Wrote That?*, which featured Barry and Cynthia singing their own songs, in hopes of moving it to Broadway. Although well received by avid fans, reviews of the show were mixed, and the show concluded its short run.

Early in the run Don Kirshner flew up to New York to see the show. Mann and Weil talked about their early days and had Kirshner stand to a rousing ovation. But a few years later, when Kirshner tried to mount his own Broadway musical based on many of the songs written at Aldon, Mann and Weil (along with King and Goffin) were reluctant to help his producers, Kirshner said, and Kirshner's show never got off the ground.

Like Kirshner, Mann and Weil were inducted into the Songwriters Hall of Fame, and the Rock and Roll Hall of Fame also recognized Barry and Cynthia's great breadth of work and inducted them in the 2010 class. Carole King introduced them, and in their own remarks they went out of their way to thank Kirshner.

"I walked into Aldon Music for the first time in 1960," Weil recalled. "Donnie Kirshner gave me a very long contract and a $50-a-week guarantee, which was a lot of money in those days 'for somebody who had never written an A side. He was the greatest publisher in the world. I have to thank him for opening the door for me."

Mann and Weil were conspicuously absent from Don Kirshner's induction in 2007 into the Songwriters Hall of Fame. Their "thank you" to Kirshner at their own Rock and Roll Hall of Fame induction was a long time coming.

Carole King and Gerry Goffin

Carole and Gerry continued to write hits through the '60s, getting the highest of all compliments when the Beatles said they aspired to write as well as Goffin and King. An even higher compliment came when the Beatles recorded a few of their songs.

The biggest hits Carole and Gerry wrote together in the post-Aldon era were "Pleasant Valley Sunday" for the Monkees and Aretha Franklin's anthem, "(You Make Me Feel Like a) Natural Woman." But by 1968, they were on their way to divorce. Goffin admits that a bout with drugs might have played a role for him in the divorce, but he felt they still had strong feelings for each other.

"It was just that we were working together and living together," said Goffin, "and she used to get all the credit, and that annoyed me. Finally I said, 'Look, you become an artist. I'm going to go my own way.' She learned how to write her own lyrics, and wound up writing one of the greatest albums of all time, *Tapestry.*"

Before *Tapestry* (and after their divorce) came an album on her own called *The Road to Nowhere*, in which Goffin co-wrote some of the songs, and he also produced the album for her. Unfortunately it never took off.

So Carole contacted Lou Adler, who now had his own label. He invited her to come to L.A. and use his office to write. The result was *Tapestry*, which was the biggest-selling album of the '70s, won four Grammy Awards, and contained the Goffin–King hits "Smackwater Jack," "Natural Woman," and "Will You Love Me Tomorrow."

It also contained the Song of the Year, "It's Too Late," which Goffin feels she wrote with him in mind. The album's success meant Carole would have to go on the road to promote. "Carole never enjoyed performing before a live audience," said Gerry, "and still doesn't to this day."

Goffin went on to write some of the greatest songs of his career, despite dealing with demons most of his life. When he was going through some very difficult emotional times in the last twenty-five years, Carole was always there for him.

"I think she wrote 'You've Got a Friend' for me," he said matter-of-factly. "And I wrote one for her after we split up, 'Do You Know Where You're Going To,' performed by Diana Ross."

He wrote the latter in '75 with composer Michael Masser, and went on to write several more blockbusters in the '80s with Masser, including: "Tonight I Celebrate My Love" ('83, sung by Roberta Flack and Peabo Bryson), "Saving All My Love for You" ('85, sung by Whitney Houston), and "Miss You Like Crazy" ('89, performed by Natalie Cole).

It became obvious over the years that Goffin had a great talent to write lyrics for women, providing Top 10 songs for the Shirelles, Aretha Franklin, Little Eva, Diana Ross, Whitney Houston, Roberta Flack, and Natalie Cole.

Even though King hit a writing slump after *Tapestry*, she still was the most decorated female songwriter according to *Billboard*, with an amazing 118 songs on their charts from 1959 through 2000.

An attempt by King and Goffin to put together a revue of their songs, called *Some Kind of Wonderful*, never reached Broadway, unfortunately. The show featured most of their hits, written separately and together. The songs were connected through a fictional storyline, similar to the way *Mamma Mia* was.

In 2011, Carole brought forth a new show called *Natural Woman*. The plot was semi-autobiographical, according to the *New York Post*. Once again their hit songs were woven throughout the story. New York backers' auditions in May and November were received warmly, the *Post* reported.

"Carole doesn't really want to talk about the '60s anymore," said Goffin, "because she's got *Tapestry*." But she had tremendous success with her Living Room tour and more recently touring with longtime friend James Taylor.

Goffin also continues to write, and he spends as much time as he can with his grandchildren. "It's funny, when my daughter was young she never liked 'Who Put the Bomp,'" he said. "But now she plays it all the time for my grandson."

"In retrospect," said Goffin in 2006, "I don't think I'd be anywhere without Carole. And I don't think I'd be anywhere without Donnie. I love them both a lot."

Tony Orlando, Toni Wine, and Ron Dante

Ron Dante had major successes, singing all the voices on a hit called "Tracy" and as the lead singer of the Archies. In years to come Dante's success would mushroom as a producer.

One day he met a wiry kid from Brooklyn who was writing and singing jingles. Dante saw the talent immediately, and the two began working together as singer and producer. The relationship lasted for over a decade as Dante steered Barry Manilow from his first hit, "Mandy," through album after album of hits.

Tony Orlando's success story is even stranger. He thought his singing career was washed up in his twenties, so he too met success producing. In fact, while producing for April Blackwood Music, one of Orlando's early scores was the signing of Barry Manilow.

Then one day, his old friends Jay Siegel and Hank Meddress from the Tokens called him. They were producing a song they needed a demo singer to record and they asked if he'd do them a favor. It was called "Knock Three Times." The result was the rebirth of Orlando's singing career.

Toni Wine continued to be an important force in his career when she wrote "Candida," his next hit, and also was one of the back-up singers as well. To this day, Toni Wine is still part of the Tony Orlando show that plays in nightclubs and casinos all over the world.

And each night in his show, he singles out Toni Wine for the hits she wrote for him and then has her perform her first big hit, "Groovy Kind of Love." Orlando is that kind of guy.

These people grew up in the business together and were thicker than any of their individual families ever were. Knowing that, no one should be surprised that in Jack Keller's final days Toni Wine and Tony Orlando were there for him.

Charles Koppelman and Don Rubin

Charles Koppelman and Don Rubin turned a songwriting job into a song-publishing career. When Morris Levy let them go, Charles and Don were forced to start their own business.

They went on to start a publishing company, which they first called Char-Don, modeling their business after Aldon. Koppelman and Rubin eventually merged with Koppelman's uncle, S. C. Swid. Later they merged with Sam LeFrak and Martin Bandier to form Swid Bandier Koppelman, otherwise known as SBK Entertainment Worldwide, Inc. In 1988, SBK sold its publishing to Thorn EMI for $320 million.

The following year, Koppelman became chairman and CEO of EMI Music Publishing. Koppelman was also inducted into the Songwriters Hall of Fame—a few years before Kirshner, it should be noted. He wanted to be bigger than Kirshner, and in the publishing world he was.

He also became Michael Jackson's advisor in his later years and recently resigned as CEO of Martha Stewart Living. Not bad for a kid from Queens with a jump shot.

Artie Kaplan

Artie Kaplan never had a big hit in the U.S. like the others, but he did wind up composing the music for several songs that were huge hits in Europe. Kaplan played sax on records with such greats as Carole King, Neil Sedaka, Van Morrison ("Brown- Eyed Girl"), and on Barry Manilow's "Mandy." He can also be heard on such hits as "The Loco-Motion" and "Sugar, Sugar."

In 1975, he recorded his own album of songs, entitled *Confessions of a Male Chauvinist Pig.* In it was a haunting tune he co-wrote with Artie Kornfeld called "Bensonhurst Blues." It was a hit in Europe in '75, and has been re-recorded and released by at least half a dozen other artists. In 2008 in France, Patricia Kass hit No. 1 with her version of it, which she renamed "Kaberet."

Kaplan is still composing, and in 2011 was in New York working on three different Off-Broadway musicals.

Lou Adler

Lou Adler can be seen in the front row of Lakers games these days, jawing with Jack Nicholson, among others. He came by his prominence the honest way. He earned it.

Adler learned the music business in California under the tutelage of Lester Sill. The same Lester Sill who saw enough promise in Phil Spector to send him to New York to apprentice with Leiber and Stoller.

Adler was sort of a smoother, more stylized version of Kirshner. Like Kirshner, he had his ear to the street and was quick to recognize who had the sound the kids wanted. Adler's ultimate success came from Carole King. He had spent many weeks in Aldon's offices in the early '60s and saw and heard firsthand what Carole could do.

After her first album, *Road to Nowhere,* failed, she turned to Adler for help. Carole needed to get away from Gerry, and she found solace in working in Adler's office. The result a year later was *Tapestry,* which she recorded on Adler's own label, Ode Records. The rest, as they say, is history.

Adler's greatest financial success, though, was yet to come. He produced a campy musical film called *The Rocky Horror Picture Show* in 1975. Now we know why he can afford those front-row Lakers seats next to Jack Nicholson.

Don Kirshner

Don Kirshner was a lot like Casey Stengel, who managed the Yankees to an amazing ten American League pennants in twelve years. But when the Yankees lost Game Seven in the 1960 World Series, 10–9, Stengel was fired. After that Game Seven loss, Mickey Mantle complained that Stengel should have started Whitey Ford in the deciding game instead of Bob Turley. Management agreed with its star and fired the man who had brought their team so much success. In a similar comparison, Screen Gems listened to the Monkees and let Kirshner go.

Since the '80s Kirshner had worked on various projects, some successful, some not. He sold his 25,000-square-foot mansion in New Jersey and moved with his wife, Sheila, to Boca Raton in South Florida. In the last few years, he had been working feverishly with producers to mount a Broadway-type show of his life, featuring many of the

The author and Kirshner exchange a few words before the ceremony.

songs he helped bring into the world. But sadly Kirshner no longer owned the rights to those songs, and his producers could not secure those rights. Both King and Goffin and Mann and Weil were writing their own shows and saving their songs for themselves.

Better late than never, the Songwriters' Hall of Fame inducted Kirshner in 2007, along with such greats as Dolly Parton, Bill Withers, and John Legend. Nearly fifty years after he first walked into Aldon's offices, Tony Orlando rearranged his tour to be there and make the most dynamic presentation speech of the evening.

I was touched that Don invited me to be at his table for the grand event.

Besides Tony Orlando, also there celebrating with Kirshner were Toni Wine and Ron Dante, the demo singers who made "Sugar, Sugar" a hit. Despite the fact that they never made a penny over scale for that song, they knew how important Kirshner had been for their careers and came to celebrate with him. The topper of the evening, however, was a surprise appearance by Neil Sedaka, who sang "Breaking Up Is Hard to Do." Kirshner was absolutely thrilled.

Also at Kirshner's table that night were (from left to right) Tony Orlando, the author, Toni Wine, and Ron Dante.

Conspicuous by their absence were Carole King, Gerry Goffin, Barry Mann, and Cynthia Weil, the people whose careers Kirshner made possible. Jack Keller had died a few months prior to the event. It's hard to believe that King, Goffin, Mann, and Weil, who all owe their careers and so much of their success to Kirshner, couldn't get there.

In September 2010, Don and Sheila celebrated their fiftieth anniversary, an amazing accomplishment. Then a few months later, he suddenly was hospitalized with an infection. Paul Shaffer, who became famous for his impression of Kirshner on *Saturday Night Live*, had stayed in touch with Don. When he heard that Kirshner was hospitalized, he immediately gave him a call.

"At first he sounded a little weak and tired," Shaffer said. "Then he realized it was me and he said, 'Hey, babe. How's everything?' It was the old Donnie again."

But the old Donnie couldn't hang on. His heart gave out on January 17, 2011. Gone far too soon at age seventy-six. The funeral was held a few days later, and once more Tony Orlando, Toni Wine, Ron Dante, and Artie Kaplan were there to honor their old boss. And once again, conspicuously missing were the songwriting teams he helped to become legends.

Carole King called Sheila Kirshner the day of the funeral and apologized for not being there. Carole's mother had also just passed away. Neil Sedaka, who invited the Kirshners to his recent South Florida appearances, was touring and sent his regrets. But as of October 2011 (nine full months after his death) Sheila had not heard from Barry Mann or Cynthia Weil. "Not a word," Sheila told me, obviously disappointed. "Not a note. Nothing."

The Rock and Roll Hall of Fame

When the Rock and Roll Hall of Fame was created in 1983 by Ahmet Ertegun and his friends, Don Kirshner expected to be an early inductee. It never happened. Despite the rocky relationship Kirshner had with Ertegun, he thought his body of work would be recognized—not only for giving us three of the greatest songwriting teams of all time, but also for masterminding rock and roll's greatest show, *Don Kirshner's Rock Concert.*

But all of that changed December 7, 2011, nearly a year after his death, when the Rock and Roll Hall of Fame announced that Don Kirshner would be among those inducted in its class of 2012. He would posthumously receive the Ahmet Ertegun (non-performer) Award.

It's hard to believe Ertegun and the Rock and Roll Hall of Fame could see fit to induct King and Goffin, and Mann and Weil, without admitting Kirshner, who stuck by them and supported and nurtured them for years before they produced a song that hit the charts. Not to mention all the other great singers and songwriters he discovered and supported over the years.

Ertegun indicated during an interview for this book that he felt the music produced at Aldon was too bubblegum-ish, and that songs written by writers like Neil Sedaka weren't worthy. Since King and Goffin had written "Natural Woman" for Aretha Franklin (who was signed by Ertegun at Atlantic) they were more worthy in his eyes.

It seemed like the Hall was Ertegun's own private club, and when you form your own club you probably have the right to let in whomever you wish. But it's gotten much bigger than that over the years, and many feel Kirshner's admission to the Hall is long overdue. Kirshner certainly felt that way before he passed away January 17, 2011, from heart failure.

"I don't want to sound like sour grapes," he told the *Washington Post* in 2004, "but I believe I should have been one of the first three or first five inducted. I mean, they've got people in there that I *trained*, and I'm not in? It bothers me, on principle."

Here's what a few rock historians had to say about the subject prior to the announcement of his induction:

Greg Shaw, who passed away in 2004, was one of the most influential rock critics ever. He was editor and publisher of *Bomp Magazine* and a frequent contributor to *Rolling Stone.* Here are a few of his comments from a 1982 profile:

"The success of New York–based rock in the early Sixties—the music often called Brill Building pop . . . without Don Kirshner, this whole style of rock music might never have happened. . . . He almost single-handedly reshaped rock 'n' roll, taking a rude music of the streets that was foundering after an initial explosive heyday, applying for the first time high standards of craft and professionalism, and moulding it into a pop industry of greater size, complexity, efficiency and profitability than ever before." (Shaw's entire profile can be found in rocksbackpages.com.)

Michael Sigman, rock critic and music publisher, in the *Huffington Post*:

"He's in the Songwriters Hall of Fame, an honor that ought to be echoed by the Rock and Roll Hall of Fame. When Kirshner dabbled in bubblegum—the Archies . . . were his creation—it was the best bubblegum. When he did a rock TV show—*Don Kirshner's Rock Concert* . . . it was *the* rock TV show. And when he was parodied, as . . . on *Saturday Night Live* by Paul Shaffer, it was a parody for the ages."

David Sanjek of BMI:

"Kirshner was a major catalyst. He's one of the pinballs that keep the machine going. One of the signposts of his career is that he had great ears for talent, that's born out by the results. He was able to recognize the capacity that people had before they could manifest it commercially, before they knew it themselves. The industry is indebted to him."

Dan Aquilante, of the *New York Post*, is one of the foremost rock critics in the country:

"Being in his early twenties, Kirshner still understood youth. He understood what was going on in a teenager's head. He understood teenagers as being a real market and that music was important to them. Kirshner first understood the power of music, and he understood that kids loved music more than almost anything.

"He helped the '60s become the '60s more than anyone else because he understood music and he understood that it was a motivator.

"And then he discovered how to use television and how to bring music to an even bigger group. MTV couldn't be MTV without what Don Kirshner did with *Rock Concert*.

"The Rock and Roll Hall of Fame is a very political organization," Aquilante continued. "Unfortunately, history has not been kind to Don Kirshner. He's not thought of as a pioneer. His name doesn't roll off of anyone's lips, possibly because he was involved with television, and that hurt his street cred or legitimacy with artists. It may be because he is a part of the pre-Beatles rock-and-roll world that he was viewed by some as an 'old fogie' by the time 1972 rolled around.

"But he absolutely should be in the Rock and Roll Hall of Fame. He's an innovator, and those are the people we put in halls of fame— people that have moved us along and have gotten us to this point. When you look at the things Kirshner did over the years, the age he did it at, and the chances he took—it's just ridiculous that he hasn't been inducted."

After his death in January 2011, there was a groundswell of support from the press for Kirshner's induction. Carole King was among those who worked hard behind the scenes to make it happen. It's too bad all the politics couldn't have been put aside years earlier so Kirshner could have been there to hear the accolades and the applause.

And I find it somewhat ironic that his award is named for the man who worked so hard to keep him out. Somewhere up there Don Kirshner is enjoying this moment.

Kirshner Looks Back

When Don Kirshner looked back on his life, he had only a few regrets. When he and Al Nevins sold Aldon Music to Columbia Screen Gems for $3 million, their timing was impeccable. It was the spring of 1963, just six months before President Kennedy's assassination and less than a year before the arrival of the Beatles and the British Invasion. And the $3 million they received is worth more than $50 million in today's money.

But one of the things they sold, along with the contracts of their star songwriters, was the publishing rights to all of those hits they published—more than 200 on *Billboard*'s charts in less than five years.

"In 1963 nobody really played oldies," Kirshner said in 2010, during one of our last conversations. "There weren't a couple of hundred radio stations in the country playing the hits of the '60s like there are today. If I had held on to the publishing [rights], they would be worth $1 billion today. Maybe more."

But before you decide he made a mistake in selling, realize this: he was the son of a tailor from a family who always struggled to get by. Three million dollars was a staggering amount to wave in front of Kirshner in 1963, not to mention how they sweetened the pot, making him director of music at Screen Gems with a big corner office and a ton of latitude. Kirshner, the Man with the Golden Ear, couldn't afford to turn down the deal.

"I believe that after I'm gone, my grandchildren will be whistling these tunes whether they know that I published them or not," Kirshner told history-of-rock.com. "Of all the legacies that I have given, personally to me, it's very important that I was able to come out of the streets of Harlem, out of my dad's tailor shop, and have the ability to create an environment where this sound will be part of American and international culture forever."

Like Gershwin and Kern and Cole Porter before them, Neil Sedaka and Carole King and Barry Mann turned out their own standards. Now, fifty years later, Kirshner reflected on what he created in that suite of cubicles on the sixth floor at 1650 Broadway:

"In a little office in New York City," he said, "these young kids were churning out the things I dreamed of when I began—turning out timeless classics that will last long after you and I are gone."

• • •

From that moment I first saw him at that record industry dinner in 1962, Don Kirshner has been an unforgettable force in my life. And like me, 60 million baby boomers will always be grateful for his perseverance.

Aldon Music Hit List

In its brief five-year existence, Aldon published more than 200 hits. Here are a few:

Debut	Song/Artist	Songwriters	Billboard Peak
06/'58	"Splish Splash"/Bobby Darin	Bobby Darin	3
08/'58	"Stupid Cupid"/Connie Francis	Sedaka/Greenfield	14
09/'58	"Forget Me Not"/ Kalin Twins	Kolber/Martin	12
10/'58	"Queen of the Hop"/Darin	Bobby Darin	9
12/'58	"The Diary"/Neil Sedaka	Sedaka/Greenfield	14
05/'59	"Dream Lover"/Darin	Bobby Darin	2
10/'59	"Oh! Carol"/Sedaka	Sedaka/Greenfield	9
10/'59	"One-Way Ticket (to the Blues)"/Sedaka	Jack Keller/Hank Hunter	1*
03/'60	"Footsteps" / Steve Lawrence	Mann/Hunter	6
04/'60	"Stairway to Heaven"/Sedaka	Sedaka/Greenfield	9
05/'60	"Everybody's Somebody's Fool"/Francis	Keller/Greenfield	1
08/'60	"My Heart Has a Mind of Its Own"/Francis	Keller/Greenfield	1
12/'60	"Will You Love Me Tomorrow"/Shirelles	Goffin/King	1
12/'60	"Calendar Girl"/Sedaka	Sedaka/Greenfield	4
01/'61	"Where the Boys Are"/Francis	Sedaka/Greenfield	4
04/'61	"Some Kind of Wonderful"/ Drifters	Goffin/King	32
04/'61	"Breaking in a Brand New Broken Heart"/Francis	Keller/Greenfield	7
05/'61	"Halfway to Paradise"/Tony Orlando	Goffin/King	16
08/'61	"Take Good Care of My Baby"/Bobby Vee	Goffin/King	1

Date	Song / Artist	Writers	Peak
09/'61	"Bless You"/Tony Orlando	Mann/Weil	15
10/'61	"I Love How You Love Me"/Paris Sisters	Mann/Kolber	5
11/'61	"Run to Him"/Bobby Vee	Goffin/Keller	2
11/'61	"Happy Birthday Sweet Sixteen"/Sedaka	Sedaka/Greenfield	6
01/'62	"Crying in the Rain"/Everly Brothers	King/Greenfield	6
04/'62	"Uptown"/Crystals	Mann/Weil	13
07/'62	"Breaking Up Is Hard to Do"/Sedaka	Sedaka/Greenfield	1
07/'62	"The Loco-Motion"/Little Eva	Goffin/King	1
08/'62	"Venus in Blue Jeans"/Jimmy Clanton	Keller/Greenfield	7
08/'62	"It Might as Well Rain Until September"/Carole King	Goffin/King	22
09/'62	"Patches"/Dickie Lee	Mann/Kolber	6
10/'62	"Next Door to an Angel"/Sedaka	Sedaka/Greenfield	5
12/'62	"Chains"/Cookies	Goffin/ King	17
12/'62	"Go Away Little Girl"/Steve Lawrence	Goffin/King	1
12/'62	"Up on the Roof"/Drifters	Goffin/King	5
02/'63	"Blame It on the Bossa Nova"/Eydie Gorme	Mann/Weil	7
03/'63	"Don't Say Nothin' Bad"/Cookies	Goffin/King	7
04/'63	"On Broadway"/Drifters	Mann/Weil/Leiber/Stoller	9
05/'63	"One Fine Day"/Chiffons	Goffin/King	5
06/'63	"Hey Girl"/Freddie Scott	Goffin/King	10
12/'64	"You've Lost That Lovin' Feelin'"**/Righteous Brothers	Mann/Weil/Spector	1

* #1 in Europe and Japan.

** Post Aldon sale; most-played song in radio history.

Acknowledgments

As described in the preface, the origin of this book started when I was a teenager, festered for years, and bubbled to the surface when I saw Mann and Weil perform their hits in 2004. Once I decided to write this book, I wondered if I could find everyone necessary to interview to make it happen.

For years I did nothing but think about the book and how to get to the key people. I even dreamed of finding Don Kirshner and that when we met he would be thrilled that I was writing this story. I also dreamed night after night of accidentally bumping into Carole King and that she'd also agree to participate. The first part became a reality, but the latter, unfortunately, didn't.

To be able to connect with more than sixty songwriters, musicians, music executives, performers, and disc jockeys, one needs a lot of help. And to put it all down and shape into an interesting, if not an exciting, read, one needs great editors.

To that end, I'd like to thank the editors who helped turn my copy into something much more readable. Sari Botton was fantastic, and her thoughts and ideas were inspirational. I couldn't have gotten here without her. Mary Caroline Powers, who edited my first draft, was also a tremendous aid in getting to the finish line, along with Jessica Burr, my editor at Hal Leonard, and Godwin Chu, my Hal Leonard copy editor. I thank them all for all their help.

I also need to thank Laurie Rosin for her suggestions, along with my friends Stuart Marland, Sue Anne Morrow, Glenn Rosenblum, Joe Valerio, Sal Marchiano, Randy Stone, and Arthur Lerner, who also lent their time and made key suggestions to help move the book forward.

In researching the book, I went into this without knowing a soul. So I need to thank those who helped me along the way, beginning with Rob Minkoff, who sent me to songwriter Patty Silversher, who put me in touch with Jeff Barry and his assistant, Laura Pinto. And Ms. Pinto, who got me in touch with Neil Sedaka's office and Ron Dante. Besides being an important character in the story, Mr. Dante put me in touch with Don Kirshner—which perhaps was the most important contact I made. He also gave me the number for Artie Kaplan, who in turn hooked me up with songwriters Gerry Goffin and Jack Keller.

Keller was fantastic. Without his never-ending memory of those days, I wouldn't have been able to write this book. He also got me in touch with Ira Howard, former *Cashbox* writer, Tony Orlando and Toni Wine, songwriter Larry Kolber, along with Keller's old friend and former songwriting partner, Paul Kaufman.

Artie Kaplan's recollections over dozens of phone calls and meetings were also critical to the completion of this book. I want to thank authors Ken Emerson and David Evanier for providing contact information to former music executives and old friends of Darin and Kirshner's. And to Mike Church, who put me in touch with Connie Francis.

I couldn't have filled in the pieces without stories from Don Kirshner's lifelong friend Joyce Becker Sugarman and Bobby Darin's adoring pal Harriet "Hesh" Wasser. Dick Lord was instrumental in retelling early stories about Don and Bobby, and Steve Blauner was most helpful in explaining why Don sold the company to Screen Gems and what led to him losing his battle with the Monkees there.

My thanks also go out to Artie Butler, whose vivid memory of Broadway in the 1958–1963 time period was of enormous help; Kenny Karen, the "surefire" singer who missed, for relaying his stories about the early days at Aldon Music; David Sanjek at BMI for his deep background information and pertinent opinions; Charlie Feldman of BMI, Jean Bennett of Melody Ram, Steve Wallach, and musicians Charlie Macey and Buddy Saltzman. Also, thanks go to Morgan Neville, the fantastic documentarian, who helped with quotes from his transcript interviewing the Aldon gang for his A&E *Biography* series.

Also to Dick Gersh, who was Kirshner's PR wizard, for all of his help and his stories; Michael David Toth for providing information on the Three Suns; Tom Noonan, former head of pop charts for *Billboard;* Dick Clark's publicist, Paul Shefrin, for getting Dick's help confirming stories about *American Bandstand;* Songwriters Steve Carlitsky and Hank Hunter, former Screen Gems head Bert Schneider, and Eric Records for making Albeth Paris available to tell what it was like to work with Phil Spector on "I Love How You Love Me." Others who helped explain what it was like at Aldon Music in the '60s include Artie Wayne, Dick Asher, Jay Siegel (of the Tokens), Artie Resnick, and Brooks Arthur. And I want to thank Randy Price for providing the *Cashbox Magazine* cover from the sale of Aldon to Screen Gems.

I also need to express my appreciation to New York's Bruce Morrow ("Cousin Brucie") and Philadelphia's Jerry Blavat for their recollections and for re-creating their introductions to a couple of Aldon's most famous songs. And to the late, great Jerry Leiber for describing his involvement with Aldon and two of their most famous songs, "On Broadway" and "Up on the Roof." Also to Lynn Lowe and Dave Appell for confirming stories about Cameo Parkway; and to *New York Post* rock critic Dan Aquilante for his thoughtful comments and to Phil Mushnick for putting me in touch with Dan.

Artists played a big part in the story, so I need to thank particularly Neil Sedaka and Leba Sedaka, Connie Francis, Bobby Vee, the late Gene Pitney, Steve Lawrence and Eydie Gorme, and especially Tony Orlando, for their vivid memories of the stories behind the songs. Also, Steve Tyrell, for filling us in about Florence Greenberg and the days he worked for Scepter Records, and Dion, who described what it was like going up to Aldon's offices.

This wouldn't be the book you see without some wonderful photos. For those I need to thank the Keller and Kirshner families, Artie Kaplan, Albeth Paris, BMI Archives, and Michael Randolph (for making the archives of his father, William "PoPsie" Randolph, available). Also, thanks go out to Michael Jurick for his digital photography expertise, and to Alan Rinde for his assistance with the Toni Wine photos.

Of course, there were those I was unable to reach and I am still disappointed their thoughts are not included. They include Paul Simon (about his college days writing with Carole King), Paul McCartney (the Beatles said they wished they could write as well as Goffin and King), and Berry Gordy (who turned me down through his secretary).

Last but not least, I want to thank my wife, Diana, and my children, Sarah and Daniel, for putting up with all the calls that took me away from them, and all the times I missed dinner during the years it took to complete this book.

Selected Bibliography

Note: Unless otherwise specified, the quotes in this book come from the many interviews I conducted over the years.

Books

Aronowitz, Al. *Bobby Darin Was a Friend of Mine*. Author House, 2004.

Bernarde, Scott R. *Stars of David—Rock 'n' Roll's Jewish Stories*. Brandeis University Press, 2003.

Dannen, Frederic. *Hit Men*. Vintage Books, 1991.

Dylan, Bob. *Chronicles*. Simon & Schuster, 2005.

Emerson, Ken. *Always Magic in the Air: The Bomp and Brilliance of the Brill Building Era*. The Penguin Group, 2005.

Evanier, David. *Roman Candle: The Life of Bobby Darin*. Rodale, Inc., 2004.

Francis, Connie. *Who's Sorry Now?* St. Martin's Press, 1984.

Gillett, Charlie. *Sound of the City: The Rise of Rock 'n' Roll*. Da Capo Press, 1996.

Hajdu, David. *Positively Fourth Street*. Picador, 2011.

Morrow, Cousin Bruce, and Laura Baudo. *Cousin Brucie: My Life in Rock 'n' Roll Radio*. Beech Tree Books, 1987.

Orlando, Tony, with Patsi Bale Cox. *Halfway to Paradise*. St. Martin's Press, 2002.

Smith, Joe. *Off the Record: An Oral History of Popular Music*. Warner Books, 1988.

Taylor, Paula. *Rock 'n' Pop Stars*. Children's Press, 1976.

Weller, Sheila. *Girls Like Us: Carole King, Joni Mitchell, Carly Simon—and the Journey of a Generation*. Atria Books, 2008.

Whitburn, Joel. *Joel Whitburn's Top Pop Singles, 1955–2002*. Record Research, Inc., 2003.

Williams, Richard. *Out of His Head: The Sound of Phil Spector*. Outerbridge & Lazard, Inc., 1972.

Articles

Aronowitz, Al. "The Dumb Sound." *Saturday Evening Post*, August 1963 (via rocksbackpages.com).

Baratta, Paul. "Neil Sedaka, Home at Last." *Songwriter Magazine*, November 1976.

Braheny, John. Barry Mann and Cynthia Weil interview. Taxi.com, 2001.

Browne, David. "Remembering Don Kirshner, Who Influenced Pop from the Brill Building to Bubble Gum." Rollingstone.com, January 18, 2011.

Kamp, David. "The Hit Factory: An Oral History of the Brill Building." *Vanity Fair*, 2004.

Lewis, Randy. "Paul Shaffer on Don Kirshner: 'He Loved the Impression.'" *Pop & Hiss* (*Los Angeles Times* music blog), January 18, 2011.

Sailer, Steve. "Q&A: Mann & Weil on Surviving as Songwriters." UPI, 2002.

Shaw, Greg. "Barry Mann: Rock 'n' Roll Survivor." *Bomp Magazine*, July 1975 (via rocksbackpages.com).

———. "Barry Mann and Cynthia Weil." *The History of Rock*, 1982 (via rocksbackpages.com).

———. "Don Kirshner: The Pop Factory." *Bomp Magazine*, 1982 (via rocksbackpages.com).

———. "Neil Sedaka: The Tra-La Days Are Back." *Phonograph Record*, December 1974 (via rocksbackpages.com).

Stewart, R. W. "The Three Suns Delight All," *New York Times*, March 2, 1947.

Other

Morgan. *The Hitmakers: The Teens Who Stole Pop Music*. A&E *Biography* (documentary series), 2004.

Online sources include the All Music Guide to Rock and Roll, history-of-rock.com, rockhall.com, rocksbackpages.com, songwritershallof-fame.org, spaceagepop.com, and tothcorp.com.

Index

Lyric Permissions and Photo Credits

PHOTO CREDITS

Courtesy of BMI Archives: 87, 162 (Award Dinner program), 165
CBS/Landov: 47
Collection of Artie Kaplan: 162 (photo of Carole King), 163
Collection of the Keller family: 101, 158